Written by a parent for parents, *Imagining Faith with Kids: Unearthing Seeds of the Gospel in Children's Stories from Peter Rabbit to Harry Potter* illustrates how keenly modern day stories reflect and interact with our Christian stories. Mary Margaret Keaton has infused this book with hope, giving us the background, confidence, and tools we need to unearth seeds of the Gospel in our culture's favorite children's stories. *Imagining Faith with Kids* will help parents who worry that the media culture is wholly incompatible with the Christian message breathe a sigh of relief.

> — *Teresa Blythe*, spiritual director and author of *Meeting God in Virtual Reality: Using Spiritual Practices with Media* and *Watching What We Watch: Prime-Time Television Through the Lens of Faith*

What a fascinating book!

The perennial challenge for Christian catechists—and this includes parents—is to enable children to "bring life to Christian faith" and "to bring Christian Faith to life." *Imagining Faith with Kids* is a masterful example of doing this effectively. Beginning with favorite children's stories, it will enable our children to move toward Christian faith and to bring their faith back to life again.

Saint Justin, Martyr, writing about A.D. 150, said that every culture holds "seeds of the Gospel," aspects that can be drawn upon for growth in Christian faith. Keaton proves that this is true today, finding points of resonance in stories for kids that can lead them into the greatest story ever told—the Good News of Jesus Christ.

> — *Thomas H. Groome*, Director of the Institute of Religious Education and Pastoral Ministry, Boston College, and author of *What Makes Us Catholic*

Mary Margaret Keaton, mother of three, has given parents and caregivers a wonderful gift—a guide to sharing story with kids that includes information about child development, moral and faith development, the value of reading, and discernment skills. Add to this a selection of favorite children's literature and how to find in them the seeds of the Gospel, and parents will gain confidence in navigating our media culture without fear, and with wisdom and joy.

> — *Rose Pacatte*, FSP, TV/Film columnist for *St. Anthony Messenger* magazine and co-author of *Lights, Camera...Faith! A Movie Lectionary*

The wisdom in this book opens the door to the wisdom of centuries past by looking deeply into stories and their messages. Helping children appreciate the power of stories, while developing a Christian lens through which to "see" media texts, provides a foundation for lifelong learning and for lives worth living. Margaret Keaton gives excellent examples of stories and guidance into how to work with children for better understanding. This book is a "must-have" for every parent and religious educator!

— *Tessa Jolls,* President and CEO, Center for Media Literacy

Increasingly, Christian preachers have rediscovered the power of story to convey the Gospel message. In so doing, they are simply following the example of the One who preached in parables that told the stories of a rich fool, a wily steward, and a silly sheep who wanders off from the flock—to mention only a few. Mary Margaret Keaton has brought together her love of God, her love of children, and her love of story to produce a book that not only encourages parents to use the books they read to or with their children as a springboard for conversations about life, virtue, and God, but she also demonstrates how it can be done.

Imagining Faith with Kids invites parents to journey together with their children into the wonderful world of children's books, and in so doing find a joy-filled way of handing on the faith.

— *Donald Heet, OSFS,* Associate Professor of Homiletics, The Catholic University of America

Not since Bettelheim's classic, *Uses of Enchantment,* has there been this thorough and readable a treatment of storytelling in the lives of children. Mary Margaret Keaton takes the development of the imagination one step further for Christian parents and teachers by integrating the insights of Piaget and Kohlberg with the simple power of the Gospels. *Imagining Faith with Kids* will send you in joyful search of both the stories of Jesus and the best literature you can find for your children. Invite them to read, fearlessly and with faith, and you prepare them for life.

— *Patrick Marrin,* editor of *Celebration,* the ecumenical worship resource of the *National Catholic Reporter.*

Imagining Faith with Kids should be required reading for all parents. It brought me back to the days when my parents read to us—one of my favorite childhood memories. It reminded me how powerful stories are, and convinced me that Gospel messages discovered in stories can bring faith, understanding, perspective, and love.

— *Haskell V. Anderson III,* actor and member of Catholics in Media Associates

Mary Margaret Keaton's biblically based *Imagining Faith with Kids* shows parents and teachers how to connect contemporary literature for young people to the faith lives of children. This easy-to-read and inspiring text is both theoretical and abundantly practical, introducing adults to the significance of story for the Christian growth of the young and not-so-young. It emphasizes the importance of respecting children's cognitive, moral, and faith development, and examines a variety of excellent stories suitable for children from preschool to grade nine.

Including her own experiences as the mother of three children, Mary Margaret pinpoints those aspects of each story that contain "seeds of the Gospel," and shows parents how to uncover opportunities for Christian growth present in the stories themselves. Texts from the Bible, the teachings of Pope John Paul II, and the *Catechism of the Catholic Church* illuminate the stories at those places where the author unearths Christian parallels and potential in her carefully-selected tales, many of them perennial favorites.

The author describes frequent occasions with her own children when enjoyable story times become holy and grace-filled moments. Her encouraging explanations invite Christian parents to delight in stories that help young listeners grow in Christian virtue, understanding, and wonder. Particularly helpful to parents is the list of stories arranged by the author according to theme and to the child's grade in school.

Every pastor, DRE, and PTA president needs this book. Mary Margaret has an unusual ability to combine a good catechetical approach with Church tradition and sensitivity to story...I wish I could visit her living room at story time!

— *Carol Dorr Clement*, Lecturer in Faith Formation, Washington
   Theological Union

Imagining Faith invites people to think sacramentally, to see beneath the surface, to recognize the sacred in the secular. It is about:

- Recognizing story as the shortest distance between the human person and Truth.
- Living the central mystery of community by sharing in the wonderful gift of imagination.
- Parenting at a much deeper level than "soccer-mom" and "taxi-dad."
- Walking with children on their Emmaus journey as they try to make sense of their world.
- Guiding children through the uncharted waters of experiences and expanding horizons.
- Rediscovering the lost sense of "wonder and amazement at the dignity of the human person" that John Paul II calls another definition of the word Gospel.
- Engaging our culture as Jesus did.

— *John Freund, CM*, Associate Professor of Theology, St. John's University,
   member of the American Association of Marriage and Family Therapists

Imagining FAITH with Kids

Unearthing Seeds of the Gospel in Children's Stories from Peter Rabbit to Harry Potter

By Mary Margaret Keaton

Illustrated by Thomas Roberts

Pauline
BOOKS & MEDIA
Boston

Library of Congress Cataloging-in-Publication Data

Keaton, Mary Margaret.

Imagining faith with kids : unearthing seeds of the Gospel in children's stories from Peter Rabbit to Harry Potter / by Mary Margaret Keaton ; illustrated by Thomas Roberts.

p. cm.

Includes bibliographical references.

ISBN 0-8198-3690-7

1. Christian education of children. 2. Christianity in literature. I. Title.

BV1475.3.K43 2005

248.8'45—dc22

2004015432

The Scripture quotations contained herein are from the *New Revised
Standard Version Bible: Catholic Edition,* copyright © 1993 and 1989 by the
Division of Christian Education of the National Council of the Churches of
Christ in the U.S.A. Used by permission. All rights reserved.

Excerpts from the English translation of the *Catechism of the Catholic
Church* for use in the United States of America, copyright © 1994, United
States Catholic Conference, Inc. —Libreria Editrice Vaticana. Used with per-
mission.

Cover art: Thomas Roberts

"P" and PAULINE are registered trademarks of the Daughters of St. Paul

Published by Pauline Books & Media, 50 Saint Paul's Avenue, Boston, MA
02130-3491.

Printed in U.S.A.

www.pauline.org

Pauline Books & Media is the publishing house of the Daughters of St. Paul,
an international congregation of women religious serving the Church with
the communications media.

1 2 3 4 5 6 7 8 9   11 10 09 08 07 06 05

For Mama

With special thanks to
Carol Dorr Clement,
who encouraged me to find
seeds of the Gospel.

Contents

Acknowledgments

E. B. White observed that writing is bad for one's health and life. He may have been on to something. By the end of the writing process, every friend and family member of the author is lurking out of view, hoping not to be asked another question or opinion about the manuscript. The poor souls upon whom this author has invited a certain purgatory can rejoice that all is now bound and on the shelf. Come out, come out, wherever you are: Fr. John Freund, C.M., who offered tremendous encouragement and great ideas to the end; Fr. Donald Heet, O.S.F.S., whose pointed questions helped direct the focus of this work; Sr. Rose Pacatte, FSP, for her inspiring suggestions and spot-on insights; and Dixie Baughn Keaton, who believed it could be done. Very special thanks are reserved for a forward-thinking editor, Sr. Madonna Ratliff, FSP, and publisher, Sr. Donna Giaimo, FSP, for transforming a journalist into an author, and to editorial assistant *par excellence,* Diane Lynch, whose lighthearted humor and superior skills kept the project moving. Most of all, the author extends her deepest gratitude to her husband, Joe, and their three children, Patrick, Diana, and Peter, for their support.

Introduction

Once upon a time I had a grandmother who read to me...and read to me...and read to me. Every day she sat with me in our living room, reading aloud from her tattered McGuffey's Reader or one of the volumes of *My Book House*, a set of green leather-bound books filled with classic poetry and prose on fragile yellowed pages. If Granny ever wished she were doing something besides snuggling on the couch reading with me, she never betrayed it. I was always welcomed and encouraged to join her on adventures into story.

A casual observer would have seen two people sitting in a house in the heart of Virginia. But Granny and I were worlds away, encountering fascinating creatures, exploring distant lands, and meeting formidable challenges as words and images transported us beyond the foothills of the Blue Ridge Mountains to places created and ruled by imagination.

In the evening the stories continued, even though my grandmother was surely exhausted from helping my mother with seven children. Granny couldn't escape my requests for stories because we shared a bedroom, so story time became our ritual. After Granny anointed her weary feet with rosewater and glycerin, and Mama tucked me in, the lights went out and the stories began. Sometimes my grandmother repeated old standards, such as *Goldilocks and the Three Bears, Hansel and Gretel,* or *The Pied Piper of Hamelin.* But the stories I loved most were those of Granny's own childhood in a log cabin in West Virginia. Her homespun patchwork of family legend and lore, embroidered with the scents and sounds of everyday life in the late nineteenth century, became an enchanting comforter that carried me like a magic carpet to another perspective. In the hills and hollows of Granny's memory we studied virtue and vice—love, family, loyalty, courage, friendship, ignorance, hatred, and the rest— before I drifted off to sleep. I don't remember whether Granny ever tried to share her wisdom with me directly in a good talking-to, but I will never forget the lessons she taught through her stories.

————•◦•————

Whether told in the unique style of a good storyteller or recorded in books or on film, stories draw us into themselves. They transport us on words and images to a different place and time, where all that we learn depends upon how much we enter into the story and allow its lessons to speak to us. I entered Granny's world of mountainfolk by following the yarn she spun into my own imagination, where I could recreate, experience, test, and enjoy the images and feelings she was presenting. In this fascinating world, I worked to understand with my mind and spirit the deeper meanings my wise old grandmother wove within the fabric of her tales: lessons of how we children of God are called to live our lives in relation to one another.

These messages took root within me and helped to form my outlook on life. They also led me to a great appreciation of story's power to lead us to God—an appreciation I hope you will come to share with me.

Story allows us to explore the realm of possibilities within human existence. When we listen attentively to the boundless combinations of plot, characterization, setting, theme, and tone, we often can hear God calling us to enter into story as whole persons, complete with intellect, emotion, imagination, reason, and spirit. Once "inside," we recreate the storyteller's world. Even though we may live in that world briefly, we will possess always the things of value we find there.

Fiction, in particular, creates a proving ground removed from real-life perils, a place where adults and children alike can explore subjects that might be too frightening, embarrassing, difficult, or dangerous to address in reality, yet should be tackled for the moral, spiritual, or personal growth that may be gained. Stories about imaginary characters offer us a comfortable distance from which we can consider life from a fresh or broader point of view.

As our children develop confidence in responding to story and entertaining the questions it poses, they become better equipped to handle real-life issues and better able to explore the richness of our faith tradition, grounded as it is in story. Eminently imbued with educational, intellectual, psychological, and spiritual benefits for our children, story is one of the best and wisest gifts we grant them.

Obviously, a good educational curriculum includes good story, and children normally enjoy this great gift during their school day. But we parents should not pass up the invaluable opportunity afforded in sharing story at home. Besides providing intellectual and scholastic benefits, engaging in story with our kids helps us build relationships with them. When our children talk about characters they love or despise, sadness or joy they've felt, suspense, surprise, humor, and more, they volunteer insights into their own desires, needs, and fears, and we get to know them better. When we, in turn, respond to their observations, they get to know us, too.

But the best part of sharing story with our kids is a joyous little secret cherished among parents who have experienced it. The truth is that "story experiences" with children are downright fun! Childhood passes much too quickly—ours *and* theirs—and story provides a refreshing oasis suspended in time where children and adults can enjoy being childlike together.

Life in the real world, as we know all too well, is not always fun. In times such as ours, fraught with global tension and turmoil, our children are burdened by anxiety and worry that they need to release. News of terrorist attacks, environmental disasters, wars and rumors of wars beleaguer our kids in ways we parents cannot always recognize. Story calls forth the questions stirring within, allowing us—parents and children alike—to begin sorting out the complexities of our twenty-first-century lives. In the process, story often helps us rediscover joy and hope.

Our youngest son, Peter, has developed a craving for a particular story in response to his fears about the world. In *The Lorax,* by Dr. Seuss, an outsider decimates a forest for his own purposes and forces its creatures to leave their home in order to survive. While Dr. Seuss intended to convey an environmental message, the tale of destruction is extremely relevant to a child since the events of September 11, 2001, and all that has followed. The scenes of obliteration address Peter's worldview, but, mostly, he looks forward to the end, when the Lorax offers the narrator a seed that will replenish the forest and restore life there. Peter breathes an unconscious but audible sigh of relief every time we reach the profound message of hope contained in that seed. And I find myself thanking God for this lesson that conquers despair.

Moments like these are among my most cherished experiences as a parent. Times that my children and I have spent together reading and watching movies or plays have enriched my own spiritual life. The clarity and purity of my three kids' reactions never fail to remind me of Jesus, who said we must "become like little children" to enter the Kingdom of God (cf. Mt 9:21). In the truth and simplicity of a child's point of view, I believe I understand what Jesus meant. Our encounters with story transcend the intellectual and the emotional. As we will explore later on, they allow us to enter into God's ongoing creation in experiences that are fully divine.

Together, my children and I have boarded a soggy ark with Noah to gather animals two by two, fought a giant named Goliath with a lad called David, and watched Jesus from a tree with a little guy named Zaccheus, who gave us pause to wonder, *"Did he look like Danny DeVito?"* We have also ridden magic carpets, followed a yellow brick road, escaped dragons, entered a strange world through a wardrobe, and boarded a train from Platform 9 3/4 to a mysterious wizarding school. Every story has offered us opportunities to discuss new subjects, come to new understandings, and learn more about ourselves and one another. And every story has given us wonderful chances to relax and enjoy each other's company, whether reading together on a bed or a couch, or sitting side by side in a darkened theater sharing a bucket of popcorn.

———•◦•———

Nevertheless, fear nearly prevented me from enjoying this wonderful part of our lives. When my oldest son discovered *Harry Potter* and began reading the books over and over again, news surfaced of concerned parents seeking to ban the books. Frightened, I wondered if I was leading my altar server astray by allowing him to read works about witchcraft and wizardry. But it was Patrick himself who proved to be the voice of reason. "Mom," he said gently, "you really ought to read the books. I think you'll like them."

It was perfect logic. I hadn't cracked open even one of these books of which I was becoming terrified and suspicious. Patrick's words also recalled for me the voice of God, inviting me to approach a beloved art form with a peaceful heart and to read the books with confidence in my critical thinking skills and with trust in the Lord, who wants only good things for us. So I decided to meet Harry Potter and identify his powers, and then determine, with both good thinking and spiritual discernment, on which side of the issue I would stand.

This book is a result of that decision. I was delighted to discover in *Harry Potter* the story of a valiant boy willing to lay down his life for his friends in the face of evil. Where I least expected to find them—tucked among the pre-teen gags, human frailties, and fantastical mythos of the books—lay "seeds" of the Gospel in themes like love, self-sacrifice, discipline, friendship, and freedom.

Many other stories express Gospel values as well. *The Chronicles of Narnia* are an obvious example, written by the revered Christian theologian, C. S. Lewis, as an allegory for our salvation in Christ. Other authors or artists may not have intended an explicit Christian message, as Lewis did, and yet, in approaching their works as Christians, we can recognize God's creative love for us in themes of good triumphing over evil and virtue over vice. In *Charlotte's Web,* a remarkable spider brings salvation and dignity to a lowly pig. *Mary Poppins* teaches stodgy Mr. Banks to remember joy, and helps two children discover an unseen world in their midst where soot-covered chimneysweeps know secrets of wonder. And an ugly duckling remains true to the way God created him, and becomes a lovely swan.

———•◦•———

We Christians base our lives on "the greatest story ever told," the story of God's limitless love for us. That story, told over and over by the writers of Sacred Scripture, finds an echo in the work of creative artists: poets, writers, filmmakers, and others who respond to inspiration and share with the world their insights into the human condition or visions of a transcendent reality.

Every story a child encounters strengthens his or her ability to reflect on meanings and search for understanding. That same ability prepares a child for grappling with the story of God's people and finding within it the path to a relationship with God in Jesus. For that reason, we needn't be afraid of stories if a child's reality is rooted in love. I truly believe, as St. Paul wrote, that "all things work together for good for those who love God..." (Rom 8:28). Stories are a wonderful, enjoyable, and, I believe, necessary part of those things. They play a role in the discipleship of thoughtful, discerning followers of Christ.

In the following pages, we will explore the role of story in a child's human growth and development, the teachings of the Church that relate to story, as well as the ways Jesus used story to spread the Good News. We will examine some examples of metaphor and story that provide good opportunities for faith sharing and some themes found in a variety of works that promote Gospel values. If this idea is new to you, I hope you will find in it an adventure into a stimulating world of wonder. All it takes is a little faith—about the size of a mustard seed—and a little imagination to enter into a refreshing spiritual experience with our God, the giver of life and love, who created the world and saw that it was good.

PART 1

Imagining Faith...

1

The Power of Story to Reveal God's Face

> I know not whether the remark is to our honor or oth-
> erwise, that lessons of wisdom have never such power
> over us as when they are wrought into the heart,
> through the ground-work of a story which engages
> the passions: is it that we are like iron and must first
> be heated before we can be wrought upon?
> — Reverend Laurence Sterne (1713–1768), author of the classic
> novel, *Tristram Shandy*

People have a basic need to share their stories with others. Just try keeping information about a new baby in the family all to yourself. It is next to impossible for the vast majority of us, because our human nature urges us to communicate! We need to share our experiences and, in doing so, to define and organize them in ways that help us find meaning in our lives.

But before we share our stories with others, we begin by sharing them with our own selves. As we go through the day and encounter the world, our senses, like on-the-spot reporters covering breaking news, tell our brains what we are experiencing. We synthesize the information with the rest of what we know as true, then sift it through our worldview filter and try to make sense of it all. Once the story has been assigned its place in our whole scheme of things, it helps to form our outlook on future events. Without doubt, we humans are complex creatures—wonderfully, marvelously made by our Creator!

A Magnificent Reality Waiting to Be Shared

Story is vital to every culture. It allows us to convey common values, pass along heritage, and express who we are, what we cherish, what we fear, and how we see ourselves in a way that captivates our imagination and stirs our very soul. Through story, we open ourselves to communicate with the divine, for God is waiting for us within each story that bears truth. The late author and scholar, Joseph Campbell, who spent a lifetime studying the stories of the world's cultures and comparing the common human experience of Truth in myth, called story a mask of God. As a mask, he explained, story shields God's "Face of Glory" while, at the same time, it reveals life beyond the visible world. "Jesus had the eye," Campbell said. "What a magnificent reality he saw in the mustard seed."[1]

It is that magnificent reality that we parents must share with children through story, encouraging its exploration as an essential part of spiritual growth and development. Just beneath the mask of bedtime tales and popular movies—indeed, all media that bear story—God awaits us. Media are, after all, gifts of God. It was God's creative power that inspired the many methods we humans have developed to communicate. Through story borne in media, we can peek at God's glorious face and learn how much we are loved.

Nobel laureate Saul Bellow, author of many wonderful stories, complained that modern times had brought on a "housecleaning of belief." Forces immeasurable by instrumentation or unobservable with the physical eye became devalued and often tossed aside as untrue and irrelevant, leaving us with little stock in mystery. And yet it is mystery and wonder that our Christian faith requires. We believe in one God in three Persons—a mystery impossible to explain with science. We believe in a Savior, born of a Virgin in a humble manger, who died on a cross and then rose from the dead to set us free from sin—a mystery that science by its nature wants to dispute and that we, through faith, know to be true. Amid fascinating scientific breakthroughs and discoveries that shed light on God's awe-inspiring creation, the human race stands yearning for wonder while simultaneously seeking concrete answers to everything under the sun.

> ## The Mustard Seed
>
> [Jesus] put before them another parable: "The kingdom of heaven is like a mustard seed that someone took and sowed in his field; it is the smallest of all the seeds, but when it has grown it is the greatest of shrubs and becomes a tree, so that the birds of the air come and make nests in its branches."
> — Matthew 13:31–32

In story, we restore the mystery that leads to intimacy with God. That face—God's face—which we seek is concealed from immediate view, and in story we venture to find it and recognize it through the power of our imaginations. When we parents share story with our children, we encourage their delight in the beauty of God's creation, which remains ongoing around us, and we foster an attitude of wonder that our children can carry with them into a mature faith.

Words Reflecting the *Word*

Story is made up of words, and that image of *Word* links us intimately with God, as the prologue of John's Gospel tells us: "In the beginning was the Word, and the Word was with God, and the Word was God" (1:1). Creation was put into motion with the Word, and creation is redeemed through the Word. God uttered the word and all things came to be: "Let there be light!" and there was light. Fashioned in the image of God, we too were uttered by God; and in words we search for God, even if we are unaware of it.

Jesus is the Word of God. He is "the Alpha and the Omega" (Rev 1:8; 21:6; 22:13)—the letters that begin and end the Greek alphabet. If we imagine what it means to "be" letters, the "stuff" of which words are made, we find a metaphor in which Jesus, as the Son of God, is both the essence of words and the Word itself. Jesus is the utterance of God, and, because we are in him and he in us (Jn 14:20), he is part of every word we communicate. Through him, with him, and in him, we are involved in a dialogue with creation.

—————⸺◆⸺—————

"I've become more and more convinced that reading aloud—parents to children or vice versa—is one of the most loving and nurturing things that any family can do. Good things come from it, they really do."
— Lloyd Alexander

—————⸺◆⸺—————

Our every word, then, written or spoken, can become prayer. Jesus is at once the message and the metaphor of God. And so are we! Created in God's image and carrying God's message within us, we are a people of the Word who participate in God's ongoing creation through words. As a result, we respond wonderfully to God in story. Mysteriously, sometimes unbeknownst to us, story slips through the matrix of mere linguistic understanding and lodges in our imagination. The imagination then brings the story into our very core and transports us to an experience of God. As Anthony de Mello, S.J., wrote:

> The master gave his teaching in parables and stories, which his disciples listened to with pleasure—and occasional frustration, for they longed for something deeper. The master was unmoved. To all their objections he would say, "You have yet to understand that the shortest distance between a human being and Truth is a story."[2]

Finding Fresh Perspective

Story carries us to a place away from our immediate reality. From that fresh outlook, and assisted by our imaginations, we can examine our own little world—filled with its personalities, situations, problems, and mysteries. We can secretly and safely sort out our feelings and ideas about life and begin to interpret them. When the themes we discover in this process help us to understand Truth and Beauty, even if it is by examining their absence in evil, story has taken us to an experience of the divine.

Story offers us a different perspective on situations, attitudes, behaviors, or philosophies that we often find hard to interpret when we're deeply involved in them. Story has the power to carry us above the proverbial forest, so we can see it as an assembly of trees, or story can take us deep into that forest to examine a particularly fascinating tree. Either way, story shifts our point of view and gives us an opportunity to compare and contrast the new viewpoint to our original one. Even if a story's message differs from Christian principles, it still holds value because it offers us an opportunity to think about what we believe and how we view the world.

Scripture offers a good example of the power of story to make things clear to us in a non-threatening, objective way. In the Second Book of Samuel, we learn about King David and his adulterous affair with the beautiful Bathsheba. When she became pregnant with David's child, David had her husband, Uriah the Hittite, killed in

> **Every genuine art form in its own way is a path to the inmost reality of man and of the world. It is therefore a wholly valid approach to the realm of faith, which gives human experience its ultimate meaning. That is why the Gospel fullness of truth was bound from the beginning to stir the interest of artists, who by their very nature are alert to every "epiphany" of the inner beauty of things.**
> — *Letter of His Holiness Pope John Paul II to Artists*, 1999

battle. After a period of mourning, David married Bathsheba, who bore their son. Then, the prophet Nathan came to David with a story:

> "There were two men in a certain city, the one rich and the other poor. The rich man had very many flocks and herds; but the poor man had nothing but one little ewe lamb, which he had bought. He brought it up, and it grew up with him and with his children; it used to eat of his meager fare, and drink from his cup, and lie in his bosom, and it was like a daughter to him. Now there came a traveler to the rich man, and he was loath to take one of his own flock or herd to prepare for the wayfarer who had come to him, but he took the poor man's lamb, and prepared that for the guest who had come to him" (2 Sam 12:1–4).

David grew very angry with the man in the story and told Nathan that the man deserved death for his behavior, saying, "...He shall restore the lamb fourfold, because he did this thing, and because he had no pity" (2 Sam 12:6). Then, Nathan clued in David and told him, "You are the man!" (2 Sam 12:7). Talk about a rude awakening!

David began to see that what he had done was terribly wrong, but not until he had looked at the injustice from a fresh perspective arrived at through Nathan's story. Even though it was a story without any specific religious overtones, when David saw clearly his own sinfulness, he turned back to God and repented.

Likewise, we can be deeply confronted and challenged by story. As adults, stories such as *Sophie's Choice* by William Styron can bring us into a fictional world unlike our own, but filled with characters whose complex needs, desires, and traits remind us of ourselves or people we know. As we travel along the plot line with the characters, we come to know them intimately and start to care about what happens to them. In *Sophie's Choice*, we grow to understand Sophie so well that, like the narrator of the story, we learn to love her. When she must make her terrible decision in a Nazi concentration camp, we feel the agony along with her. Transported across time and space into the Poland of World War II, we too experience the heartrending inhumanity of Auschwitz. We ask ourselves what we would do if we were in Sophie's place. We exercise our moral imagination, and wonder whether we would despair or find hope in the aftermath.

Sophie's story moves us to compassion and conversion— without physically leaving our own reality. Even though hers is not a story about faith or religion, it is a story about morality and human dignity—subjects that are, in essence, all about God. In reflecting upon them, we open ourselves to profound spiritual experiences.

Story works on children in the same way. The only difference is thematic—kids need tales appropriate to their ages and developmental levels. *Sophie's Choice* is strictly adult fare, dealing with grown-up situations, but wonderful opportunities to study the human condition await our children across a wide panorama of artistic expressions. Such expressions can tap into their imaginations and draw forth responses that we parents can help them examine and understand in light of our faith as they begin to develop skills for making their own life choices.

Movement Through Metaphor

American author Ursula Le Guin, who has written many popular children's books, explains, "The unread story is not a story; it is little black marks on wood pulp. The reader, reading it, makes it live: a live thing, a story."

As already noted, we enter into story through our imaginations, and, as Le Guin says, allow it to come alive for us. The vehicle that accomplishes that movement of words from the page or screen into our imaginations is called *metaphor*. Metaphor is a figure of speech in which a word or phrase that literally denotes one kind of object or idea is used in place of another to suggest a likeness between them (as in drowning in sorrow, money, or debt). Metaphor enhances the true meaning of a message and makes it more understandable, while its literal meaning becomes less understandable or false.

A classic example of metaphor comes from William Shakespeare's *Julius Caesar:* "Friends, Romans, countrymen, lend me your ears." We immediately understand that Antony is not asking the crowd to yank off their ears so he can borrow them; we realize that he wants his audience to listen for a moment. Our ability to visualize and transfer this imagery in our minds is part of what makes us human, created in the image of God; our imaginations find the literal meaning and carry it from the part of our brains that processes that type of information to another area, where we can compare and contrast the implications.

⟾◈⟸

"When we read a story, we inhabit it."
— John Berger, *In Keeping a Rendezvous*

⟾◈⟸

Metaphor captures our attention in a teasingly charming and colorful way and involves us in its story. It engages us by tapping into our emotions and bringing our human person into its little game of hide-and-seek. The more striking the difference between the literal meaning and the figure of speech, the more emotionally involved we become.

Consider the emotional undertones in these two sentences:

My dentist is a butcher.

My brother-in-law Pete is a butcher.

In the first sentence, by juxtaposing two seemingly irreconcilable images (cleavers vs. dental tools, livestock vs. people), the writer creates tension that evokes an emotional response. We cringe at the thought of the dentist! However, at face value, the second sentence doesn't attach a negative association to "butcher"—and we're not sure what Pete does for a living—so the sentence causes no tension or emotional response in us.[3]

The Master Storyteller

Jesus created tension in his metaphors to call us to conversion. A master storyteller, the Lord used metaphor in ways that continue to fascinate and invite us to contemplation. In his ministry of preaching, his striking imagery piqued his followers' interest and drew many into the mystery of God's love. For example, John's Gospel records several compelling metaphors, such as, "I am the vine, you are the branches" (15:5); "I am the gate for the sheep" (10:7); "I am the good shepherd" (10:14); "I am the light of the world" (8:12).

These descriptions demand our imagination to consider their implications; for example, we have to visualize and conjure up in our minds a vine with branches, then think about how it grows, what happens when vine and branch are separated, the sameness of the branches along the vine, and their common source of nourishment and life. When we apply the idea of Jesus as Messiah to that conjured image and make a leap within our consciousness, we get to know Jesus better and understand more clearly our intended relationship with him.

Similarly, Jesus captured the Samaritan woman's imagination by saying of the well water: "Everyone who drinks of this water will be thirsty again, but those who drink of the water that I will give them will never be thirsty. The water that I will give will become in them a spring of water gushing up to eternal life" (Jn 4:13–14). The woman replied, "Sir, give me this water, so that I may never be thirsty or have to keep coming here to draw water" (Jn 4:15). She responded emotionally, with desire, because she was still thinking literally about water, a precious commodity in Palestine. Living water, or spring water, was even more valued than water collected in a cistern and stored for the long rainless months because it tasted fresh and clean.[4] The Samaritan woman didn't yet understand Jesus' metaphor—that living water represented the Holy Spirit, who comes to those who accept divine revelation.

So Jesus further engaged the woman in conversation and showed her a sign of his power by telling her about her own past. She eventually understood what he meant by living water, as we learn in this one simple phrase: "...the woman left her water jar" (Jn 4:28). She had made the leap from literal to figurative, and let the metaphor tap beneath emotion into her soul. She could then envision another way of being, a transcendent reality of communion with God. This led her to "put down" the literal meaning of water along with her jar, and set out toward her hometown as a missionary for Christ.

The Aristotelian Perspective

In the classic work **Poetics,** Aristotle suggests that an audience's level of involvement in a story is an excellent indicator of the story's universal appeal. When people get involved in story, Aristotle wrote, it causes catharsis or emotional cleansing—or, from a Christian perspective, reconciliation and redemption. The reader or viewer is not only witness to the act of redemption described for the protagonist, but also co-participant along with him or her in the healing.

Throughout the Gospels, Jesus invites us, like the Samaritan woman, to use our imaginations and become involved in his stories. In his parables, he used examples of ordinary people and events familiar to the listeners of his day to engage their imaginations and lead them to a deeper understanding of Christian truths. He didn't talk about people involved in religious practices to make his points. Instead, he used secular examples—those having to do with farming or business— to invite the men and women of his time to think about ordinary realities in terms of faith, to challenge them to enter into the Kingdom of God and the choices that lifestyle requires.

Entering into Christ's Imagery

The English word "parable" comes from the Greek word *parabole,* meaning "to place alongside." A parable, as a story that uses metaphor, compares one thing to another. It is not an example of something Jesus is trying to explain; it *is* the explanation.

Let's take a look at the parable of the talents, found in Matthew's Gospel (25:14–30):

> "For it is as if a man, going on a journey, summoned his slaves and entrusted his property to them; to one he gave

five talents, to another two, to another one, to each according to his ability. Then he went away. The one who had received the five talents went off at once and traded with them, and made five more talents. In the same way, the one who had the two talents made two more talents. But the one who had received the one talent went off and dug a hole in the ground and hid his master's money.

"After a long time the master of those slaves came and settled accounts with them. Then the one who had received the five talents came forward, bringing five more talents, saying, 'Master, you handed over to me five talents; see, I have made five more talents.' His master said to him, 'Well done, good and trustworthy slave; you have been trustworthy in a few things, I will put you in charge of many things; enter into the joy of your master.'

"And the one with the two talents also came forward, saying, 'Master, you handed over to me two talents; see, I have made two more talents.' His master said to him, 'Well done, good and trustworthy slave; you have been trustworthy in a few things, I will put you in charge of many things; enter into the joy of your master.'

"Then the one who had received the one talent also came forward, saying, 'Master, I knew that you were a harsh man, reaping where you did not sow, and gathering where you did not scatter seed; so I was afraid, and I went and hid your talent in the ground. Here you have what is yours.'

"But his master replied, 'You wicked and lazy slave! You knew, did you, that I reap where I did not sow, and gather where I did not scatter? Then you ought to have invested my money with the bankers, and on my return I would have received what was my own with interest. So take the talent from him, and give it to the one with the ten talents. For to all those who have, more will be given, and they will have an abundance; but from those who have nothing, even what they have will be taken away. As for this worthless slave, throw him into the outer darkness, where there will be weeping and gnashing of teeth.' "

In this story, Jesus uses the imagery of the master distributing talents to three servants to demonstrate that we are stewards of our gifts—and that we are held accountable for the way we use what we receive. It also represents a call to hope: the first two servants acted optimistically, investing and increasing the talents, while the third servant let fear keep him from an abundant life. The metaphor is far more powerful and easier to remember than if Jesus had said, "Christian life demands that you use your gifts to build the Kingdom of God."

By engaging our creative imaginations, Jesus invites us to work toward an understanding of what he means in his parables. We can either throw up our hands in confusion or take time to enter into the picture he created. Once we are inside the metaphor and the imagery is lodged within the secret recesses of our selves, we are completely vulnerable to the message—and it can rock us to the core, especially when it presents a way of living and thinking that is radically different from what one may be comfortable with.

⟹·◈·⟸

"Like dreaming, reading performs the prodigious task of carrying us off to other worlds."
— Victor Null, *Lost in a Book: The Psychology of Reading for Pleasure*

⟹·◈·⟸

The story of the prodigal son is one of the most familiar of all Jesus' stories. In it, we meet a father with two sons—one dutiful, the other prodigal or reckless. The dutiful son stays with his father, working their land. But the prodigal son asks for his inheritance up front, then takes off to lead "the good life" he imagines. He ends up bankrupt by a debauched life and decides to go home, hoping his father will allow him to work as a hired hand. The prodigal son returns in complete humility. To his utter dismay, his father *runs* to meet him, offers complete forgiveness, and throws a party for him! The father's behavior flies in the face of the social mores of the time. The father is as recklessly extravagant with his love as the prodigal son was with his money. And we are left with an image of the unconditional love that God the Father has for his children, and the opportunity for redemption no matter how far from grace one wanders.

But Jesus leaves us hanging at the end of this story. The dutiful son becomes incensed, understandably, when their father throws a party for his ne'er-do-well brother who has suddenly shown up, the big loser.... We are left to wonder what this "faithful son" might do in his anger and frustration. In wrestling with the possibilities, we can recognize and contemplate issues we ourselves may have with relatives and friends—and the power of story has transported us once more to a new perspective. Moreover, it has penetrated our inner world and again rocked our core.

Today's Parables

Jesus told stories about the real world and all of its glorious messiness. People used, saved, lost, and squandered money. Employers treated workers unfairly. People danced, drank wine, ate food, performed chores, had jobs, got angry, felt afraid, ignored other people's needs, held prejudice, harbored grudges, fought wars, paid taxes, made mistakes, and offered forgiveness. They were people just like us in situations not so different from our own, despite the socio-political changes that have transpired over the two millennia since Jesus' birth.

The fact that Jesus told stories about imperfect people doing everyday, ordinary things indicates that God calls us in the midst of our messiness and flawed humanity. Jesus told stories to which people could relate...and they flocked to him and begged for more. Jesus touched their hearts with stories of people like themselves, and their lives were transformed by the truth.

The Spirit continues to speak to us through story. In today's popular culture, the Spirit calls us through story contained in books, movies, and more. Many of today's storytellers continue to share the message of God's love and redeeming grace through tales of characters and circumstances we can understand. Our challenge is to see, hear, and discern the Spirit's voice amidst the noise, and to pass along that gift to our children.

A Message of Love

One good example of a piece of pop culture that bears a message of love and redemption is the story, *Shrek*, by William Steig. While the film version is markedly different from the delightful children's book, both renderings are charming and have merit.

In the movie, the lovable ogre must complete a quest to recover his swamp from the evil Lord Farquad. Shrek is used to living alone, without the complexities of relationships and the compromises they demand. Along the journey, Shrek finds friendship with a donkey and falls in love with a princess, and his simple quest becomes a challenging series of complications. In the process, Shrek learns about forgiveness and the transforming power of love.

In the book, Shrek goes in search of an ugly princess that a witch predicted he would marry. When they find one another, they fall in love. And the great lesson for all is this: Shrek loves himself, therefore he can love another. Just as the ogre delights in himself despite his repulsiveness, we are called to take pleasure in our own flawed humanity because we are children of God. And that is a message of hope we can share readily with our kids.

So, which is better: book or movie? Both are great vehicles for sharing Gospel values with our kids: love, joy, and discovering truth along our journey.

2

How Do We Engage Our Media Culture?

Today's kids are so bathed in bits that they think technology is part of the natural landscape.

— Don Tapscott,
author of *Growing Up Digital*

Scientific and technological advancements during the twentieth century have changed the way people live on Earth, particularly the way they communicate. Inventions such as satellites, fiber optics, and the Internet have made rapid communications commonplace, maybe even taken for granted. When my husband's travels took him high into the Himalayas in Nepal, we both were genuinely amazed that we could communicate by e-mail and cell phone from the other side of the planet. Funny we should have been surprised, though, having watched television emissions from the moon as kids!

As communications have become easier, the world has become smaller. Politics aside, the world, from a communications point of view, is much like the beautiful orb we witnessed with the astronauts from space: water and landforms without boundaries. As a result, opportunities exist as never before to experience stories of diverse peoples and find new avenues toward mutual understanding among members of the human family. How humanity responds to this call to hope will likely determine the story of the twenty-first century.

The question we Christian parents need to ask ourselves is whether the ease with which we can communicate has improved our ability to do so. Do we share the stories of our own lives with our children and invite them to share their stories with us? Do we take time to contemplate the stories we encounter? Are we alert to Gospel values present within story? Do we contribute views based on our Christian perspective to conversation about story, pointing to messages of redemption and love—or their absence—that we recognize? As Christians, we have a voice and point of view to share based on the Good News. And the best place to start is at home—with our children!

—————◈—————

"The real purpose of books is to trap the mind into doing its own thinking."

— Christopher Morley

—————◈—————

Engaging Our Culture As Jesus Did

Many stories, even those written by authors from other faith traditions and beliefs, speak to our Gospel values. These stories can enhance our faith life, even if they challenge us, because we emerge stronger and more certain of our beliefs after successfully grappling with them. By the same token, some stories do offer messages that are contrary to our beliefs. Although it may be tempting to try to make fortresses of our homes that keep out offending messages and allow only strictly Christian influences to enter, Jesus didn't set that example. If we are going to imitate Christ, we must engage our culture, understand it, and respond to it.

Wrestling with Story

Have you ever read a story or seen a movie that settles deep within and bothers you? Sometimes tales upset us in a way that calls us to conversion, pointing out areas where we need to reform our lives. Other times, upon reflection, we may find that a story's basic message conflicts with our beliefs or values.

When I was a teenager, William Golding's *Lord of the Flies* disturbed me, but I was too young to figure out exactly why. Now I see that the story affronts my belief in the basic goodness of people. Of course we are sinners— but we are not inherently evil. In his tale of stranded boys who descend into savagery, Golding sends the opposite message: we're all just horrible animals under a civilized veneer.

Contemplating the characters' behaviors in this novel forced me to wrestle with what Golding was saying between the lines. Ultimately, I realized that the story's theme of abject pessimism was not consistent with the Christian perspective. Yet it did me good to wrestle with it, because I emerged from the exercise more convinced of the goodness of creation, especially of human persons, created in God's own image.

Jesus shared the Good News by meeting his disciples exactly where they were and addressing them in ways that made sense to them. When he saw the brothers, Simon Peter and Andrew, fishing in the Sea of Galilee, he didn't say, "Come be construction workers for the Kingdom of God!" Instead, he met them where they were, in the midst of their nets and fish stories, and spoke in a way that appealed to them: "Come after me, and I will make you fishers of people" (cf. Mt 4:19). A delightful play on words, the call acknowledged their everyday circumstances and invited them to bring their identities and skills as fishermen to the task of evangelization, but to redirect the focus of their catch. No nets were needed for this new way of fishing, so the brothers left them behind and followed Jesus.

In a similar way, Jesus addressed the Samaritan woman at the well (cf. Jn 4:4–42). On their way through Samaria, Jesus and his disciples arrived in Sychar, where Jacob's well is located. While the disciples went into town to buy food, Jesus sat down at the well to rest. Along came a Samaritan woman, whom Jesus asked for a drink. She was shocked because Jesus was a Jew, forbidden by Jewish law to drink from cups handled by Samaritans, who were considered ritually impure. Moreover, she was shocked because he, a man, publicly spoke to her, a woman—contrary to the religious and social norms of the time.

Jesus engaged the woman in conversation and demonstrated his understanding of her Samaritan ways and beliefs: "You worship what you do not know" (Jn 4:22). Even though he knew her personal life was fraught with problems and shared that knowledge with her, Jesus afforded her dignity and spoke directly to her as a complete and intelligent person, capable of accepting the Word. When, after their conversation, he identified himself as the Messiah, she was convinced. She freely and immediately set out to share the Good News, and "many Samaritans from that city believed in him because of the woman's testimony" (Jn 4:39).

Jesus approached the woman in her everyday routine. He didn't try to communicate with her in a language she didn't understand. Instead, he met her where she was—at the well, a place shared in common with the entire community—and spoke the truth in a way that she could grasp. He captured her attention! Undoubtedly, she shared the Good News in the same way she had received it—in a language her people could grasp and in a way that made them take notice.

Drawing from Our Twenty-First Century "Well"

Just as Jesus engaged Simon Peter and Andrew and the woman at the well, we need to meet people right where they are and share that same Good News in a language they can understand. But where is our "well," our common meeting place, in the twenty-first century? And in what language will our children best recognize their encounters with Christ?

One well around which our kids are already gathered, drawing waters with other kids all over the world, is the media. And our kids are drinking heartily! In fact, media are commonplace aspects of life for this generation, the first to grow up surrounded by digital media.[5] For our kids, CD-ROMs, DVDs, broadband Internet connections, Instant Messaging, scanners, digital cameras, and cell phones are nothing to get excited about; they're part of the natural landscape. "Old" to them means VCRs—just when we parents had almost figured out how to program them! Indeed, our kids are growing up in a media culture that social scientists believe will radically change the fabric of society in this century.

Computer and Internet experiences make up a large portion of our kids' media usage today. But television remains a prime source of entertainment. According to a 1999 Nielsen Media Research report, almost every home in America (98 percent) has at least one television set, and the average household has at least two TVs. Also in 1999, a Kaiser Family Foundation study, "Kids & Media," found that 88 percent of families had more than one television set and that the average American child grows up in a home with three TVs, two VCRs, three tape players, three radios, two CD players, one video game system, and one computer.

A survey, "Media in the Home," conducted in 2000 by the Annenberg Public Policy Center at the University of Pennsylvania found that, in homes with children between the ages of 2 and 17:

- 97 percent had a VCR;
- 70 percent had a computer;
- 68 percent had video game equipment;
- 52 percent had Internet access;
- 42 percent had a newspaper subscription.

Almost half of the families with children (48 percent) had all four media staples: television, VCR or DVD, video game equipment, and computer.

The survey also investigated *where* in the home media are available to children, and found that in the bedrooms of American kids aged 2–16:

- 57 percent had a television set;
- 39 percent had video game equipment;
- 30 percent had a VCR;
- 20 percent had a computer.

While studies aren't perfect indicators, these results clearly point to television shows, movies, and websites as major influences on our families and media "wells" of our century. It is important to note that one very influential medium, books, was not assessed in this study; yet we can see from the record-breaking sales of author J. K. Rowling's *Harry Potter* series that books—to the delight of

---

From the U.S. Department of Education's National Center for Education Statistics, "Computer and Internet Use by Children and Adolescents in 2001," published in October 2003:

- **About 90 percent of children and adolescents ages 5–17 use computers, and about 59 percent use the Internet.**

- **About 75 percent of 5-year-olds use computers, and over 90 percent of teens (ages 13–17) do so.**

- **About 25 percent of 5-year-olds use the Internet, and this number rises to over 50 percent by age 9 and to at least 75 percent by ages 15–17.**

- **In contrast to the 1990s, when boys were more likely to use computers and the Internet than girls were, overall computer and Internet use rates for boys and girls are now about the same.**

http://nces.ed.gov/pubsearch/pubsinfo.asp?pubid=2004014

parents, teachers, and librarians around the world—remain an important medium for children, especially when the story captures their imaginations.

These statistics also provide plenty of food for personal thought and prayer, allowing us to examine our consciences about the way we use media. Why not take a moment to think about our families and analyze media usage in our own homes?

What would a survey say about your media consumption? How much time are you spending watching TV or on the computer?

_____

_____

_____

Are you a critical media consumer or a basic omnivore?

_____

_____

_____

Do you take time to enjoy your media? How?

_____

_____

_____

Do you take time to digest what you have consumed? How?

_____

_____

_____

Roughly speaking, how many books, magazines, television shows, movies, computer programs, electronic games, websites, and radio shows do each of your children "consume" each day at home?

_____

_____

_____

_____

How much time are they spending on the computer or in front of the TV?

_____

_____

What kinds of shows are they watching on TV?

_____

_____

_____

What kinds of websites do they visit?

_____

_____

_____

What about the time they are away from home? Do you know what kinds of media experiences they are engaging in?

_____

_____

_____

What about computer and video games your kids play? Do you know the structure and goal of these games, how a player "wins"? What messages emerge from the games played in your home?

_____

_____

_____

_____

How much time does each child spend, generally, playing these games? Compare that amount to time spent playing outdoors and time spent reading.

_____

_____

_____

How are you engaged in media with your children? Are they experiencing these communications alone?

_____

_____

_____

What do you think about your answers? Is God calling you to a new way of interacting with media?

_____

_____

_____

_____

Media are gifts of God, borne of the creative spirit God has instilled in humanity. As with all gifts entrusted to our care, we need to learn to use media within the context of our faith. Like anything wonderfully rich that is available in massive quantities, media need to be consumed in a spirit of moderation and with an eye toward the big picture—that is, we need to be attuned to how our engagement in media is affecting our journey toward communion with God and, as Christian parents, how it is affecting our mission to witness to and teach our children about the faith.

"Literature is the Thought of thinking Souls."

— Sir Walter Scott

Equipping Kids for Media Encounters

In an ideal world, professional communicators responsible for media would serve the human family in a way that generally promotes the values we hold dear. But economic and ideological pressures exerted by various segments of the information and entertainment industry lead decision-makers to choices that do not always meet the moral and ethical standards required by our Christian faith.[6] As long as sex and violence "sell," that's what we'll find in many of the movies, television shows, even computer games aimed at our kids. Program sponsors naturally want a good return on their advertising investment in the form of higher product sales. Since our children are spending a great deal of time taking in messages that are sometimes compromised by these choices, we parents have an obligation to become involved and to be ready to help them interpret these messages according to our faith. To do this, we must know what our chil-

The Principles of Media Literacy for Families

These principles can help parents develop critical thinking skills to use in approaching media at home:

- **Media offerings are created by human beings.** People make the movies, television programs, computer and video games, books, etc., that we experience. The world portrayed in media may not be like ours, so kids need to learn to tell the difference.

- **Media influence the way we think and behave**—and we need to be aware of their impact on ourselves and our kids.

- **Media use techniques to influence our thinking.** Newspapers use bold headlines to draw our attention to certain stories; movies and TV shows use sound effects and music to enhance mood and make us feel happy or sad or scared. We must train ourselves to recognize these techniques and reflect on their influence.

- **Audiences react differently to media.** Parents and kids can see, hear, or read the same thing and understand it differently, depending on maturity and perspective.

- **Media messages contain many shades of values and viewpoints.** Some will differ from Christian values and the Christian perspective. Discussions will help families clarify their own values together.

- **Media messages have social and political consequences** because they can undermine those taught by Church and family, so we need to be aware of their influence and talk about it with our kids.

- **Media are part of a profit-driven industry.** Most of the entertainment industry is in business to make money. We need to concern ourselves with the impact of that goal on our families.

"Media Concepts"; Media Beware website; *Ontario Ministry of Education (1989) Media Literacy Resources Guide: Intermediate and Senior Divisions,* www.educ.uvic.ca/Faculty/sockenden/edb363/students/MichelleDaly/media-concepts.html.

Considine, David. "Some Principles of Media Literacy," 1995; *Telemedium, The Journal of Media Literacy,* Fall 1995, Volume 41, Number 2, dren are encountering in media and, as much as possible, encounter it with them and question it through conversation.

Ironically, media reflect the very culture they help to create.[7] When we engage in media, we identify with certain things the characters experience or with how they behave. In turn, we pick up new words and phrases, ideas, images, and social cues that can become part of our own behaviors and language. These new factors influence our wants and desires, and media, in turn, cater to them and fuel them in content and advertising. As a result, we are inevitably drawn into this irony.

Certainly, we can and should protect our families to a degree within our culture. My husband and I do turn off the TV or change the channel when objectionable shows come on. We consider the appropriateness of movies we rent or go to see in theaters. We place limits

---

"There's trouble right here in River City...why, the boys are out back of the corn crib reading *Capt'n Billy's Whiz Bang.*" — a line from *The Music Man*

It is no longer enough to look with studied criticism at the content of media and ask questions about its effects.

The advent of each new technology in history has produced changes beyond the anticipation of its inventors, dreams of its investors, or hopes of those who sought to possess it. The television set was brought into the home for entertainment. In the last thirty-five years it has come to displace, or accompany, seven hours a day of activity in the average home.

On the way to that statistic, TV has changed our furniture arrangements, eating habits, language, political process, public agendas, and the nature of questions about the birds and the bees.

— Rev. George Conklin, media and computer consultant, from "Video Values: Questions for the Reflective Viewer"
www.medialit.org/reading_room/article286.html#top

on Internet surfing, but we are finding that this is much more difficult—and, apparently, we're not alone. The Annenberg "Media in the
Home" study indicates that most parents (88 percent) supervise television viewing at home, but that parental supervision drops dramatically for all other forms of media.

Meanwhile, our kids experience some media moments that
we can't possibly supervise—while visiting friends, for example.
Media influences that shape the lives of our children's peers will
influence our own children in some way. Someone at some point is
going to share with our kids "the good parts" of a trashy novel or
quote a line from a movie that we have not allowed them to see. A
well-meaning mom who doesn't share our spiritual goals is going to
show a video, not imagining any objections on our part, and introduce a new experience of violence or more to our children. In
response, we parents can try to shelter our kids, or we can work to
equip them with tools to deal with what they encounter. Having
learned from experience, I believe it is best to equip our children with
certain important media literacy education skills, especially by creating an atmosphere at home in which kids know they can bring up
their questions and deal with them with us until, one day, they are
able to sort through such issues on their own.

Focus on the Big Picture

In our efforts to provide beneficial media consumption, it's also
important to consider our kids' overall intake. An hour spent watching a documentary about sharks will offer different lessons than an
hour spent with the underwater cartoon character, SpongeBob
SquarePants, or an hour spent reading Jules Verne's *20,000 Leagues
Under the Sea*. Each form of underwater adventure through media
has its attributes. In almost all respects, SpongeBob pales in compar-
ison to the other two ways of passing moments of childhood, but the
offbeat little program offers something the other two do not: humor.
While SpongeBob might not be the right choice for every family, the
need to kick back, relax, and laugh at nonsense once in a while is uni-

versal. As it is written in Ecclesiastes, there is an appointed time for everything (3:18), which includes striking a balance in our media diet in the same way we balance our dinner plates.

Again, the temptation is great to create a defense tower rising high above the madding crowd to keep our families safe from the barrage of questionable messages they meet in media. We parents naturally want to safeguard our kids, but part of our mission as Christians is to bring the Good News to the world. Our faith doesn't call us to hide away in a narrow, insular tower. Instead, in order to follow Jesus, we must go out to meet people—our children included—where they are, in the context of today's media culture, to share this great message of love and redemption. Then, in the fluency of this culture, our children will be equipped to continue the work of building the Kingdom of God by making the Gospel message relevant to their peers.

⟹◈⟸

"A house without books is like a room without windows."
— Horace Mann

⟹◈⟸

Since part of parenting is teaching children how to manage their lives, a healthy attitude toward media usage and an ability to make choices about media are important parts of our children's upbringing. Kids need to learn how to interpret from the Christian perspective what they experience, and decide how media messages fit or don't fit into their walk with God. As parents, one of the best ways we can help our children to do this is through a mutual experience of story.

Becoming a Discerning Audience

If our children learn to become discerning and acquire critical thinking skills from a Christian perspective, they will be more ready to handle media experiences and to assess media messages within the context of what it means to be a Christian. With parental guidance and the grace of God, children will learn when to switch a channel or discount a notion that doesn't uphold Judeo-Christian values. I once overheard my oldest child telling my other children, "We can't watch this. Mom wouldn't like it." While he hadn't developed his own reasons for changing the TV channel at that point, I was glad he knew that I would object to the content. Now a teenager, he recently

Media Skills for Every Family

- **Set a good example** when consuming media. Children are watching us, so let's examine habits and set the right tone.
- **Experience media with kids** and ask questions about content. For example, talk about violence and the use of stunt actors, special effects, and editing techniques. Is the violence meant to be funny? Exciting? Is the violent character punished or rewarded? What about the victim? How would that family feel in real life?
- **Point out advertisements** on TV and radio and what they are hawking. Ask about these products: have the kids seen them, played with them, tasted them? Are the commercials' claims true?
- **Teach kids the purpose** of advertising: to pay for programming.
- **Ask kids what they think** about what they are experiencing. They have a different perspective than you.
- **Point out different values** expressed in media offerings. Tell kids what you like and don't like and why. Ask them what they like. Talk about it!
- **Find positive media experiences** to share, such as books, movies, and television programs that you can comment on positively.

brought up a couple of subjects he found disturbing while reading Oscar Wilde's *The Picture of Dorian Gray,* indicating to me that he has developed an awareness of content and that he understands basic Christian principles and can compare them to messages he encounters in media.

The Church encourages parents to set an example of media discernment. In *Ethics in Communication,* the Pontifical Council for Social Communications teaches:

> For their children's sake, as well as their own, parents must learn and practice the skills of discerning viewers and listeners and readers, acting as models of prudent use of media in the home. According to their age and circumstances, children and young people should be open to formation regarding media, resisting the easy path of uncritical passivity, peer pressure, and commercial exploitation. Families—parents and children together—will find it helpful to come together in groups to study and discuss the problems and opportunities created by social communication.[8]

A discerning outlook, which we parents convey to our children, will become the primary piece of equipment they need in a media culture toolbox. If we can teach them to approach media from the Christian perspective—that is, the point of view from which we *as Christians* view the world—they will be able to use this perspective to filter what they encounter in the media and elsewhere.

3

The Christian Perspective

The Gospel does not lead to the impoverishment or
extinction of those things which every individual, people, and nation and every culture throughout history
recognizes and brings into being as goodness, truth,
and beauty.

— Pope John Paul II

Having expressed the need to approach media with a discerning
eye, focused with the Christian perspective, it's important to explore
what that means and what the Church teaches us about it. And the
best place to begin is in the beginning, when God created the heav-
ens and the Earth. In the wonderful creation story in the first chapter
of Genesis, we learn that God created light, water, plants, day and
night, fish and fowl, cattle and wild animals. When "God saw how
good it was" (1:25), God created human beings, saying, "Let us make
man in our image, after our likeness" (1:26). God chose to share the
love that *is* God by creating us. Created from love and for love, we

were made to be like God and to share in God's ongoing creation. We were made to be creative as God is creative!

God Found It Very Good

Scripture goes on to tell us that "God looked at everything he had made, and he found it very good" (1:31). God delighted in humanity and in the world created for us. Unfortunately, humans brought sin into the picture and created avenues for corrupting that creation, and sin and its effects are with us still. Nevertheless, God intended that we enjoy what we've been given. Redeemed in Christ, we are free to recognize and avoid evil present in the world, but also to focus our attention on the blessings we find here. God wants us to delight in our humanity and carry this hopeful spirit throughout the world.

⟫◆⟪

"The purifying, healing influence of literature, the dissipating of passions by knowledge and the written word, literature as the path to understanding, forgiveness, and love, the redeeming might of the word, the literary spirit as the noblest manifestation of the spirit of man, the writer as perfected type, as saint."

— Thomas Mann, *The Magic Mountain*

⟫◆⟪

An undue focus on evil creates negativity that leads to anxiety and fear. Our attention, then, must be on God as we look for the truth and beauty present in creation. While Jesus recognized and addressed evil and sin, he also enjoyed living in his culture and relished the beauty of humanity. He went to weddings, had dinner with people, even hung around with seedy types like prostitutes and tax collectors, bringing the same message of love wherever he went, to everyone he met. He wasn't afraid of evil because he knew he had dominion over it. And he won that same freedom for us through his life, death, and resurrection.

Perspective and Worldview

In the way of Jesus, we are called to see the world from this Christian perspective. We already know what *Christian* means. *Perspective,* or point of view, is the way we look at things. But that perspective is colored by our *worldview*—how we see the world and all that happens within it. Each of us has a unique worldview that has been affected by the location of our homes, by our family relationships, cultural traditions, hobbies, interests, education, friends, and by the places and faces we have encountered on our journeys. The knowledge we glean through various experiences helps mold and detail our own particular way of looking at the world and understanding the stories we encounter.

———◈———

"Storytelling with children is a vehicle through which God works. It teaches children to listen to the spirit. It trains the heart to be open."

— Jane Reehorst, BVM

———◈———

As an illustration of *worldview*, imagine that an event occurs in Thailand, and three people together watch a television news report about it in the United States. One person grew up in Thailand, one visited Bangkok for three days long ago, and one has never left his hometown but learned about Thailand from the movie version of *The King and I,* the famous Rodgers and Hammerstein musical about a Thai king who falls in love with an English governess—a story many Thai people find highly offensive because they believe their king is portrayed as a buffoon. Even though all three television viewers in this scenario hear the same words and see the same images in the news report about Thailand, each perceives the news event differently because of his or her own personal worldview. The unique filter each uses to sift through the story will impact the way each person understands that news.

Blessed Are the Pure in Heart

As Christians, we are called to a develop a worldview with loving lenses, colored by the hopefulness of the Christian perspective that springs from the belief that God loves us and wants only the best for us. In the Beatitudes, found in Matthew's Gospel in Jesus' Sermon on the Mount, Jesus calls this perspective on creation being "pure in heart." Those who have such a way of looking at things will receive the ultimate Christian "perspective": they shall see God!

The Beatitudes form the central message of Jesus' teaching because they reveal the secret of happiness. Saints and scholars throughout Christian history have contemplated the simple yet profound message that articulates the goal of human existence: finding happiness in God's love. Most of us are still working on becoming pure in heart, trying to get in sync with God's will, attuning mind and

The Beatitudes

The eight Beatitudes, Jesus' teachings to his disciples, are from the Gospel of St. Matthew (5:3–10), and, along with the Ten Commandments, are regarded as essential guidelines for Christian living.

Blessed are the poor in spirit, for theirs is the kingdom of heaven.

Blessed are those who mourn, for they will be comforted.

Blessed are the meek, for they will inherit the earth.

Blessed are those who hunger and thirst for righteousness, for they will be filled.

Blessed are the merciful, for they will receive mercy.

Blessed are the pure in heart, for they will see God.

Blessed are the peacemakers, for they will be called children of God.

Blessed are those who are persecuted for righteousness' sake, for theirs is the kingdom of heaven.

spirit to the call to holiness. Meanwhile, we enjoy moments of grace that allow us to see "according to God."[9] In such moments, we can see God in our neighbor and ourselves and recognize God in our midst. These glimpses of heaven, when we see the divine in our everyday lives, encourage us with gifts of hope and joy, strengthen our faith, and help us to open those eyes of love toward a worldview consistent with Christian values.

When we recognize and believe that God loves us, we can see truth and beauty all around us, even though evil exists. I once met a missionary stationed in Haiti who related the powerful Christian perspective of the people he lived among. While many in his care live in misery, malnourished and ravaged with disease, not a single suicide has ever been documented in the community because, as he says, the people believe God has a better place waiting for them, "so they have a thousand reasons for getting up each morning and facing the day. They recognize that in spite of their immediate misery, they can still enjoy the splendor of a Caribbean sunset and hear children laughing at play. They see beauty in their lives and deem it worth remembering. And it works the same way for us all. Even though things look gloomy sometimes, we know that some-where else a symphony is being created, and God's love remains."

Aligning Our Worldview

Perhaps it's time to ask ourselves whether our worldview is consis-tent with that of the Church. As Catholic Christians, we are blessed to have not only Sacred Scripture, but also the rich resources of eccle-sial writings to help us in our discernment.

Vatican II's Pastoral Constitution on the Church in the Modern World, *Gaudium et Spes,* for example, offers a good assess-ment of the Church's worldview to which we can compare our own. The world, according to the Council's teaching, means "the entire human family considered in the context of all realities; the world which is the theater of human history and which bears the marks of humanity's struggles, its defeats, and its victories; the world which Christians believe has been created and is sustained by the

A Spirituality for Communications

If we tell the story of Jesus [...] through the arts, music, and the social means of communications, we become apostles for our time and utilize the means that human ingenuity has developed for the good of the Gospel.

When media are used to corrupt and seduce the human spirit, it is a betrayal of human genius and an instrument of degradation. When the media are used to tell the story of Jesus, however, the human spirit is uplifted. The person who is dedicated to truth in media will reach those who are open to the truth and will show those willing to learn how to live lives of heroic love.

— Fr. Jeffrey Mickler, SSP, Ph.D., from "A Spirituality for Communications," *The Pauline Cooperator,* Vol. IV, No. 1.

Creator's love, a world enslaved by sin but liberated by the crucified and resurrected Christ in order to defeat evil, and destined, according to the divine plan, to be transformed and to reach its fulfillment."[10]

What a hopeful, loving, wonderfully optimistic way of looking at the world! The worldview of the Church, then, is a wide-angle lens that encompasses everyone in every culture and way of life and filters the scene through the eyes of love—as our Creator would see it. All that we do, all that we create is part of our movement toward transformation and fulfillment. God is at work in the world! And God is communicating with us through the world.

Pope John Paul II uses this point from *Gaudium et Spes* to explain a Christian worldview in his book, *Crossing the Threshold of Hope:*

> For Christians, the world is God's creation, redeemed by Christ. It is in the world that man meets God. Therefore, he does not need to attain such an absolute detachment in order to find himself in the mystery of his deepest self. For Christianity, it does

not make sense to speak of the world as a "radical" evil, since at the beginning of the world we find God the Creator who loves his creation, a God who "gave his only son so that everyone who believes in him might not perish but might have eternal life" (Jn 3:16).[11]

Knowing that in the world they will find God, Christians see the world as a field ripe with opportunities for building the Kingdom. "The Church is always looking toward the future," writes John Paul II. "She constantly goes out to meet new generations."[12] These new generations, our children's generation, are actively engaged in today's culture, and the Church calls us all to meet them there, to bring the Church's faith-based, hope-filled, loving worldview into society, using media as a tool to connect with others.

A Sense of Adventure

The Church is asking us to bring a sense of adventure to our interactions with media culture. In an address to the Pontifical Council on Social Communications, Pope John Paul II said:

> If the Church holds back from culture, the Gospel itself falls silent. Therefore, we must be fearless in crossing the cultural threshold of the communications and information revolution taking place. Like the new frontiers of other times, this one too is full of the interplay of danger and promise, and not without the sense of adventure which marked other great periods of change. For the Church, the adventure is to bring the truth of Christ to bear upon this new world, with all its promise and all its searching and questioning. This will especially involve the promotion of a genuinely human ethic which can build communion rather than enmity between peoples.[13]

We are called to behave like missionaries, venturing into parts unknown to bring the message of salvation. And these new frontiers are closer than our own backyards; they are in our very homes! Our kids are already out there in uncharted territory, surfing the Internet, enjoying entertainment with a mix of influences and messages, communicating in ways we sometimes don't even understand. Out there—and yet right under our noses. While we can learn about their world and participate in new communications, we may feel unable to catch up with our kids on their turf, but we can effectively share the Gospel with them in our homes, and build connections between the faith and media culture through the power of story. Our adventures in fictional worlds will hone tools of discernment that our kids can use in their new frontiers to keep the Gospel alive. The call is urgent because the alternative is unacceptable from a believer's perspective; therefore the Church is telling us to become proactive and find ways to make the Good News relevant. I believe that sharing story is an effective way to carry out our baptismal commitment.

The Church Encourages Media Enjoyment

Sharing story in the variety of media available in today's culture is completely in line with Church teaching. The Church encourages media enjoyment, saying media "offer people access to literature, drama, music, and art otherwise unavailable to them, and so promote human development in respect to knowledge and wisdom and beauty. We speak not only of presentations of classic works and the fruits of scholarship, but also of wholesome *popular entertainment* and useful information that draw families together, help people solve everyday problems, raise the spirits of the sick, shut-ins, and the elderly, and *relieve the tedium of life.* "[14]

The Church is not only saying it is fine to enjoy movies and books in today's world. The Church is saying *to find* good movies and books to enjoy—*and to enjoy them!* The Church's worldview promotes a stress-free attitude toward enjoying works of art, the fruits of our culture, and learning to recognize the aesthetic, educational, moral, and ethical aspects of these works and how they compare to our Christian faith. We bring the Word of God to our culture, and we hear that Word through expressions of popular culture. Part of God's ongoing creation is an ongoing dialogue through the Holy Spirit!

As poet, playwright, writer, and actor, Pope John Paul II offers particular insight into the value of enjoying today's artistic expression in our walk with Christ. In his *Letter to Artists,* he asks us to allay fears about experiencing culture, even when content is upsetting: "As fruit of an imagination which rises about the everyday, art is by its nature a kind of appeal to mystery. Even when they explore the darkest depths of the soul or the most unsettling aspects of evil, artists give voice in a way to the universal desire for redemption" (no. 10).

Virtues for the Internet

The following list of virtues for the Internet is adapted from *The Church and Internet,* by the Pontifical Council for Social Communications, February 22, 2002:

- **Prudence** is necessary in order to see the implications—the potential for good and evil—in this new medium and to respond creatively to its challenges and opportunities.

- **Justice** is needed, especially to close the digital divide, the gap between the information-rich and the information-poor in today's world. Justice requires a commitment to the international common good, no less than the "globalization of solidarity."

- **Fortitude,** courage, is necessary to stand up for truth in the face of religious and moral relativism, for altruism and generosity in the face of individualistic consumerism, for decency in the face of sensuality and sin.

- **Temperance** is needed—a self-disciplined approach to this remarkable technological instrument, the Internet, so that we use it wisely and only for good.

"I see a far more intimate and
immediate connection between the true life of
Christ and the true life of the artist."
— Oscar Wilde, *De Profundis*

With a healthy dose of informed prudence, common sense, and trust in God, we can move forward into our culture with confidence that "all things work together for good for those who love God" (Rom 8:28). Even when we encounter material that challenges our beliefs or explores the pain of human living, we can use it to help

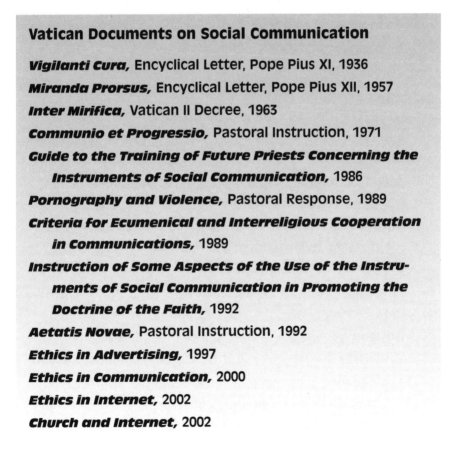

Vatican Documents on Social Communication

Vigilanti Cura, Encyclical Letter, Pope Pius XI, 1936

Miranda Prorsus, Encyclical Letter, Pope Pius XII, 1957

Inter Mirifica, Vatican II Decree, 1963

Communio et Progressio, Pastoral Instruction, 1971

Guide to the Training of Future Priests Concerning the Instruments of Social Communication, 1986

Pornography and Violence, Pastoral Response, 1989

Criteria for Ecumenical and Interreligious Cooperation in Communications, 1989

Instruction of Some Aspects of the Use of the Instruments of Social Communication in Promoting the Doctrine of the Faith, 1992

Aetatis Novae, Pastoral Instruction, 1992

Ethics in Advertising, 1997

Ethics in Communication, 2000

Ethics in Internet, 2002

Church and Internet, 2002

us consider where we stand with God and where we need to grow. Or in material that explores the dark side of humanity, we can recognize within ourselves a desire to move from sin into the loving arms of God. With developed critical thinking skills and tools for evaluating what we encounter, we can open our spiritual lives to a stimulating and refreshing change of pace.

We are challenged to trust in Jesus, who said, "Hear me, all of you, and understand: nothing that enters one from outside can defile that person, but the things that come out from within are what defile" (Mk 7:14–16). Stories will not harm us if kept in proper perspective—the Christian perspective. In fact, many stories will help us on our journey and lead to a lovely experience of God that can strengthen our faith. And the Church itself is inviting us to come to these waters, here at the well, and join with the whole human family for a refreshing drink.

PART 2

...With Kids

4

A Child's Growing Need for Wonder

If a child is to keep alive his inborn sense of wonder,
he needs the companionship of at least one adult
who can share it, rediscovering with him the joy,
excitement, and mystery of the world we live in.
— Rachel Carson, author of *A Sense of Wonder* and *The Sea Around Us*

We parents know, deep in our hearts, that children need stories. We know, by some gift of parental instinct, that cuddling with a child to share a special book or to watch a movie or television program together is right and good. When we take that time to share story with our families, and go where it leads us in conversation, we feel affirmation from God that we are spending our time wisely and well.

Our way of worship as Catholic Christians underscores this conviction. Just look at the two components of our Eucharistic liturgy: we share stories from Sacred Scripture, and we break bread together around the table of the Lord. Our Church demonstrates in worship that story is an essential part of our Christian life. Within our individual families, story becomes a sacrament of the domestic church.

Parents today also enjoy the affirmation of secular experts, who have found that story is not only important but also necessary in the life of a healthy child. Certain well-known theories of child development, constructed during the twentieth century, give us insight into the inner lives of our children by describing the normal metamorphosis over a child's years of maturation. These dramatic changes from birth to adolescence affect a child's experience of story and the meanings they glean from a tale. It also helps parents to understand what sort of material is appropriate in various developmental stages. For those of us interested in nourishing a child's faith life through imagination, these theories are well worth examining before we delve into the practicalities of sharing story with kids.

Understanding Our Children's Development

Piaget and Kohlberg

Swiss psychologist Jean Piaget spent a lifetime studying the moral lives of children and how knowledge develops in the human organism. With a background in both biology and philosophy, he called the basic framework of his studies "genetic epistemology." He concluded that humans experi-

---

Nurturing Your Toddler's Emergent Literacy

- **Read aloud only as long as your toddler is willing to listen.**
- **Point to things in picture books and name them. As children learn to talk, ask them to "point and say."**
- **Set aside at least one regularly scheduled time each day for reading.**
- **Take toddlers to the library or bookstore for story hour.**
- **Recite nursery rhymes and sing songs. Rhymes help develop a young child's ear for language.**

— Adapted from *Reading Is Fundamental, Inc.*, www.rif.org/parents

ence patterns of physical or mental action that underlie intelligent behavior. These patterns, or "cognitive structures," correspond to normal stages in human growth and development. Piaget believed that these cognitive structures change as humans adapt to their environment. And he maintained that all people move through four main stages of cognitive development in life, which he termed *sensorimotor, preoperational, concrete operational,* and *formal operational.* Within each of these stages, Piaget identified dozens of distinct substructures, such as concepts of time, spatial relationships, movement, and numbers. Because Piaget's work has profoundly affected the understanding of child development, we'll explore his "four stages" concept in some detail.

Sensorimotor Stage

The sensorimotor stage is pre-verbal, before children can communicate in words; when knowledge is gained through touching, smelling, seeing, hearing, and tasting the people and things around them. A book presented to a very young child is tasted, chewed, sniffed, and generally thrown around—until the child learns that books carry other wonders to enjoy, such as pictures to see or stories to hear.

When my daughter Diana was small, she loved a book called *Pat the Bunny* by Dorothy Kunhardt. As I read to her, Diana could see the pictures *and* feel the fuzzy fake fur included in the book. Sometimes we never made it past the fuzziness, because Diana wanted to keep on patting the bunny, but that was fine. Our purpose was to learn to enjoy stories together...and we were just at the beginning of our journey!

At the same time, we were building a relationship with one another. While parents and kids can't share faith verbally during this stage, we can do a lot to lay the foundation for a child's developing faith by encouraging trust, sharing time and laughter, and allowing some exploration and imagination when we play together. Since our faith tradition includes word and sacrament—tangible manifestations of our encounter with God—these early encounters with story that are accompanied by tangible moments of sharing together will provide the first connection between faith and life. They will help establish in our kids an attitude of listening and a delight in the transcendent moments afforded by story. Later, it is listening and delight that will nourish the gift of faith.

Pre-Operational Stage

Following the sensorimotor stage, Piaget theorized that children enter a pre-operational stage in which they begin to use language, thought, and symbols. In this stage, children believe that all stories are true. Talking animals? No problem, even though such creatures are never encountered in children's everyday living. If they can imagine it, it is true for them.

When my oldest, Patrick, was about three years old, my husband was deployed on a Navy ship far from home. One night, at the end of *Snow White and the Seven Dwarfs,* Patrick, who was probably thinking about his dad, asked, "Do you think the dwarfs miss Snow White? She left them, and they love her." Without thinking, I committed a grievous parental error and absently replied, "Well, Snow White isn't real, honey."

Confusion momentarily crossed Patrick's little face—followed by vehement denial. "She is *so* real, Mama!" he argued while, at the same time, a forthright friend who was visiting murmured to me, "What are you trying to do? Ruin his childhood?"

"Oh, I don't know what I was thinking!" I told them both, scrambling for a better response. "You know, I'll bet they *do* miss her—terribly! And I'll bet *she* misses *them*, too. Don't you think so?"

Patrick was no worse for the wear. Because he was pre-operational in Piaget's lexicon, he accepted fiction as reality and never really doubted the characters' existence. As a result, my appalling comment had fallen upon deaf ears. We were able to rebound with a nice discussion (based on an assumption that Snow White exists!) in which Patrick revealed his longing to see his dad and his hope that Dad missed him in return—just like the scenario he imagined for the story characters.

My youngest, Peter, has never heard me say fictional characters are not real, because Patrick's reaction reminded me that characters we get to know in fiction *are* real. They exist in our imagination and become part of our "reality"—even when we've moved beyond the pre-operational stage. So, when Peter put a knitted glove in the backyard one evening "for the animals to live in," I blithely went along, knowing that the idea sprang from a story we had shared—a Ukrainian folk tale called *The Mitten*, about a menagerie that moves into a little boy's lost mitten. (Author Jan Brett created a

Building Literacy Skills

With Your Preschooler:

- Encourage your child to join in while you read. Pause to let him or her fill in a rhyming word or repeating line.
- Ask open-ended questions, such as, "What do you think is going to happen next?" or "Why do you think she did that?"
- Move your finger under the words as you read aloud. This helps preschoolers connect printed words to spoken words.

With Your Beginning Reader (Grades K–2):

- Let your child gradually share some of the reading aloud. You read a sentence, paragraph, or page, then it's your child's turn. Take over if your beginner seems tired or discouraged to ensure that reading is always fun, not hard work.
- If your child can't sound out a word, suggest skipping it, reading the rest of the sentence, and deciding what word would make sense.
- Leave notes on the refrigerator or in a lunch bag for your child to discover and read.
- Take your new reader to the library to sign up for his or her own library card.

— Adapted from *Reading Is Fundamental, Inc.*, www.rif.org/parents

beautifully illustrated version of the story that we like to read, but an older, slightly different version by Alvin Tresselt remains enjoyable as well.)

Peter, during this pre-operational stage, delighted in the silliness and surprise of so many animals, each one larger than the next, cramming themselves into a little boy's mitten. Each time he thought a bigger animal would eat the rest, that animal peaceably got into the mitten, and the grandmother's sturdy stitches stretched to allow it in. In the end, the littlest thing caused them to break apart: a mouse made the bear sneeze, and all of the animals went flying!

Since Peter is a hopeful person, I believe this story, which he still enjoys, appeals to his anticipation and belief that wonderful, marvelous things are possible. The morning after he left his own glove in our yard, he expected to find animals in it. When he found none, he concluded that they had been there, "but had to go home a minute ago." I didn't dare dispute it, for a sense of wonder and a belief in things that elude the eye are building blocks of our faith life, precious attributes to be cherished and encouraged. As Jesus said after his encounter with a doubting Thomas, "Blessed are those who have not seen and yet have come to believe" (Jn 20:29).

Children in the pre-operational stage like to hear stories about themselves and their own world, just as they love nonsense, like Mother Goose nursery rhymes or Jack Pretlusky poetry. Peter identifies with the hopefulness and optimism of *The Mitten's* main character, and he enjoys the absurdity of various animals squeezing together in a glove. Both draw him into the story. Additionally, the story sparks his desire for wondrous things to occur. When the little boy asks his grandmother to knit him a white mitten, she warns him that white mittens are difficult to find in the snow. Still, he wants white. He discovers that his Baba is right: white *is* difficult to find in snow! But miracles happen. A surprising bit of grace reunites the boy with his mitten, larger now and stretched out, but still in tact because of the grandmother's skillful knitting.

"I wonder how that mitten stretched so far!" we might say to a child in the pre-operational stage—and then listen to the reply. Answers to comments such as these can astonish us with their creativity, insightfulness, and innocent trust in the wonder of creation. As parents, we are called to encourage these things in our children so that they will be able to trust in God and open themselves later to respond to the gift of faith.

Entwined in *The Mitten* is a marvelous metaphor that may appeal to children on a deeper level, although it is unlikely that they will grasp it consciously at this stage. We parents can enjoy it and use it as a springboard to prayer at the same time that we begin to plant in our children the seed that deeper meanings await us in story.

The mitten begins as a pure white, exquisitely crafted article of clothing for a little boy who, predictably, loses it. Out in the drifts of snow, the mitten, although fashioned to protect and warm a small hand, becomes shelter for all sorts of creatures who stretch it and stretch it and stretch it still more. No matter how far its yarns extend, the mitten remains whole, giving warmth and togetherness to a wild and wooly menagerie. As each animal seeks the hospitality of the mitten, we think, "Surely, it can't handle anymore. It's going to burst!" But the mitten surprises us and lets them in. In the end, the mitten is changed by the numerous and unexpected creatures who found refuge within it. And it gives the grandmother and the boy pause to wonder, to use their imaginations to contemplate the mitten's transformation.

I believe that the mitten expanded to mythic proportions because of the grandmother's love. Her true and steadfast love for the little boy certainly found its way into every stitch. And that love made the mitten able to take on much more than anyone could expect. It became miraculous.

Another splendid storyteller, Margaret Wise Brown, created several wonderful books for children in this stage of development. My children never seemed to get enough of *Goodnight Moon,* the story of a bedtime ritual in which a sleepy little bunny says goodnight to everything in his great green room. Their favorite page was the blank one midway through the story that simply said, "Goodnight, nobody!" In our home, Brown's whimsy was guaranteed to elicit peals of laughter and fervent begging, "Do it again, do it again!" It was delightful and perpetually surprising to encounter the blank page, but something was also believable about saying goodnight to an unseen entity...for the children instinctively suspected that Someone *was* there, perhaps because we said bedtime prayers to God, whom we cannot see. Besides being great fun, Brown's quirky insertion appealed to the children's sense of awe and recognition of mystery in our lives.

⟐

**"Each reader derives his own meaning
from a work through direct participation;
another's explanation remains a hazy outline until
the images become clear firsthand."**
— Bernice Cullinan, author, professor of children's literature

⟐

In another Brown story, *Home for a Bunny,* a rabbit looks high and low for a woodland home, until, at last, he finds a place and another bunny to make his home with. God has a place and people for each of us, too, and we need to journey until we find them. We could mention to our children how grateful we are that God sent them to our homes and our families—and wait to see what kind of response that suggestion draws out. Also, we could mention that God prepared a special place for us where God also sent friends and loved ones for us to cherish and enjoy.

Recently, I came across a wonderful resource written for Jewish parents. In *Teaching Your Children About God,* Rabbi David

Wolpe asserts that nothing is more important to a child than feeling loved and understood. This gift, called *Bitachon* in Hebrew, is "a sense of confidence that runs deep inside because it flows from above."[15] Trust, teaches the rabbi, is a priceless legacy that parents give their children, a gift that offers them security in a perplexing world. In return, he says, parents learn through their children to become more trusted and, maybe, more trusting.

Basic trust begins in the sensorimotor stage of development, and it grows stronger in the pre-operational stage. A child's sense of story also develops in the pre-operational stage. In sharing story with our kids, we can nurture their spirituality by exploring the trust we have in others, in the order of things, and in God's love for us as we talk about story characters and their situations. Our exploration may remain on the level of bunnies and bears and mittens for a long while, but good stories that offer life-giving messages and affirmation will set the stage for a fulfilling faith life in the future.

Concrete Operational

When children become able to distinguish between reality and fiction in story, they have entered a stage that Piaget called concrete operational.

I remember how, as a small child of five or six, I believed that L. Frank Baum's story about Dorothy in *The Wizard of Oz* had really happened. I fully expected to get swept up like Dorothy in a tornado and have my own Glenda present me with ruby slippers—until my sudden epiphany several years later. While enjoying the movie's annual network broadcast on my Uncle Robert's color TV (the transition from dull Kansas to Technicolor *Oz* was more enthralling there than on our own rabbit-eared, black-and-white Zenith), I remember the exact moment when I began to realize that Dorothy could have dreamed the whole Yellow Brick Road thing. *Dreamed it!*

My mother gave me a wonderful gift in response to my dismay. When I asked her if Dorothy's journey to Oz was a dream or if she "really went there," Mama replied, "Well, we don't know, do we? It could have been a dream, but maybe it wasn't."

Building Literacy Skills with Your Developing Reader (Grades 2–3):

- When your children read aloud, help them catch and correct their own mistakes by asking guiding questions. For example, you might ask, "Does that word really make sense here? What letter does it start with? What do you think the word could be?"
- Talk about the books you read together and about the books your children are reading on their own.
- Don't stop reading aloud! Developing readers can read simple chapter books alone, but they still need you to help read the kinds of books that will challenge their thinking and build their vocabularies.
- Suggest that your child read to a younger brother, sister, or neighbor. It will be good practice, a chance to show off skills, and an inspiration for the younger listener.

— Adapted from *Reading Is Fundamental, Inc.,* www.rif.org/parents

Even though my mother could have told me that Oz wasn't real, and at that age I might have simply accepted it, instead she granted my imagination full permission to soar. At the same time, she planted a seed containing the notion that stories can have layers of meaning and are well worth mulling over because she had invited me to spend time examining the possibilities within this story. Now, Mama won't admit to any particular genius in this regard, but her open-ended response about Dorothy was both brilliant and exemplary. Perhaps, as she suggests today, she didn't know what to say at the end of a long day. But she never discouraged me from asking questions or tossing around ideas about story.

Today, I can see that my Dorothy epiphany was precisely about layers of meaning and my awakening ability to discern them. I still thought Dorothy was real, but not her experience of Oz. This is typical of kids who are emerging from a pre-operational stage and moving into a concrete operational stage, where they usually remain for about four years. It is important to note that reactions to story can be quite different at the beginning of this stage than they are at the end, and that all the stages tend to overlap one another, with children regressing periodically before fully advancing in these stages.

In the concrete operational stage, children with a rich experience of story develop expectations about them and become able to predict endings.[16] A certain nine-year-old in our house often blurts out the endings of books, once he has figured them out, and loses interest in reading further. "Blah, blah, blah," he'll say about such stories. A tough critic he is, to be sure, but he has experienced a lot of story, so his standards are getting higher as his facility for concrete operations increases. If I am familiar with the story and know that something delightful, intriguing, or surprising awaits him, I encourage him to continue. And sometimes it works!

———•◦•———

I remember well one evening, when I was about seven, talking to my mother about the story of Noah's Ark, from Genesis 5–9. When I suggested that we must be related to Noah, since everyone else was wiped out by the Great Flood, she entertained the notion and asked me a few more questions—how did I think Noah felt losing his friends; what it must have been like on the ark with the smells and noises of all of those animals; how Noah and his family felt when the dove returned with the olive branch; how they felt when they saw the rainbow. Mama wasn't quick to supply answers, but let me think aloud and encouraged me by listening and probing. I consider this her greatest gift to me because it fostered a lifelong enjoyment of story and an attitude of looking deeper into story and finding nuggets of wisdom there. By including Bible stories with well-written children's literature, she helped me develop an aesthetic appreciation for story, including that which is contained in our sacred texts.

A wonderful English professor once told me that teachers "beat the poetry out of their students" in elementary language arts curricula by focusing on reason and information at the expense of figurative language and imagination. Reading comprehension in the early grades is determined by responding to questions aimed at literal meanings: Where did Charlotte spin her web? What did Mary do in the secret garden? How did Lucy get into Narnia?

While many experts suggest that children do not recognize metaphor and symbolism in the concrete operational stage, perhaps it is simply that they aren't asked the right questions.[17] Often, kids are not confronted with queries that seek out imaginative connections and deeper meanings. *Where* Charlotte spun her web, for example, is much less important to a child's sense of story and growing faith than *why* and *how* she did it. Those lines of questioning can lead to discussions about God and miracles, for a spider composing and spinning words in her web is something miraculous indeed. With practice, a child in the concrete operational stage *can* begin to tap into that richness, and we parents can augment our child's experience of story if we learn to draw out deeper meanings in the way we ask our questions. (We'll delve into some practical ways to do this in chapter six.)

Formal Operational

By the pre-teen years, around age eleven or so (nowadays called the "tweens"), most kids can reason, consider alternatives, deal with abstract concepts, and accept ambiguity in story. That is, they have entered the formal operational stage of development. At this stage, according to Piaget's theory, children can enjoy metaphor as well as complications and dilemmas within story. As they develop, kids glean more and more insights into the moral complexities of the story. They look for stories that validate their own experiences of life, their feelings that they are on their own.[18] Children also begin to understand mortality at this age. As a result, stories of orphans and lost children hold tremendous appeal as kids approach and enter the formal operational stage.

One evening, I began reading *Midnight for Charlie Bone* with my son Peter. The book, by British author Jenny Nimmo, is the first in a series about Charlie Bone, who, like Harry Potter, finds himself in a

Building Literacy Skills with Your Independent Reader (ages 9–12):

- Continue reading aloud books that challenge your child's listening vocabulary and thinking skills. Reading books that are above your child's reading level will help him or her grow as a reader.
- Encourage your child's independent reading by providing a steady flow of books and conversation about them.
- Help a child who seems to have lost interest in reading find the time to read at home for pleasure. Make sure that her life hasn't become overly scheduled.
- Help your child find more reasons to write. Enlist him in taking messages, making the shopping list, writing letters, and answering email.

— Adapted from *Reading Is Fundamental, Inc.,,* www.rif.org/parents

special school because of his mysterious gifts. Since Peter is bright, a librarian had suggested the series because other young readers seemed to like it, even though at eight, Peter was decidedly and appropriately "concrete operational," rather than "formal operational." I went against my gut instinct that this story wouldn't work for Peter and started reading it with him. By page 27, I wished I had followed my intuition. "Oh, no," Peter complained. "Why do so many 'chapter books' have kids with dead parents?"

Orphans and lost children *didn't* appeal to Peter—at least not in this stage of development. While Peter could handle the vocabulary and story line of books appropriate for older children, the theme was somewhat over his head, or at least out of his interest range then. (After *Charlie Bone,* I tried to remember "concrete operational" when looking for books for the two of us to read!)

Frankly, Peter's experience makes a great point about a good deal of literature (and movies, for that matter!) created for tweens and teens in the formal operational stage: many of these stories involve death and dying. And even though these recurrent themes can appeal to a formal operational child and provide much food for thought and conversation, parents may want to attempt to balance their child's reading materials by offering, at least once in a while, humorous and heartwarming stories that don't involve overly dark story lines.

One example of a good *and* humorous book is Norton Juster's charming masterpiece, *The Phantom Tollbooth.* This delightful adventure, in which a bored boy is transformed into a celebrant of life's richness and variety, is especially wonderful for kids aged eleven and up because they can appreciate and enjoy interesting, figurative language. Far from uninspiring silliness, this laugh-out-loud story offers a clever metaphor of our journey through life, a journey fraught with mistakes and learning experiences, as well as invitations to marvel at creation and all that happens within it. The novel's nuances of meaning and nuggets of wisdom remind all of us of our call to be childlike and to enjoy God's wondrous creation.

The story centers on the journey of Milo, a little boy who receives a toy tollbooth in the mail and drives through it in his electric car to the Lands Beyond, a Wonderland-Oz-type of place filled with curious, tongue-in-cheek characters and scenes—the Island of Conclusions, for example: to get there, one must "jump."

The Reluctant Teen Reader

Web resources to explore:

Young Adult Library Services Association, an American Library Association website: http://www.ala.org/yalsa

Teen Reads, commentary, news, interviews, and reviews from leading authors for teen readers: http://www.teenreads.com

TeenHoopla, sponsored by the American Library Association. This Internet guide for teens provides book reviews, and lets older students share books and book-related websites: http://www.ala.org/teenhoopla

— Adapted from *Reading Is Fundamental, Inc.,* www.rif.org/parents

As he travels with two amusing companions, Tock and the Humbug, on a quest to find the princesses of Sweet Rhyme and Pure Reason, Milo makes many mistakes, but also increases in both wisdom and joy.

When he finally finds the princesses, Milo is sorry for the blunders he has made along his journey. In return, Reason offers him a seed of the Gospel when she says he "must never feel badly about making mistakes...as long as [he takes] the trouble to learn from them." The advice echoes Jesus, who taught us to not only forgive others, but also ourselves, to love our neighbors *as* we love ourselves.

Rhyme, in her turn, offers another Gospel seed about the Kingdom at hand, suggesting that "many places you would like to see are just off the map and many things you want to know are just out of sight or a little beyond your reach. But someday you'll reach them all, for what you learn today, for no reason at all, will help you discover all the wonderful secrets of tomorrow." What a splendid message of hope and of trust in Providence—right there in the pages of a side-splitting fantasy tale!

Kids in this stage love mystery and adventure as well. Around age eleven or twelve, one of my favorite books was *A Wrinkle in Time* by Madeleine L'Engle. Long after I had read it and put it away on my shelf, the story of two kids who go with their neighbor on a harrowing journey through space and time to find their lost father seeped deep within and invited me to ponder. When my daughter Diana was in fifth grade, I read it again with her, and, to my great delight, the story enthralled us both with its call to imagine.

In the story, the children discover a repressed, uniform society on planet Camazotz, controlled by evil incarnated in a disembodied brain called IT. When Meg must free her brother, Charles Wallace, from IT, she discovers the power of love, for it is love that sets him free. Moreover, she learns that understanding everything is unnecessary; rather, accepting mystery is essential. Both of these lessons—filtered through a piece of pop culture—come directly from the Gospel, and both strike a chord with our souls that can lead us to God. And, happily, I noticed in the week that followed our reading of the story that Diana was especially kind to her own little brother, indicating that the Gospel seed planted by Madeleine L'Engle had begun to take root.

Returning to *The Wizard of Oz,* in ninth grade I wrote a paper about the metaphor of Dorothy and her journey, including insights gleaned from Baum's books in addition to MGM's classic film version of the story. (The books are markedly different in places from the movie starring Judy Garland.) As I explored the meaning of Dorothy's story, I experienced yet another epiphany. This time, I discovered a sacred message in the story of a child who loves deeply and is transported to a place where she learns that all she ever needed was already in her midst. Just as I had been shocked to realize that Dorothy could have only dreamed about Oz, so now I was surprised and delighted to find satisfaction in exploring metaphor within the depiction of Dorothy's journey. As Piaget had predicted, I had developed a deeper understanding of story that would continue to grow and to foster joy in years to come.

In 1969, using Piaget's basic construct, Harvard-based psychologist Lawrence Kohlberg expanded the four stages of moral reasoning into six stages. Kohlberg theorized that children move from a self-centered way of existence to one focused on community and family, then to one concerned with society as a whole. In the fifth and sixth stages, he attested, people make moral and ethical judgments based on principles of fairness rather than on cultural or societal law. While Kohlberg was not a great promoter of story, he saw value in tales that present moral dilemmas for discussion.

Later theorists have criticized Piaget and Kohlberg's work for neglecting to explore the role of imagination and symbols in early learning and for limiting definitions of imagination to mere fantasy in the very early years. Their notions have even been termed "simplistic."

Nevertheless, their studies remain valuable for parents because they offer food for thought about the way God created us. We can expect our children to move through stages of understanding that are common to all humans. Moreover, the theories ultimately emphasize children's genuine need to develop strong imaginations as they journey to adulthood.

Given the example of Jesus in his extensive use of parable and story, Christian parents can feel confident in the importance of imagination in developing faith as well. By creating an atmosphere of appreciation for story in our homes, we help our children prepare to accept the gift of faith when they are truly ready and to receive the word of God as it whispers to us in our daily lives.

Vygotsky

Another theory on human cognitive development that offers interesting insights for parents wishing to encourage a child's imagination and sense of story surfaced amidst the turmoil of early twentieth-century Russia. In contrast to Piaget, who believed that cognitive development follows normal human patterns that are influenced by a child's environment, Lev Vygotsky (1896–1934) maintained that children learn to form concepts—to think—through language and communication. His theory becomes intriguing to families because of the importance he placed upon relationships in the development of a child's intellectual capacities.

Because Vygotsky was a Marxist, in many ways a product of his times in Russia, some of his ideas hold no merit for Christian parents. Yet, his work on human intelligence opened new doors in the quest to understand the way we learn, and his ideas on the crucial role of parent-child communications offer fascinating insights for parents and teachers.

Ironically, Vygotsky's thinking was viewed as inflammatory and dangerous to the Soviet State; as a result, Lenin silenced him. Vygotsky became *persona non grata* in his own country until his untimely death from tuberculosis in 1934, the debut of Stalin's regime. Stalin ordered Vygotsky's work kept under lock and key.

Because of this repression, Piaget learned of Vygotsky's criticism of his work much later. In 1962, Piaget published a paper addressing some of Vygotsky's concerns, agreeing with certain points, and expressing deep regret over denied possibilities to put heads together with such a brilliant colleague.[19] Since the dissolution of the Soviet Union, Vygotsky's writings have resurfaced, and theorists have discovered in them wisdom worth some reflection.

Piaget believed that a child's ability to do "abstract symbolic reasoning" and create concepts develops from biological and physical interaction with the world; in other words, for Piaget, both normal human development and the environment in which we live determine the way our thinking develops. Vygotsky, who studied the psychology of art and fables as well as child psychology, believed that the ability to form concepts comes from language development. In addition, Vygotsky held that one of the main tasks of childhood is to learn to assimilate the intellectual and cognitive tools humans have developed, such as music, art, mathematics, and language, and that

Vygotsky's Zone of Proximal Development

Lev Vygotsky focused on the social or communicative interaction between a child and its mother, peers, and others as the first ways that children come to know and learn to behave. Picture a mother or father leaning over a child's crib and engaging in chatter, smiles, tickles...and the child responding. That space between parent and child is Vygotsky's "zone of proximal development" (proximal meaning *very near*) where words, concepts, values, and understanding are created and communicated. As time goes on, and other people enter the world of the maturing child, that space expands as does the child's vocabulary and understanding of narrative. Story becomes extremely important in maintaining a family's "zone" and for building trust that facilitates a child's cognitive, faith, and moral development.

— Rose Pacatte, M.Ed. Media Studies

learning to use these tools is essential to becoming truly educated, a full human being. The role of story for Vygotsky, then, is paramount to a child's intellectual development and socialization.

Vygotsky also believed in the importance of "reflection" in the development of full human potential. Since we are entertaining the notion of experiencing story through media together with children, and then thinking and talking about them, a little reflection on this concept is worth our while as parents.

Vygotsky believed that cognitive development begins when we interact and communicate with others; but he also believed that conscious, purposeful reflection on the significance of what we have learned or experienced is essential. From that point, according to Vygotsky, new perspectives must be integrated into our personal body of knowledge to inform our ideas, actions, and abilities.[20]

Meeting Human Needs

Abraham Maslow, an American psychologist who pioneered the study of human motivations, also added to the theories of human growth and development, noting that story and imagination are basic human needs. His work includes the famous triangular diagram of the hierarchy of shared human needs.

According to Maslow, appreciation of beauty and order—things we experience in story—can only be gained after more basic human needs are met. Physiological needs—the need for food, warmth, clothing, and shelter—must be satisfied first. Then we need to experience love and a sense of belonging. From there we must develop competencies that lead to self-esteem. Only after these needs are met can we truly address our need for truth, beauty, justice, and cognitive knowledge—the stuff of story. In fulfilling all of these needs, we reach what Maslow termed *self-actualization*.

Maslow noted certain characteristics of self-actualized people: they can distinguish the false from the genuine; they see problems as things to be solved, not sources of angst and sorrow; and they see the journey as more important than the destination in life. Self-actualizers need privacy, rely on their own judgments, resist

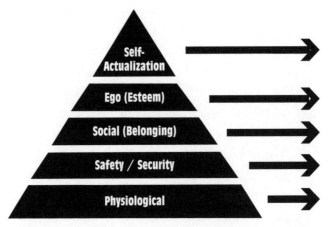

Maslow's diagram of the hierarchy of human needs.

social pressure to conform, show compassion, celebrate variety in the human race, and have a few very close friends. They also possess a sense of humor that is not hostile, accept themselves and others as they are, act spontaneously, cherish simplicity, view the ordinary with wonder, think and act creatively, and have experiences in which they feel at one with God.[21]

From a Christian perspective, a self-actualized person is someone who has become the person God created him or her to be. Maslow selected a list of historical figures that he felt met the standard of self-actualization: Abraham Lincoln, Thomas Jefferson, Mahatma Gandhi, Albert Einstein, Eleanor Roosevelt. I would add Blessed Teresa of Calcutta as well as someone not quite so well known: Bill Stott, a man in my parish church.

Bill is clearly a fully realized person, confident of his creation in the image of God and living as an excellent steward of his personal gifts and resources. Having spent a successful career in academia as an English professor, he offers a college-level course in Scripture as literature in our parish—free of charge. The group of people who attend the class each week benefit from the educational and spiritual nourishment they receive from Bill's good graces. In addition, Bill offers his time and energy to other parish and community projects while continuing to write poetry, teach ornithology, and enjoy the company of Peggy, his spouse of forty-plus years, their five children, and many grandchildren. From my point of view, Bill, through faith, hope, and love, discovered and developed his personal gifts to become the person he was called to be.

The Jesus of the Gospels brings to mind Maslow's theory of a hierarchy of needs. He came to Earth as a baby and learned humanity from parents who cared for his basic needs and loved him. He lived in a well-established society with a strong sense of family and cultural belonging. After gaining competence in carpentry, reading, and Scripture, he began his mission of preaching and healing, relying heavily upon story and imagery to convey his message of peace, love, and justice, and inviting believers to belong to the community of disciples.

The story of the loaves and fish, found in the Gospels of Matthew and Mark, perhaps best illustrates how Jesus recognized a human hierarchy of needs. Sensitive to the physical needs of his followers, Jesus multiplied five loaves and two fish into enough food to satisfy five thousand men—plus an uncounted number of women and children—with twelve baskets of food left over (cf. Mt 14:15–21). In addition, Jesus fed the people numerous parables to satisfy their need to think and wrestle with the deeper meaning of human existence in God. He showed us that we need story just as we need food.

Parents help children to begin their spiritual journeys toward communion with Christ by feeding and cuddling them, addressing their most basic needs, preparing them to accept love and belonging. When we share story and snuggle with our kids over a book or during a movie, we nurture that sense of belonging. A child's increasing skill in deciphering story, characters, plots, vocabulary, and themes leads to competence and a sense of accomplishment, as well as to knowledge and appreciation of the truth and beauty conveyed in various works of art. Clearly, story facilitates progress toward healthy "self-actualization."

And isn't that what every parent hopes and prays for in their children? We dream that our kids will become the wonderful adults God created them to be and to realize their full potential. By encouraging their imaginations through rich experiences in story, we open a door to endless possibilities that they can explore as they journey to discover God's hopes for their lives.

—————⟹◈⟸—————

"Noticing what is wonderful and allowing it to seep into our consciousness is the beginning of cultivating a sense of wonder."
— Rabbi David Wolpe

—————⟹◈⟸—————

Stages of Faith Development

During the 1990s, taking certain ideas from Piaget and Kohlberg, the-ologian James Fowler, a Methodist minister and director of the Center for Research on Faith and Moral Development at Emory University, delineated the normal pattern of faith development, asserting that one's faith matures in a predictable succession of stages. Particularly important to parents is Fowler's notion that early faith experiences impact the way an adult faith life develops, includ-ing the potential to experience profound faith.

Fowler maintained that, before entering the first stage of faith, children learn basic trust or mistrust from their parents or care-givers. All that follows in their faith life depends on how they believe they should react to the world! A person whose infancy experiences lead to a basic worldview of mistrust must first learn and accept basic trust in order to develop fidelity to belief systems. Persons who begin life with a sense of trust, however, are prepared early on to embark upon a wonderful journey toward true faith.[22]

Stage One: Intuitive/Projective Faith

According to Fowler, a child forms "pre-images of God" dur-ing infancy. Around age two, the child enters the first faith stage. This initial stage lasts until the age of reason (usually around age six or seven), and is marked by an expanding imagination. Although the child doesn't question fantasies or perceptions, the experiences and images encountered during this phase will impact the adult faith to come through the developing senses of intuition and of how the world operates.

During this stage, children become aware of death and sex—and of cultural or family taboos surrounding these powerful subjects. Two of my earliest and most vivid memories involve death: watching the news coverage of John F. Kennedy's assassination when I was barely four, and seeing my Grandma Keaton in her coffin when I was five. In contrast to the attitude of celebration with which Christians are called to regard death, these experiences, for whatever reasons, made me fearful of death well into my adulthood, until my experience of my father's death changed that attitude. As Fowler said: "It is striking how many times in our interviews we find that experiences and images that occur and take form before the child is six have powerful and long-lasting effects on the life of faith both positive and negative."[23]

Stage Two: Mythic/Literal Faith

The ability to create story emerges in the second stage of faith. Children can create or retell stories that express their experience of the world and what that experience might mean. But the child isn't ready to step outside of story to reflect on a deeper meaning. In this phase, children mainly take story at face value. However, Fowler points out that story may touch or move the child in this stage at a deeper level, even if the child is unaware.

For example, when my youngest was eight years old, he told me heaven is cold. When I asked why, he replied that hell is hot, so heaven, as its opposite, has to be cold. "See," he added, "hell is like Florida. Up in heaven, angels wear those long suits because they're trying to stay warm." He picked up these images of the afterlife somewhere, and, with all due respect to Floridians, put it into terms he related to his own body of knowledge. I listened to what he had to say and learned that he had been discussing opposites at school that day. He had also heard the expression "hotter than hell" during hot summer days. In addition, since our family has experienced a number of deaths in the past few years, the subject of heaven comes up fairly frequently. Now he is trying to put together some images that make sense to him based on what he knows.

Children often surprise us with comments and questions we don't expect. The French artist, writer, and filmmaker Jean Cocteau told of his niece and her indifference on the day a new baby brother arrived. Cocteau asked her, "You know, an angel has brought you a little brother. Aren't you curious? Don't you want to see him?" "No," the girl replied, "but I'd like to see the angel."

Fowler says children in this stage work hard to sort out reality from make-believe and often seek proof of things presented to them as fact. Stories become increasingly important to a child because they "extend their experience and understanding of life."[24] Children normally can't step back in this stage to reflect on stories and their meanings, yet they can be "affected deeply and powerfully by symbolic and dramatic materials."[25]

Parents, then, can help along a child's growing faith by providing good story experiences that include a wide-ranging variety. While we ask questions about the material to tap into their reactions to symbolism and dramatic elements, we also help our children by simply entertaining their own questions and encouraging them to think about the stories they encounter. In the long run, their faith will benefit from learning to struggle with questions and ambiguities. As Rabbi Wolpe wrote: "Learners of all ages should be taught to wrestle. Children do not have to believe what we believe when we believe it. They can struggle with ideas on their own level in their own way."[26]

Stage Three: Synthetic/Conventional Faith

Adolescence marks the entrance into a stage that involves the formal operational thinking described by Piaget. Young people can begin to think about their own views and synthesize images and ideas into their own identities. God is understood in terms of interpersonal relationships—a friend or companion who values the teenager and understands him or her. In this stage, story would provide a sort of mirror to help kids explore who they are and where they are going as persons of God. Faith helps adolescents synthesize values and information and helps shape the outlook on life that they will carry with them into the future.[27] Encouraging good literature with well-rounded characters and themes of moral decision-making is especially important and valuable during these formative years.

Stages Four Through Six

We experience the later stages delineated by Fowler when we are adults, so here we will only mention them. Stage Four, Individuative/Projective Faith, is usually experienced in early adulthood, when a person reflects on his or her own role in the world and what he or she believes. Stage Five, Conjunctive Faith, embraces the mystery of God, how God can be both seemingly unavailable and yet within our midst.

According to Fowler, only a few persons move into Stage Six, Universalizing Faith, during their lifetime. Fowler believes that persons who reach this level behave as if the Kingdom of God is at hand, with a hallmark simplicity and attitude of true freedom. He cites Thomas Merton and Mother Teresa of Calcutta as modern-day examples. These are persons recognized for their consummate faith and holiness of life.

Enchanted Transport

The preeminent theories in human intellectual, psychological, and spiritual development strongly suggest that story plays a vital role in our lives, addressing many needs. More than escapist entertainment, story carries us beyond daily living to a place where we can plumb the depths of our humanity. Through story, we discover inroads into self-knowledge, understanding, imagination, and compassion as we get to know the characters and sort out the complexities surrounding them. We become more and more able to imagine places, people, and situations unlike our own and to recognize within them what is common to us all.

Story also hints at questions stirring within us. During the opening days of the war in Iraq, my eight-year-old commented, "If the world blows up, God will send a big spaceship down, and we'll go to another world, right?"

Knowing that the fantasy gave him some comfort in a frightening time, I asked how he imagined "another world." He described a place where everyone likes one another and plays kickball together without breaking rules or fighting; where the weather is always nice and people eat lots of chocolate. Sure sounds heavenly to me!

Even though I made an effort to watch the news and listen to the radio when the children were out of earshot, the war was very much on their minds. They knew people fighting there, they heard stories from their friends, they saw an occasional headline, and we talked about the situation whenever it came up in conversation. In response to his fear, Peter craved sitting close together to read books or watch movies together. And no matter what we read, the theme always wound back to war—first, discussing good guys versus bad guys; later, fantasizing about life in the setting described in the story we encountered. Although our discussions betrayed his anxiety, they also brought hope as we imagined a better world—such as the one we are called to bring forth as Christians. While Peter is certainly not ready for deep theology, I believe that encouraging him now to imagine other ways of being will lay the groundwork for openness to the message of the Kingdom of God.

Story also helps us deal with ordinary problems closer to home, such as friendships, sibling rivalry, school woes, and the like. It allows us to consider alternate behaviors and attitudes as we react to characters and their plights. As we sift through their relationships, we scrutinize, sometimes unconsciously, our own lives and begin to gain insights into ourselves and others.

Discovering Life's Meaning

Bruno Bettelheim (1903–1990), a Viennese psychoanalyst who was interred in the Nazi concentration camps at Dachau and Buchenwald in 1938 and emigrated to the United States in 1939, spent his career helping troubled children rediscover meaning in their lives and writing about influences that affect a child's development. He argued that children need story that is appropriate to their developmental stage and that suggest a deeper meaning because it helps them make sense of the world. To be valuable to the child, Bettelheim maintained, story must stimulate imagination, help develop intellect and clarify emotions, be attuned to anxieties and aspirations, give full recognition to difficulties, and suggest solutions to perturbing problems—all in a way that never condescends.[28]

Fairy tales and certain Bible stories, complete with violence and sin, speak to the inner terrors that kids carry around with them, according to Bettelheim. These stories offer models of virtue and vice and the triumph of good over evil, and their realism helps children to externalize their fears and begin to deal with them.[29] Fowler, it is significant to note, agrees with Bettelheim about the value of these stories in developing faith, and encourages parents to expose their children to death, poverty, treachery, and maliciousness *through story* and to test and share together the feelings they elicit. However, Fowler insists that exposure to television violence, materialism, and "sexploitation" in certain TV shows and cartoons do not offer this kind of value.[30]

While Bettelheim makes a good point, experience teaches me that other stories prove valuable in the lives of children as well. Robert Coles, the famed pediatrician, child psychiatrist, scholar, professor, and writer, said that "the call of stories"—many stories—leads to profound experiences of meaning throughout our lives.[31] Jesus imparted the same message in his abundance of intriguing parables that stimulate imagination and promote reflection on meanings woven within each one. Knowing that we were created with a need for wonder, Jesus fed us with the Word of God, filled with myriad complexities and, paradoxically, profound simplicity. The greater our facility in deciphering story, the greater becomes our understanding of Sacred Scripture and our relationship with Jesus.

As Christian parents, our goal is to prepare our children to encounter Christ and help them begin their journey. Knowing that our children not only desire but require story to become the persons they were created to be and to have the relationship with God to which we are all called, we must bring good story into their lives. It doesn't require a degree in English literature or certification to teach. It calls for a willingness to be transported by words and images, to entertain the questions that arise—without worrying about having the answers—and to marvel at just how much God loves us to offer us something so good as the opportunity to relax and enjoy the company of our children.

Witness to the Power of Story

Reasons offered by educators, pediatricians, psychologists, linguists, and other experts to encourage story in a child's life are plentiful and convincing. But I have one very personal example from my parenting portfolio to share, in which story played an essential role in helping one of my children overcome a tremendous hurdle.

Patrick was nearly four years old before our second child came along, so his early years were filled with many experiences in story. We lived overseas, and I was a stay-at-home mom with abundant enthusiasm for story. As a result, we read together for hours on end. When it was time for household chores, Patrick was usually content to play, but he didn't seem to enjoy his toys half as much as he loved playing with my Tupperware and a box of tissues. So I was happy to give him some basic household objects to let his imagination roam wild, transforming tissues pinched between fingers into people, and pasta servers into carriages for them—with nary a "bibbidy, bobbidy, boo"! The creative play strengthened his imagination and attention span for stories, while the stories fueled a desire for more creative play.

This good-natured little fellow, now a prayerful and thoughtful young man with a rapid-fire imagination and completely fearless approach to art, was going to benefit more than I could have imagined from our time engaged in story and his imaginative play. Despite his keen intelligence, Patrick struggled in school and had begun to dread it. Thorough testing in third grade revealed that he was severely dyslexic. Because we had enjoyed story extensively, he had developed an intuition about plots and characters that helped him fake an ability to read. When his teachers asked questions about story, he was often able to guess correctly at the answers and, therefore, camouflage the problem. But his teachers and I knew that something wasn't right when such a bright kid could not come near the scholastic level of his peers.

Once testing had pinpointed the nature of Patrick's particular dyslexia, a tutor developed a one-on-one program to teach him to read. Patrick's path to becoming an educated young man would be more difficult for him than for most. Yet his tutor said something I'll never forget: "Thank God you fed this beautiful imagination of his. He is an extremely creative thinker with an excellent vocabulary. That will be a great strength for him in dealing with the way he learns."

———⟫◆⟪———

"Woe to the man whose heart has not learned while young to hope, to love—and to put its trust in life."
— Joseph Conrad, *Victory*

———⟫◆⟪———

The tutor was correct, and together we tackled Patrick's education. She worked intensively on his reading and math skills, while I handled the rest by home-schooling him that year. Knowing how much Patrick loved story—something I could offer him with confidence—I created study units based on other cultures. We covered a different culture every month with geography, literature, and field trips to plays and museums, plus games, movies, and food. When we studied Japan, we read Japanese stories, saw a Japanese watercolor exhibit, attended a Japanese puppet show, and watched one video of Gilbert and Sullivan's *The Mikado* and another on sumo wrestling. We learned about St. Francis Xavier, Japan's first Christian missionary. At the end of the three-week unit, we enjoyed a meal of sushi, miso soup, and green tea with our next-door neighbors on their

Japanese dishes, then watched a Japanese movie—*Godzilla!* I don't know which of us had more fun, but Patrick was enjoying learning again through the power of story.

The following year, Patrick enrolled in a school with dynamic and effective teachers. He made rapid progress during the first year, but still balked at reading for pleasure. Then, along came *Harry Potter.* For the first time in his life, Patrick wanted to read. I was delighted as he read the first, second, and third of J. K. Rowling's books without so much as a squawk about their length. Then, he read them again and again. Clearly he had crashed through a learning barrier that opened like a floodgate. At age eleven, Patrick became a reader—and an avid one at that! And, of course, that was only the beginning.

So, I invite you on an adventure to indulge in story, and through story, in all the good things God wants for us! The power of story made a difference in my family, and I believe all families can benefit, regardless of special needs or circumstances. In the next chapters, we'll explore Christian values and themes found in several well-known works, including *Harry Potter.* If some of the insights are too advanced to share with your children right now, just smile and enjoy the fruits of the Spirit for yourself, remembering that we must become like children to enter the Kingdom of God.

5

Grappling with Story

Reading a good story is like wrestling with angels—
you do not expect to win, but you should expect to
come away from the experience changed.

— Jane Yolen, author

One evening at bedtime, I tried to read a story to my eight-year-old.
I tried, but he interrupted at least once per page. Every sentence
seemed to remind Peter of something important he needed to tell me.
After the fourth or fifth interruption, I put down the book and chatted
with him for a while, then picked it back up and tried again. Another
interruption. "Do you like this story?" I finally asked.

"Oh, sure!" he immediately replied. "But it's not really a
story, is it?"

Out of the mouths of babes....

The children's book, filled with beautiful illustrations, contained lovely lyrical language about a chipmunk in the forest. But
Peter was right: there wasn't much of a story to it, just a succession

of sentences. So we looked at the rest of the pictures and soon closed the book. "*Now* can you read me a story?" Peter asked.

Kids need and deserve story with good plot, well-developed characters, and quality narrative. Recognizing the difference between good story and mediocre to poor to non-existent story is an ability that develops through exposure to well-written story. The more we read to and with our children and delve into story in other media, such as television and film, the more we will be able to discern quality—and the more enjoyable the experience will become for our kids and for us. After all, as C. S. Lewis noted: "No book is really worth reading at the age of ten which is not equally worth reading at the age of fifty." I think the same is true for other media.

Fortunately, many well-written stories with memorable characters and meaningful messages await us that can engage our imaginations and speak to our Gospel values. Whether we experience them for the first time with our children or for the first time since our own childhood, good stories carry seeds of challenge and change that cry out to be nurtured within us. These stories take root and help develop the landscape of our spirituality by bringing us to examine our own attitudes, behaviors, prejudices, and relationships. Oftentimes story encourages us to open ourselves to virtue and grace—even when the story is not explicitly about God. But be prepared for unexpected adventures: the experience might just bring on a breath of fresh air that could carry you away!

A Few Guidelines for Entering into Story

Before we unearth a few seeds of the Gospel in the works of some well-known authors, you might want to consider a few guidelines for sharing story with kids.

Movies are great, but don't minimize the value of good, old-fashioned reading!

I love all sorts of media. Having worked in radio, television, newspapers, magazines, and the World Wide Web, I know various media "from the inside" and enjoy them for what they are and what they offer. I am also a genuine "movie nut," with a love of film as an art form as well as a vehicle for prayer and spiritual refreshment. But for parents and kids who want and need to spend time together and desire to be transported by story, nothing compares to the medium you hold in your hands right now.

Since we're highlighting great books to read with kids, I've contacted the experts in my own home for some interesting ideas. Look in this chapter for lists my own three children compiled highlighting their favorite stories—Patrick's Top Twenty-Five Titles, Diana's Favorite Fiction, and Peter's Picks.

Books demand our complete attention and imagination. When read aloud in a quiet room, story brings new experiences to a child through a voice he or she knows and loves. Instead of focusing on a screen that looms prominently and allows a certain amount of viewer passivity, books draw us into ourselves, where we must construct the vision of the author. Humble ink-dotted papers wield significant power unrivaled by TV and film. While here I offer suggestions for sharing story through other media, which I continue to enjoy and love, I really feel that, for parents and kids, books are best for building relationships while enjoying story.

Enjoy the media experience together.

It may sound simplistic, but the first part of this process is to enjoy media *together:* read together and watch movies and television together. Snuggle, get comfortable, and relax! This is supposed to be fun! And when watching films or TV programs together, fight the temptation to gaze passively at the screen; make viewing an active experience by talking about it afterward (or during commercial breaks!).

Remember, though, to ask open-ended questions. If we ask kids if they liked the story, they'll probably say yes—or, sometimes, no—and that's about all. So, it works better to start off with something such as: "Wasn't it funny when..." or "Gosh, it surprised me

Peter is an elementary school student with very discriminating taste!

Peter's Picks

Where the Red Fern Grows by Wilson Rawls

The Lorax by Dr. Seuss

Shiloh by Phyllis Reynolds Naylor

Horton Hatches the Egg by Dr. Seuss

The 500 Hats of Bartholomew Cubbins by Dr. Seuss

Charlotte's Web by E. B. White

Frindle by Andrew Clements

The *Robert* series by Barbara Seuling

Mr. Popper's Penguins by Richard and Florence Atwater

Jumanji by Chris Van Allsburg

that..." or "I just loved the part where..." or "That part about... reminded me of the time...." Don't worry if your attempts don't elicit much of a response at first. Just keep trying; one day your child will have something to say...and that moment is likely to fill you with joy!

I still laugh when I think of my daughter's reaction to P. L. Travers' *Mary Poppins*. "I don't like her," Diana staunchly declared. "She's so rude." *Good for her,* I thought, *now she's involved in the story.* And our conversation was very lively that evening!

Whether the story comes to life in a book, magazine, film, or TV show, remember to ask children what they think about the story they are encountering.

Preparation pays off in selecting good story.

It takes effort to choose story that offers a good plot, interesting characters, and valuable lessons. Many resources are available to help you select books and movies to share with your kids, including your local librarian as well as the list provided at the end of this book in chapter ten. But the best ideas might be resting inside of you. Take a moment to think back, and then write your answers below:

My favorite book as a child:

_____

I loved it because:

_____

Other books I loved:

_____

My favorite movie as a child:

_____

I loved it because:

_____

Other movies I loved:

_____

My favorite TV show as a child:

_____

I loved it because:

_____

Other shows I loved:

_____

Share what you loved as a child with your own kids. Your enthusiasm will make the experience better for everyone—and that enthusiasm may be contagious! Be sure to ask your kids about their favorite stories. Perhaps they have encountered at school or with a friend a story that they would like to share with you. Go together to the library or bookstore and find books or movies you can enjoy together.

When kids are older and read independently, keep talking about story. One of the best experiences of connectedness I've had with my daughter happened one evening when I heard her crying in her room. I peeked in to see my then-nine-year-old dabbing her eyes with a tissue. In her other hand she was holding an opened copy of

Diana is a middle school student who loves mystery most. These are her all-time faves.

Diana's Favorite Fiction

Because of Winn Dixie by Kate DiCamillo

War Comes to Willy Freeman by Christopher Collier

Bingo Brown, Gypsy Lover by Betsy Byars

Harry Potter and the Prisoner of Azkaban by J. K. Rowling

Harry Potter and the Chamber of Secrets by J. K. Rowling

Harry Potter and the Sorcerer's Stone by J. K. Rowling

Chrysanthemum by Kevin Henkes

Lily's Purple Plastic Purse by Kevin Henkes

Little Women by Louisa May Alcott

Mr. Popper's Penguins by Richard and Florence Atwater

A Wrinkle in Time by Madeleine L'Engle

Charlotte's Web by E. B. White

Goodnight Moon by Margaret Wise Brown

Lily's Crossing by Patricia Reilly Giff

Mary Poppins by Pamela L. Travers

The Last Silk Dress by Ann Rinaldi

Nancy Drew series by Carolyn Keene

The Haunting by Joan Lowery Nixon

The Water Babies by Charles Kingsley

The Secret Garden by Frances Hodgson Burnett

Louisa May Alcott's *Little Women.* Immediately I knew. "Is it Beth?" I asked sympathetically.

"Oh, Mom! She died! Beth died! I can't believe it!" We talked about that wonderful story for a long, long time. It was, in fact, my favorite story when I was my daughter's age. Even though we didn't read that particular story aloud together, we enjoyed discussing it and sharing with one another our impressions.

⚯

"Whatever is felt upon the page without being specifically named there— that, we may say, is created."
— Willa Cather

⚯

Diana particularly enjoyed the spunkiness of Jo, the main character, probably because Diana is a spunky, vivacious girl herself. As she experienced Jo's struggles and triumphs throughout the story, she came to admire the character's tenacious, yet tender nature. She related to the friction arising from sibling rivalry between Jo and Amy, the youngest of the "little women." And she found hope in Jo's ultimate success and happiness. Our sharing gave me greater insights into Diana's character and it delighted her to know that we enjoyed the same story. Loving the story is something we have in common that serves as a touchstone in our experiences together. (On a cultural note, it's interesting that this story, which we find wholesome enough today to encourage all young women to read, was once the subject of hot debate. The author of *Little Women,* Louisa May Alcott, was severely criticized by fundamentalist leaders when her book was published in 1868 because it was deemed "too worldly.")

Another time, Diana was laboring over a book report for school. I remember her genuine surprise and delight when I began to discuss the story with her. "I didn't know you had read this book!" she exclaimed. "Well, I saw that you were reading it, so I got a copy to read, too."

We then talked about various aspects of the book, especially parts she just didn't "get." I asked her a few questions about it until, lo and behold, Diana's face lit up in a sudden epiphany. Something in the story finally made sense to her. But if I hadn't read the book, I wouldn't have been much help in bringing about this *Aha!* moment. Moreover, if I hadn't read the story, I wouldn't have known that Diana was bothered by certain parts of the book, which ultimately gave me insights into what was going on inside of her.

While it requires our time—often seemingly impossible to set aside—it is really worth the effort to read what our kids are reading and watch what our kids are watching, even when we're not doing it together. The payoff is tremendous in helping us connect with our kids and becoming aware of media influences in their lives.

Ask open-ended questions.

Avoid questions with right and wrong or yes and no answers. Ask how and why and what do kids think, rather than who, what, when, and where about the story, if you want discussions to contain any substance and lead to any faith sharing. The idea is to use story as a springboard to conversation, to listen to what your kids are thinking, feeling, and experiencing, and to create opportunities to share seeds of the Gospel.

It's okay to react—and to let your kids see your reaction.

If the story is funny, laugh; if you have a lump in your throat, go ahead and cry. Kids need to know that you are moved by story and that emotions are okay. My children still remember, years after the fact, that Diana and I cried during the movie *Mighty Joe Young,* about an enormous but beloved gorilla that is gravely injured. They remember how we all laughed during parts of each and every *Harry Potter* book we've read together.

I have giggled with all of my children over Chris Riddell's story, *Humphrey's New Trousers,* about a hippo that needs new pants. Humphrey tries to buy a pair of pants, but can't find anything to fit his generous hippo hips. He is forced to turn to an upholsterer, who fashions trousers with Humphrey's old red draperies and tells the hippo he is shaped just like an armchair. It is wonderfully silly—and a great and healthy way for us to share a laugh. Kids enjoy discovering that parents laugh about things they themselves find funny!

No anxiety allowed!

Remember the anecdote about my mother and *The Wizard of Oz?* Don't worry if you can't answer all of your child's questions about a story. My mother didn't answer my questions about Dorothy, and look where that dazzling ambiguity led—a whole book about finding meaning in stories!

——◈——

"There is then creative reading as well as creative writing."

— Ralph Waldo Emerson

——◈——

The most important part of sharing story is exposing honest reactions. "I don't know" is an acceptable answer that can be followed by ideas, suggestions, or, if the question concerns fact, a peek in the encyclopedia or an Internet search. If you think of something later, you can always bring it up: "Remember when you asked me about such-and-such? Well, I was thinking...." It just might lead to a great conversation.

Gauge your child's spiritual maturity.

Just as you gauge a child's emotional maturity, listening skills, attention span, and, sometimes, reading ability when choosing stories to share, try to gauge his or her "spiritual maturity" before launching into the kind of "God-talk" suggested in the following chapters. Sometimes a simple word may be enough, while other times demand we say nothing, and still others may open windows for wonderful conversations about the faith, complete with explanations of Christian principles. Each of us must determine how much and

Patrick is the oldest kid in our household, a teenager and an avid reader with so many favorite books that he had difficulty reducing his list to a mere twenty-five!

Patrick's Top Twenty-Five Titles

The Odyssey by Homer (Robert Fitzgerald translation)

The Giver by Lois Lowry

Harry Potter and the Order of the Phoenix by J. K. Rowling

Harry Potter and the Goblet of Fire by J. K. Rowling

Harry Potter and the Prisoner of Azkaban by J. K. Rowling

Harry Potter and the Chamber of Secrets by J. K. Rowling

Harry Potter and the Philosopher's Stone by J. K. Rowling

The Hobbit by J. R. R. Tolkien

Shiloh by Barry Moser

Tuck Everlasting by Natalie Babbitt

The Phantom Tollbooth by Norton Juster

Tangerine by Edward Bloor

Holes by Louis Sachar

The Outsiders by S. E. Hinton

The Watsons Go to Birmingham—1963 by Christopher Paul Curtis

The Once and Future King by T. H. White

The Magician's Nephew by C. S. Lewis

The Lion, the Witch, and the Wardrobe by C. S. Lewis

Among the Hidden by Margaret Peterson Haddix

Charlie and the Great Glass Elevator by Roald Dahl

How to Eat Fried Worms by Thomas Rockwell

Jumanji by Chris Van Allsburg

Ben and Me by Robert Lawson

Where the Wild Things Are by Maurice Sendak

Curious George by H. A. and Margret Rey

what kind of spirituality and conversation about God our own child is ready for, based on our knowledge of the child and our relationship with him or her. The most important part is not to force such moments, but to relax and wait for the right moments to arise.

Barbara Joosse, author of many popular stories, including *Mama, Do You Love Me?* (featured here in chapter six), shared with me an insightful anecdote about inviting her son, Rob, to pray as a boy:

> When Rob went to church with me, I'd tell him, "Rob, first you kneel down and say hello to God."
>
> "What should I say, Mom?"
>
> "Say anything you want. God likes to hear it all."
>
> A few moments later he was kneeling and laughing. "What's so funny?" I asked him.
>
> "I just told God a joke and he really liked it!"
>
> Rob's initial adventure with faith was so pure. He heard God's voice. God was a buddy. I've tried to learn this from my son.

Keep it fun!

Sometimes this is the hardest part. Make sure kids are in the mood to talk about stories when you try this in your own family. Since no one knows your child better than you, trust your instincts about timing. Sometimes the time is right to talk about a story weeks after you've read it; other times, the right time is immediately, after the last word. No matter when the time is right, make sure the experience is enjoyable! Try not to seem rushed or bothered and just relax.

Seeking Seeds of the Gospel

In the following chapters, we'll take a look at stories created for children that contain Christian principles or messages. Chapter six focuses on books for a very young audience, kids aged two to six, and explores some of the seeds of the Gospel that await us there. Chapter seven has stories for elementary school-aged kids, and chapter eight covers tales for kids in middle school and junior high. One of the most intriguing contemporary literary characters—Harry Potter—has a section all his own in chapter nine.

Besides the stories themselves, the chapters offer some suggestions for unearthing the seeds of the Gospel contained in the stories and ideas for planting them in the hearts of our children through parent-child conversation about the literature. These suggestions are meant to promote an enjoyable experience for families to share together. So...sit back, relax and have fun while spiritually nourishing your kids (and yourselves!) with the Gospel seeds that await you!

6

Gospel Seeds Planted

Imagination is more important than knowledge.
— Albert Einstein

Beginning in the very earliest years, we read to our children. When we can get a child to sit with us and enjoy the pages of a book, we begin to unlock a world of wonder through reading. The most important thing to remember in beginning this wonderful way to connect with our children is that every child is different. A child's interest in story as well as a child's attention span affect the approach you will take and the amount of time you can spend sharing story. As the parent, you will know when the time is right to try to talk about our faith with your child, especially the themes that emerge from children's story, presented in this book.

When I was nearing the end of my pregnancy with our first child, who is now a teenager, I remember reading an article about a Japanese woman with a brood of geniuses. She believed the secret to producing *wunderkind* is to read to them in the womb. And not just any old story: she read her children Shakespeare—*in utero!* I felt woefully inadequate. I had let an entire pregnancy slide by without so much as reciting "to be or not to be." Did it matter? *That* is the question.

For me, the answer is no. So, I don't have "Shakespearian geniuses." My kids can appear on *Oprah* some day and complain about it if they like. On the other hand, I do have bright, fun-loving children who genuinely like one another. Every single one of them has a vivid imagination and enjoys "thinking out of the box." If Albert Einstein is correct in saying "imagination is more important than knowledge," then I believe I have done some good in nurturing the greater gift.

While many imagination-builders are required to produce a healthy imagination, such as exposure to art, music, and theater, free time to play, and encouragement to experiment and try new things, a major ingredient—perhaps the most essential of all—is story. Sharing story is essential to fostering imagination. And a good imagination is key to the kind of open spirit that allows a faith life to grow. While we want our kids to do well in school and create successful lives that bring them happiness, it is their relationship with God that remains most important.

It's never too late in a child's development to start reading together—nor is it too early. As soon as kids are ready to listen, the time is right. But it may take a little perseverance. Remember that first time you introduced vegetables or meat to your baby? If your kids are like ours, it didn't always go over so well... When Patrick was a baby, he balked at green beans the first time I served them. But I never gave up; week after week, I tried to give him a spoonful of beans until finally he ate them—and enjoyed them! It may be a similar experience with reading together. Don't worry about initial fidgety moments or a child wandering off after a page or two at the beginning. Just keep trying, and eventually you and your child will be deep into story, enjoying moments of togetherness and fun.

The most basic picture books and stories for very early reading experiences—for example, *Pat the Bunny, Mother Goose,* and alphabet books—are not really flush with seeds of the Gospel, and kids who read them are not really ready for more than the most basic God-talk. Before you know it, though, kids are ready to develop a concept of God as well as a healthy imagination that will later serve their faith. Until that time, simply work to set the stage by introducing story time, establishing a habit of sitting down together with books, and reading together as much as possible.

When both you and your child are ready, begin unearthing Gospel seeds that await you in story and planting them deeply within your child's heart. On the following pages, you'll find lots of ideas from popular children's literature to get you on your way.

Curious George by Margret and H. A. Rey

Margret and Hans Augusto Rey were born in Hamburg, Germany, around the turn of the twentieth century. On a trip to Brazil in 1935, Hans was reunited with his childhood acquaintance, Margarete Waldstein, in Rio de Janeiro, where she was living to escape the political climate of Nazi Germany. They fell in love, married only months later, and honeymooned in Paris, where they decided to live. As a cartoonist for a Parisian newspaper, Hans drew a giraffe that caught the eye of a book publisher, who asked him to create a children's story around the drawing. In the story, a curious little monkey named George appeared.

Background: The Reys thought George deserved a book of his own and worked together on the manuscript. Before it could be published, the Nazis were poised to invade Paris. The Reys demonstrated a resourcefulness as great as that of Curious George: Hans cobbled together two bicycles out of spare parts, and in the early hours of June 14, 1940, the day the Nazis seized Paris, the two fled the city and biked to Spain in four days. They took with them a little food, warm coats, and five manuscripts, including *Curious George.* In

Spain, they sold their bicycles for train fare to Lisbon, Portugal, and eventually made it to New York City. In 1941, Houghton Mifflin published *Curious George*—a book so popular that it has never been out of print. Although we will only look at the original book, six other stories by the Reys are equally delightful.

Synopsis: George is a little monkey whose curiosity leads him to be captured by a nice man in a yellow hat. Before the man can take him to a zoo, George causes all kinds of mischief and ends up in prison! George manages to escape, but soon gets into more mischief, snatching a bunch of balloons and sailing high into the sky. Frightened, George holds on tight until he finally lands on top of a traffic light. The man carries George to safety, pays the balloon man, and takes George to the zoo, where all of the animals enjoy his balloons, and George is happy.

Seeds of the Gospel: George's curiosity gets him into lots of trouble. But how does the man in the yellow hat react? He is firm with George, but kind, and, most of all, forgiving. He understands George's curious nature and, although it causes him problems, he still cares about George. "How do you think George feels when he gets into trouble?" you might ask. The answers will undoubtedly reflect some feelings your child has had in similar situations.

Ask kids about the man in the yellow hat: "Do you think he worried about George?" Use this opportunity to tell kids how much they are loved, even when they get into mischief. Time spent with this story could help a child comprehend that parents understand curiosity, but that rules can be good for them, too, because they help kids stay healthy and strong, physically, emotionally, and spiritually.

You might want to bring up the subject of rules and why parents and caregivers create and enforce rules to teach their children and keep them safe. "What did George do that wasn't safe?" you might ask. You could try to elicit an answer by talking about the tightrope, the balloons, or leaning over the side of the boat. "Why do you think we're not allowed to lean over the side of a boat?" you might suggest.

Compare George's experiences to something closer to home, too, substituting, for example: "Do you know why you have to wear a bicycle helmet?" Talk about how the helmet keeps your child safe and that it's a parent's job to help kids stay safe. Young children might not be able or want to talk about rules that help them learn proper behavior, but safety rules are generally easy to bring up. I once talked about safety by mentioning that God has a special job for each of us and God wants us to be careful so we can grow up and still be able to do it. The response was a wide-eyed expression and a delighted reply: "God has something for *me* to do?" The moment encouraged my child's self-worth and left us both in pleasant wonder about the idea.

Mama, Do You Love Me? by Barbara M. Joosse

Barbara M. Joosse is the author of many children's books, including *The Thinking Place* and *I Love You the Purplest*. She is the mother of three grown children and lives in Cedarburg, Wisconsin. She dedicated *Mama, Do You Love Me?* to a priest, "Fr. Jose Valdez, friend and guide on a remarkable journey." That piqued my curiosity, so I contacted the author and asked her for the story behind the dedication, which she kindly shared:

> I hadn't gone to (Catholic) church for many years, then had a real awakening experience, so decided to see a priest. Fr. Valdez was newly ordained. I walked in, but left one foot out the door...just in case. There were so many things he could have said that would have sent me running. Instead, he said, "Never confuse anger with the Church with God." Right. So I stayed. We began an amazing spiritual adventure together. As thanks for that adventure, I dedicated the book to him.

Background: This story celebrates Inuit culture in the Arctic with interesting vocabulary, animals, and beautiful illustrations. Joosse got the idea for the story when she was reading Margaret Wise Brown's *The Runaway Bunny* together with her then-two-year-old son, Robby. "He threw the book across the room, a big statement for an author's son," Joosse said. "I wondered why? I decided that this story, while reassuring for many children, was my son's worst nightmare. With two hovering big sisters, and a totally loving mom, his job was to gain his own independence. Yet, as a two-year-old, he was testing his limits constantly. I decided that I wanted to write a reassuring book that told Robby about my unconditional love, while celebrating his adventuresome spirit."

Synopsis: A little girl asks her mother in many different scenarios what would happen if she made mischief or mistakes or ran away. The mother steadfastly replies that no matter what naughty or crazy things her child does, or how angry or disappointed she becomes because of them, the mother will always love her child.

Seeds of the Gospel: The Gospel message is easy to find in this story, for it's all about love. The mother loves her child unconditionally in the same way God loves us. This wonderfully illustrated book calls to mind the words of Mother Teresa of Calcutta in her message to the Fourth United Nations Women's Conference in Beijing: "A woman's love is one image of the love of God." Use this book to tell your child how much you love him or her and enjoy the moment.

Sometimes, after reading this book, kids will mention a time when parents became angry or upset with them. If you are blessed to have that happen, use that bit of grace to talk about it and to remind kids that even though you were angry, you never stopped loving your child. Try adding: "Did you know that God loves us that way, too? No matter what we do, God will forgive us and love us! What do you think about that?"

———◆◆✕◆●———

Grandpa's Face by Eloise Greenfield

Eloise Greenfield is an award-winning poet and author living in Washington, D.C. Born in 1929 in Parmele, North Carolina, Greenfield and her family moved only months after her birth to a public housing project in Washington called Langston Terrace. In that multicultural, impoverished neighborhood, Greenfield enjoyed a happy childhood within a close-knit community of families who looked out for one another. She became a mother and grandmother, but, as a civil servant, didn't expect to become a writer. Fortunately for us, one day some thirty years ago, Greenfield sat down and started to write, launching a very successful career in children's literature that led to thirty-two books and numerous awards. The author's work often portrays strong, loving African-American families, like her own. In 1999, she was inducted into the National Literary Hall of Fame for Writers of African Descent.

Synopsis: Tamika and her grandpa have a close, loving relationship. She loves his expressive face, his stories, and especially their "talk-walks" around the neighborhood. Grandpa's face always shows love for Tamika, even when he's angry. One day, Tamika sees Grandpa rehearsing for a play, using a cold, hard face that frightens her. She broods and worries that he might look at her that way one day. When she acts out at dinnertime, Grandpa discovers what is upsetting Tamika and reassures her that he will always love her.

Seeds of the Gospel: Tamika's story calls to mind one of King David's psalms: "Let your face shine upon your servant; save me in your steadfast love" (31:16). Tamika counts on her Grandpa's love and needs his face to shine upon her. She can't bear to imagine him looking at her without a loving expression on his face. "Why do you think Tamika is so interested in Grandpa's face?" you could ask. "What was he doing when Tamika saw Grandpa looking so mean? Why did Tamika get so upset?"

Talk about Tamika's emotions in this story: "How does Tamika feel when Grandpa tells her that nothing she does will ever make him look at her with that mean face?" And explore the notion of mercy and forgiveness: "Do you think Grandpa will always forgive Tamika? Why?" Our relationships as parents, grandparents, and caregivers of children have a deep impact on their spiritual lives. Use the opportunity to plant a seed of the Gospel about God's everlasting love: "Did you know that God loves us just like Grandpa loves Tamika? Nothing will ever make God too angry to love us! What do you think of that?"

———⟫•◇•⟪———

When asked how to develop intelligence in young people, Einstein answered: "Read fairy tales. Then read more fairy tales."

———⟫•◇•⟪———

Grandpa's love soothes and comforts Tamika and makes her feel special. When Tamika puts his love to the test and acts up at the dinner table, Grandpa tells her nothing could ever make him stop loving her. In the same way, nothing we do can ever cause God to stop loving us. Consider the seed of the Gospel as expressed by St. Paul in his letter to the Romans: "For I am convinced that neither death, nor life, nor angels, nor rulers, nor things present, nor things to come, nor powers, nor height, nor depth, nor anything else in all creation, will be able to separate us from the love of God in Christ Jesus our Lord" (8:38–39).

Tamika acts badly at the dinner table because she is worried about something else. Wise Grandpa figures this out, but we don't always recognize the true source of a child's behavior problems when they arise. Talk about the relationship between Tamika and her grandpa, and the trust they have developed in one another: "Why did Tamika act like that at the dinner table? How did Grandpa figure out what was really bothering her?" you might ask. "What do you think about Tamika's grandpa?"

Talk about Grandpa's "talk-walks" with Tamika and how conversations help them sort things out and get to know one another better. "Why does Tamika like the talk-walks so much?" you might begin. Point out that Grandpa showed Tamika his love for her in his face and also in his taking time to be with her and find out what is on her mind. This attention calls to mind a passage from St. Paul's letter to the Ephesians: "Let no evil talk come out of your mouths, but only what is useful for building up, as there is need, so that your words may give grace to those who hear" (4:29). Enjoy your own talk-walks in celebration of the message of love we find in Greenfield's book, the celebration of familial bonds, and love's power to heal.

The Tale of Peter Rabbit by Beatrix Potter

Beatrix Potter was born in London in 1866 to a well-to-do family. As a child, she began to study and draw animals. When a young woman, she had no success in publishing her scientific drawings and, in her thirties, began writing and illustrating her wonderful children's stories. She married late in life, became Mrs. William Heelis—a sheep farmer, antique collector, and preservationist of the English Lake District where they lived—and never wrote again. She died in 1943.

Background: Several publishers rejected Beatrix Potter's first book, *The Tale of Peter Rabbit.* When it was finally published in 1902 by F. Warne and Company, the book was an immediate hit that launched the author's career in children's literature. She went on to write twenty-nine other volumes about little animals in the English countryside.

Synopsis: Peter Rabbit is a mischievous bunny that disobeys his mother and sneaks into Mr. McGregor's garden to munch on vegetables growing there. Mr. McGregor finds Peter and chases him with a rake. Frightened, Peter rushes through the garden and gets caught in a gooseberry net. When Peter begins to sob in despair, some friendly sparrows encourage him to try harder to escape. He wriggles out of his new blue jacket and hides in a watering can. Peter catches cold in the water and sneezes, so Mr. McGregor again chases him around the garden. At last, Peter reaches his rabbit hole, where Mother Rabbit puts him to bed with a spoonful of chamomile tea. Meanwhile, the other little rabbits that listened to their mother's instructions enjoy blackberries and milk for supper.

Seeds of the Gospel: This is a cautionary tale about obedience and rewards.

Peter isn't punished harshly for disobeying the rules; he has punished himself enough with the stress and terror of his day, as well as the cold he has caught while in the watering can. This aspect of the story provides a springboard to share with kids why parents set limits on behavior. *Discipline* is part of our Christian call to be *disciples,* words that share the same root. While it is our least desirable job as parents, the letter to the Hebrews tells us, "Discipline always seems painful rather than pleasant at the time, but later it yields the peaceful fruit of righteousness to those who have been trained by it" (12:11). Try to talk about Peter Rabbit's antics by saying: "I wonder why Peter went into the garden. He knew it was dangerous!" You might point out that Mother Rabbit set limits because she loves Peter and doesn't want to lose him or see him get hurt. "We can't always do everything we want to do, can we?" you might add to plant that Gospel seed of discipline.

Although little bunnies love to hop into gardens and munch on leaves, Peter knew he shouldn't do it. His mother had stressed the danger of going into the garden, but Peter was stealing from Mr. McGregor as well. Use this opportunity to talk about one of the Ten Commandments: "You shall not steal" (Ex 20:15). Talk about respecting the property of others, comparing what we should do to what Peter Rabbit did. For example, try asking: "Peter took that food from the garden without permission. How did Mr. McGregor feel when he saw Peter stealing his food? Why was Mr. McGregor so angry?" You might point out how hard Mr. McGregor works in his garden and how much time he spends there so that he can provide for his family.

Also, talk about the little sparrows that encourage Peter when he is trapped in the net and about to give up. "I like those birds!" you might mention. "How did they help Peter?" While children this age may not have had enough experiences to share their own stories about helping others, you can praise the birds for their gift of encouragement and plant another seed of the Gospel articulated by St. Paul: "Therefore encourage one another and build each other up, as indeed you are doing"(1 Thes 5:11).

Horton Hatches the Egg by Dr. Seuss

Theodore Seuss Geisel intended to become a literature professor, but fell in love while studying for his doctorate at Oxford University. He married and returned to the United States in 1927 to begin writing for the leading American humor magazine of the time, *Judge.* In 1936, he wrote *And to Think That I Saw It on Mulberry Street,* rejected by forty-three publishers before making it into print. He wrote four more children's books before World War II, when the Army assigned him to Hollywood to create documentaries for Frank Capra's Signal Corps Unit, for which he won two Academy Awards as well as the Legion of Merit. Later, he won an Oscar for a cartoon he created called *Gerald McBoing-Boing* (1951). In 1954, *Life* magazine published a report, "Why Johnny Can't Read," about illiteracy among school children. The report said kids were having trouble reading because their books were boring. A publisher sent Geisel a list of important words for kids and asked him to use them in writing a reading primer. The result was an instant and enduring hit, *The Cat in the Hat,* that used only 220 words, and catapulted Geisel to fame as Dr. Seuss in a prolific career that led to fifty-four books in all. Geisel died in 1991.

Background: The last book Dr. Seuss published before joining the Army was *Horton Hatches the Egg,* released by Random House in

1940. In 1954, Dr. Seuss produced another book about the lovable elephant, *Horton Hears a Who.*

Synopsis: A lazy bird named Mayzie tires of sitting on her egg, waiting for it to hatch. She asks Horton to take over to give her a short break. Horton, an elephant, kindly agrees and takes pains to get his heavy self gently onto the nest in a tree. Faithful to his promise to guard the egg, he stays there from fall to spring. Other animals poke fun, but Horton perseveres. Meanwhile, Mayzie is traveling the world having fun, not caring about the egg at all! One day, hunters prepare to shoot Horton, but he throws out his chest and stays on the nest. They decide to capture Horton and put him in a circus, where he becomes very unhappy, but remains true to his promise. Mayzie runs into Horton at the very moment the egg hatches. Although she claims the new baby bird, to everyone's surprise, it undoubtedly belongs to Horton, with ears, tail, and trunk just like his!

Seeds of the Gospel: Horton keeps his promise in spite of great personal sacrifice, reminiscent of a passage in the book of Sirach: "Be sincere of heart and steadfast, undisturbed in time of adversity" (2:2). Horton accepts the task because Mayzie promises not to be gone long. She breaks her promise, but Horton will not leave the egg. He values his promise and he values the life inside the egg. In talking about this story, plant a Gospel seed about commitment: "Why do you think Horton stays on the nest?" "Why is keeping a promise important?"

Older children may be ready to compare and contrast values in this story as well. Talk about the bird and her selfishness, perhaps asking: "Why did Mayzie stay away so long?" "How did the bird treat Horton when they met up at the circus? How did that make Horton feel?" Explore some of the ideas and feelings that surface, especially if they remind your child of someone in real life.

Talk about Horton, who put his own wants and needs aside to do something important and life-giving. "Did you ever make someone else happy by doing something hard? How did you feel afterward?"

Horton exemplifies respect for life, an attitude to which we are all called as Christians. Plant a seed of the Gospel about the importance of each life by asking: "What was in the egg? How did Horton know that protecting the egg was important?" When the egg hatches, the bird resembles an elephant because of Horton's devotion and love. Ask: "Why did Mayzie's baby bird look like Horton?"

The Little Engine That Could by Watty Piper

Watty Piper never existed. The publishing firm of Platt & Munk used the pseudonym on many children's books in the early twentieth century for in-house projects. In 1949, an Arizona woman began to write publishers claiming her cousin, Frances M. Ford, then ninety-five years old, wrote the *Little Engine* story in 1910 under the pen name of "Uncle Nat." In 1955, *The New York Times* published an article with samples of several "Little Switch Engine" stories that Mrs. Ford wrote, convincing most that she was indeed the author of *The Little Engine That Could*. But Platt & Munk vigorously defended their claim to the story and won the publishing rights in court. Mrs. Ford died at the age of 102.[32]

Background: As far as scholars can tell, the original story of a train with can-do spirit appeared in print in 1908 in a Sunday school leaflet designed to encourage kindness and hopefulness among Christian readers. The train story has been compared to Jesus' parable of the Good Samaritan (Lk 10:25–37), because in both, the "least likely" character becomes the "hero" of the story.

Synopsis: On its way to the city on the other side of the mountain, a train full of toys and good food gets stuck. The dolls and toys cry out to other engines to pull their cars over the mountain. A shiny new engine says it only pulls passenger cars and would never pull the likes of *their* train. A big strong engine refuses because he claims to be a very important freight train with essential machines to carry. A rusty old engine says he's too weary for the job.

At last a little blue engine comes along and listens to their plight. She points out that she is only used to switch trains in the yard and has never been over the mountain, but she wants to help. She says, "I think I can. I think I can. I think I can." Soon she is over the mountain, happy with herself for her accomplishment. The dolls and toys are grateful to *the little engine that could* because the boys and girls in the valley will have toys and good food, thanks to her generosity.

Seeds of the Gospel: The parallel of the Good Samaritan is a good place to begin.

In *The Little Engine That Could,* the engines that refuse to help are like the people in the Good Samaritan parable who passed by the man who was beaten and half-dead on the side of the road, ignoring his need for assistance. In contrast, the little blue engine is like the Good Samaritan who dresses the poor man's wounds and takes care of him. Talk about each of the engines. About each engine that wouldn't help the train, ask: "Why wouldn't that engine help?" Then, ask about the little engine that did help. "What made that little blue engine help?" Encourage conversation about helping others and being ready to help when we're called upon.

The can-do spirit is an attribute that serves any child well. "How did the little engine do this hard job? How did she keep her mind on what she was doing?" you might ask. Also, ask: "Why did she keep trying?" When tough jobs come up, remind your child of *the little engine that could* and encourage the power of positive thinking with a suggestion to repeat: "I think I can, I think I can."

Even though we often hear the old Benjamin Franklin adage from *Poor Richard's Almanac,* "God helps them that help themselves,"as Christians, we are called to *confidence* that we can handle the difficult situations placed before us, because God is with us and helps us. You might suggest that your child pray for God's help before a hard task and then try repeating, "I think *we* can, I think *we* can, I think *we* can," to remind him or her that together with God, we can do great things!

❖◦◉◦❖

Where the Wild Things Are by Maurice Sendak

Maurice Sendak, son of Polish Jewish immigrants to America, is an award-winning, self-taught artist and storyteller who grew up in Brooklyn, New York. Because he spent a lot of his childhood indoors, Sendak began to draw and let his imagination run free. At age twelve, his family took him to see Walt Disney's *Fantasia,* which made a deep impression on the budding artist. Sendak considers Disney's art, as well as the images evoked by the poetry of William Blake, to be his greatest influences. His long and prosperous career began in high school, when he worked for All-American Comics on the *Mutt and Jeff* comic strip.

As author of nearly fifty children's stories in fifty years, he considers story the most important part of children's books because art alone is not enough to make them good books. Sendak's work has won numerous awards, including the Caldecott Medal, the Hans Christian Andersen Award, the Lewis Carroll Shelf Award, and others throughout the world. Sendak lives and works in Connecticut.

Background: *Where the Wild Things Are,* published in 1963, is Sendak's best-known fantasy. When it was first published, its monsters concerned parents, but it soon became a best-seller...and has remained in print and extremely popular ever since.

Synopsis: Max is sent to his room for being mischievous and enters into a world of imagination, where he is king of all wild things and sends the beasts to bed without their supper. But Max gets tired of being king (and perhaps of being wild, too) and wants to be where "someone loves him best of all." He "returns" to his room and finds supper waiting for him...and it's still hot!

Seeds of the Gospel: Max learns that being wild and having power mean nothing compared to being loved. Even though Max needs to be disciplined for mischief, his mother still loves him and nurtures him, which the author demonstrates through warm food. "How do you think Max felt when he found that dinner?" you could begin.

While this book presents a perfect opportunity for parents to reinforce the notion that we love our kids unconditionally, no matter how many wild things they do, the story also offers an opportunity to find out how your child feels about being a kid. "Why do you think Max wanted to go where the wild things are?" you might ask, and: "How do you think he felt to be king?" Conversation may offer some insights into things that are bothering her or things he may find unfair. If anything comes up, use the opportunity to reinforce the truth that parents impose rules because they love their children and want them to be safe and happy. Part of becoming happy is becoming disciplined.

If your child is afraid of monsters, Max may be a surprisingly good role model. After sharing the story, you could mention that the monsters are afraid of Max and point out that he becomes king of all wild things. "How do you think Max feels when the monsters make him king? Why do they listen to him?" you might ask. A possible thread of conversation could be that Max conjures the monsters with his own imagination, so he remains in charge of them at all times.

Or, if your child won't accept that monsters are imaginary—and we want to encourage imagination—simply point out that, like Max, little children are able to command monsters to behave and even have fun with them and make friends with them, so there's no reason to fear them. This aspect of the story contains a seed of the Gospel expressed in St. Paul's second letter to Timothy: "God did not give us a spirit of cowardice, but rather a spirit of power and of love and of self-discipline" (1:7). By taming the beasts, Max learns a little about the importance of self-discipline, and then returns home, where he is loved.

———— •••• ————

Little Bear's Trousers by Jane Hissey

Jane Hissey is a British author who taught art in a college until she had children. Staying at home with two boys and a girl, Hissey began to work on drawings of her own childhood toys and to create stories about them, using her children's ideas. In 1988, she published *Old Bear,* followed by a succession of wonderful picture books as well as an animated television series about her toys. She lives in East Sussex, England, with her kids and her husband, Ivan. Earlier in her life, she tells a funny story of the encouragement her father gave her when she learned to read:

> The day I learned to read, my father fell through the floor! I remember running the half-mile home from school that day, clutching my reading book "The, big, red, lorry, went, up, the, hill. The, pots, and, pans, went, up, the, hill. The, pots, and, pans, were, in, the, big, red, lorry!" My father, home on leave from the navy, was trying to mend a rotten floor in a room at the back of the house. I dashed in calling, "Listen to me, Daddy, I can read!" and began to recount the story of the big red lorry. As I started to read there was the sound of splintering wood, and my father disappeared into the black hole under the floor that had probably not been visited for 200 years. To give him his due, he emerged from the darkness of the underfloor world filthy and cobweb-covered but smiling (probably desperate not to dampen my enthusiasm for literature!). I, for my part, decided that this was a suitably dramatic reaction to my good news and that reading was obviously going to be very exciting.[33]

Background: Jane Hissey's drawings are based on toys in her own home. Little Bear and Bramwell Brown are teddy bears given to her oldest son, Owen; Old Bear is the author's own childhood teddy.

Synopsis: Little Bear wakes up one morning and can't find his trousers. He sets out on a quest through the house to find them, and discovers that his trousers are leading a life of their own! Camel used them for hump warmers, then Sailor, a sea-faring doll, used them for sails. But Sailor didn't like them because they looked too much like trousers. "That's because they *are* trousers," Little Bear tells him. Dog took them next for a "two-bone holder," but the bones kept falling out. So, Rabbit took them to use as a ski hat, but they fell over his eyes and he crashed. Zebra took the trousers to carry blocks for a house he was building, and then gave them to Duck for a sandcastle flag. Duck passed them along to Bramwell Brown, who filled them with icing to use as a pastry bag that makes two stripes at once. Poor Little Bear is very upset to find his pants full of icing, so Bramwell makes a Trousers Day cake, which all of the toys enjoy while Little Bear's freshly washed trousers are drying.

Seeds of the Gospel: Little Bear woke up with plans to "do something different," and he did. But he wasn't counting on spending the day looking for his trousers and discovering that everyone used them without recognizing they are his, which makes him feel cross, exasperated, and, I think, overlooked. When at last he finds his britches, he can't even put them on and tries hard not to cry. He has reached his emotional limit. "I wonder how it would feel to have a day like that!" you might say...and wait for a response. If nothing comes up, try: "What made Little Bear so upset?"

One subject this book addresses well is respect for personal property. When Camel finds the pants, he assumes they are hump warmers without trying to find out if they belong to anyone, and thus begins the odyssey of Little Bear's trousers. "What do we do when we want to use something and we don't know whose it is?" you can ask. Reinforce the idea that we *ask* before we borrow things at home or in school or at someone else's house out of respect for the person to whom the things belong.

By the same token, the book is also an invitation to mention that Little Bear didn't put away his trousers before he went to bed, so Camel didn't know what they were. If not putting away toys or clothes is a problem, this might be a good way to broach the subject. Try asking: "What should Little Bear have done with his trousers before he went to bed? Why do you think he left them where they were?" If the answer is that he forgot, suggest gently that Little Bear needs to try harder to take care of his things. This is a seed of the Gospel known as stewardship. If everything we have is a gift from God, then we are called to take care of what we are given—an idea Jesus shared in the parable of the talents (Mt 25:14–30), which you will find on page 19. The servant who could be trusted in small matters was later trusted with greater things, just as we prepare our kids for responsibility by building trust in small matters such as cleaning up after themselves or completing chores.

Another great seed of the Gospel in this story that you can discuss with kids is the Eucharistic theme of reconciliation and thanksgiving presented at the end. Little Bear can't recognize the creative spirit around him as he is led from one animal to the next, and he feels hurt and dejected. When he finally locates his trousers, Old Bear comes to console him and set things right by having the pants washed. Little Bear feels grateful to Old Bear for understanding and is thankful to have his trousers again. All is forgiven, and the animals gather to celebrate a moment of reconciliation with a special cake for a remarkable day. What was lost has been found— the trousers as well as Little Bear's feeling of belonging. "How do you think Little Bear feels when he finds his trousers?" you could ask. "How does he feel at the end of the story? What makes him feel that way?"

As parents, we all feel like Little Bear sometimes: getting up to greet the day with a vision of something new and wonderful, and then getting the new, but not seeing its wonder. All the animals imagined ways to use the trousers that make us laugh. Their creativity is astounding! But Little Bear is frustrated. His mind is focused on one goal, which his friends' ingenuity keeps him from reaching. As a parent, I have used this story as a prayer to remind me to keep my sense of humor when my own little bears found "funny new ways" to use my things that dashed previous big plans for the day—like decorating my dining room chairs with lipstick or the massive overflow caused by "someone" flushing a whole roll of toilet paper. However you use this story, you're sure to find ways to apply its lessons to real life in your home that help cultivate its seeds of the Gospel.

———◦•◦◦•◦———

Adelita: A Mexican Cinderella Story by Tomie dePaola

Tomie dePaola was born in Meriden, Connecticut, in 1934, and grew up in an Irish-Italian Catholic family. At age four, he announced that he would write and illustrate children's books, which he loved because his mother read to him every day. He studied art at Pratt Institute in Brooklyn, New York, and graduated in 1956. Several years later, dePaola's first book, *The Wonderful Dragon of Timlin,* was published. The author began a dual career in 1962 when he became an art professor at Newton College of the Sacred Heart in Massachusetts. After several years, dePaola moved to San Francisco for a teaching position at Lone Mountain College, using the opportunity to earn his Master of Fine Arts degree from the California College of Arts and Crafts in 1969, and his doctoral equivalency from Lone Mountain in 1970. He returned to New England in 1972, teaching at several colleges throughout the 1970s before focusing solely on his writing career. Author of more than 100 stories for children and illustrator of more than 200 books, dePaola works today in his New London, New Hampshire studio, attached to a renovated 200-year-old barn.

Synopsis: Adelita is a beautiful child whose mother dies. Her father raises her with the help of Esperanza, a kind, loving nanny. Adelita's father remarries a widow with two ugly daughters. When Adelita's father dies, the stepmother's true colors show: she fires Esperanza, relegates Adelita to the attic, and forces her to work as the maid. An invitation arrives for a fiesta celebrating the homecoming of Javier, who was a childhood friend of Adelita and is rumored to be seeking a bride. Doña Micaela refuses to include Adelita, but, after the stepfamily leaves for the fiesta, Esperanza

Tomie dePaola

In addition to fictional stories from popular culture, parents will want to include Bible stories and anecdotes from the lives of the saints in encouraging a child's spiritual growth. Artist and author Tomie dePaola has created a wonderful array of stories that Catholic families will enjoy. Titles include:

Clown of God

The Christmas Pageant: Text from the Stories of Matthew and Luke

The Lady of Guadalupe

The Legend of Old Befana

The Little Friar Who Flew (author Patricia Lee Gauch)

Francis: Poor Man of Assisi

The Story of the Three Wise Kings

Noah and the Ark

David and Goliath

The Miracles of Jesus

The Parables of Jesus

Tomie dePaola's Book of Bible Stories

My First Easter

Patrick: Patron Saint of Ireland

The Great Adventure of Christopher Columbus

Legend of the Poinsettia

Christopher: The Holy Giant

Mary, Mother of Jesus

Tomie dePaola's Book of the Old Testament

Holy Twins: Benedict and Scholastica (author Kathleen Norris)

Pascual and the Kitchen Angels

arrives, having learned Adelita's plight in a dream. She leads Adelita to a beautiful white dress and red *rebozo,* or shawl, that belonged to Adelita's mother. When the stunning Adelita arrives at the party, Javier falls in love at first sight. Afraid his parents will refuse to allow him to marry a kitchen maid, Adelita flees the fiesta. The next day, Javier searches for his love. From her attic room, Adelita hangs her *rebozo* from the window; Javier sees it and dashes to find her. Doña Micaela says no one but her daughters are there, but Adelita enters, wearing her dress and *rebozo,* to the stepmother's shock and Javier's delight. Graciously, Adelita includes the horrible stepfamily in the wedding, and the couple lives happily ever after.

Seeds of the Gospel: Every Cinderella story contains a message of hope and human dignity that bears the seeds of the Gospel. Tomie dePaola's Mexican version of the story is especially charming with its touching illustrations, many references to Latin American culture, and the inclusion of Spanish words and phrases in the text. Catholic families will enjoy pointing out symbols of our faith within the illustrations of Adelita's home, such as the crucifix and the portrait of Mary that resembles Our Lady of Sorrows.

After Doña Micaela denies Adelita's request to attend Javier's fiesta, the girl, utterly dejected, carries dirty dishes back to the kitchen, passing the Blessed Mother's portrait. The sorrowful Mary seems to be looking at Adelita and praying for her in her suffering. "Do you know who that is in that picture?" you might ask. If your child isn't familiar with the image of Mary, talk about the Blessed Mother: "That's Mary, Jesus' mother! She must be praying for Adelita. What do you suppose Mary is asking God to do for Adelita? Why does God listen to Mary? Did you know she prays for us, too?" Mary is the Mother of God, the *Theotokos,* but her spiritual motherhood extends to all God's children. As our spiritual Mother, she prays for us and stands ready to listen to our concerns.

Esperanza is the name of Adelita's nanny, but the word *"esperanza"* means "hope" in Spanish. When Adelita loses her privileged life

Our Lady of Sorrows

Our Lady of Sorrows, a representation of Mary, Mother of Christ, dates to apostolic times. Traditionally robed in black with seven swords piercing her heart, this image represents the Blessed Mother who suffered, especially at the foot of the cross as her son and her God died in agony.

Devotion to Our Lady of Sorrows flowered in the Middle Ages, when the hymn *Stabat Mater* was composed:

At the Cross her station keeping,
Stood the mournful Mother weeping
Close to Jesus to the last.

The Church formally recognized the title "Our Lady of Sorrows" in the fourteenth century and encouraged contemplation on the seven dolors of Mary, who, as the first and greatest disciple of Jesus, participated most intimately in his redemptive suffering. Based in Scripture, the dolors include:

The prophecy of Simeon (Lk 2:34–35);

The flight into Egypt (Mt 2:13–21);

The loss of the Child Jesus for three days (Lk 2:41–50);

Meeting Jesus on his way to Calvary (Jn 19:17);

Jesus' crucifixion and death (Jn 19:18–30);

Jesus taken down from the cross (Jn 19:39–40);

Jesus laid in the tomb (Jn 19:40–42).

In 1499, Michelangelo depicted this image in the *Pietà*, now at St. Peter's Basilica, the Vatican. Devotion to Our Lady of Sorrows encourages the faithful to share our own sufferings with Mary, who understands, and to do penance for the pain caused by our sins.

— Adapted from an article by John O'Connell in *The Catholic Faith*, March/April 1998. www.catholic.net/rcc/Periodicals/Faith/1998-03-04/sorrows.html

and becomes the kitchen maid for her stepfamily, she also loses Esperanza, the woman who mothered and loved her since birth. When the stepmother and stepsisters attend the fiesta without her, Adelita loses *"esperanza"* as well. At that moment of mourning and weeping, Esperanza arrives to restore Adelita's hope of a happy future and provides a plan to help her get to the fiesta. "How did Esperanza know that Adelita needed her?" you might ask. Talk to your child about the dreams Joseph had during the events of the Nativity, described in the Gospel of Matthew: Joseph wanted to end his engagement to Mary until he learned in a dream that she was telling the truth about her virgin motherhood; and he learned in a dream that they should flee to Egypt with baby Jesus (Mt 1:20; 2:13–16). Throughout Christian history, many saints also learned God's will through dreams. "Sometimes God talks to saints through dreams," you might venture. "Why do you think God might do that?" If the subject of bad dreams arises, talk about them, but remind kids that God wouldn't send a nightmare, only a dream that reminds us we are loved.

> ## Liturgical Colors
>
> **The variety of liturgical colors in the Church arose from the mystical meaning attached to them. Thus white, the symbol of light, typifies innocence and purity, joy and glory; red, the language of fire and blood, indicates burning charity and the martyrs' generous sacrifice; green, the hue of plants and trees, bespeaks the hope of life eternal; violet, the [penitential] cast of the mortified, denotes affliction and melancholy.**
>
> www.newadvent.org/cathen/ 04134a.htm

Esperanza leads Adelita to an old-fashioned white garment and a beautiful red shawl—colors deeply symbolic for the Church. White, symbolizing new life, is the color we wear when we are baptized. In the Church, as in art, white represents reverence, purity, innocence, simplicity, and humility. Red is the liturgical color for the celebration of a martyr's feast day, and also the color used on Good

Friday. Red marks the descent of the Holy Spirit on Pentecost and in the sacrament of confirmation, coming to the baptized in a special way, strengthening our union with Christ and equipping us for full participation in the life of the Church. In art, red represents passion, life, and vitality, a sensual color associated with our most profound urges and impulses. Talk about Adelita's outfit: "Why did Esperanza show Adelita the new dress?" you could begin. "How do you think Adelita felt in her mother's clothes? How do you think she felt when she arrived at the fiesta?" If your child can handle a discussion about color symbolism, ask about the white dress: "What does that white dress remind you of?" Answers will likely include a wedding dress, First Communion dress, or christening gown. Talk about the reasons for wearing white gowns during the sacraments of marriage, first Eucharist, and Baptism to mark newness in our lives and what that might mean in this story.

Adelita puts on the clothes of a woman ready for full participation in the fiesta and in life. She arrives at the celebration in radiance and splendor—and captures Javier's heart. No one recognizes Adelita as this "new creature," a scene that calls forth the words of St. Paul in his letter to the Ephesians: "You were taught to put away your former way of life, your old self...to be renewed in the spirit of your minds, and to clothe yourselves with the new self, created according to the likeness of God in true righteousness and holiness" (4:22–24). Adelita gains abundant love in her new life—even to the point of forgiving her horrible stepfamily for their transgressions. "What changes for Adelita?" you might ask. "What stays the same?"

Talk about Adelita's kind heart: "Do you think it was hard for Adelita to forgive her stepfamily for all that they did to her?" Adelita's family tried to prevent her from attaining joy and dignity. Esperanza, instead, attended to Adelita's quiet suffering in a way that shocked (and humiliated) her stepfamily at first. She turned Adelita's mourning for the lost fiesta experience into joy, the kind expressed in King David's psalms: "You have turned my mourning into dancing; you have taken off my sackcloth and clothed me with joy" (Ps 30:11).

Adelita's generosity and mercy toward her stepfamily is a wonderful way to plant the Gospel seed of love of enemies in a way that children can understand: "Love your enemies, pray for those who persecute you" (Mt 5:43–44).

Adelita is a model of virtue for young story lovers that kids of all ages will enjoy.

———◆◆◆◆———

Pedro and the Monkey by Robert D. San Souci

Robert D. San Souci has written more than eighty children's books, mainly retelling traditional folk tales from various cultures. A native Californian who lives in San Francisco, the author says his goal in bringing these stories to today's children is to help them discover "how much we share in common with people around the world, while underscoring just how rich, unique, and wise many of these sometimes unfamiliar cultures are in their diverse histories and traditions."

For the illustration of his work, San Souci has collaborated with artists from Moscow to Mexico City. Nonetheless, his favorite illustrator remains Daniel San Souci, his brother. Together, they have published nine books, including *Two Bear Cubs,* a Miwok legend about bears in California's Yosemite Valley.

Robert San Souci wrote the script for the Disney animated film, *Mulan,* as well as a book about the story, *Fa Mulan,* his own original, historically-based retelling of the ancient Chinese legend about a girl who disguises herself as a man to preserve her family's honor. His book, *The Talking Eggs,* illustrated by Jerry Pinkney, received Caldecott and Coretta Scott King honors.

Background: This version of the classic "Puss 'n Boots" story is well known throughout the Philippines. Folklorists believe the story arrived with colonists from Spain. Rather than a clever cat, though, this tale features a clever monkey. (In Siberia and Mongolia, the animal is a fox, and in India, a jackal.) The author made significant efforts to include Filipino culture in his retelling.

Synopsis: A poor farmer in the Philippines traps a pesky monkey that shocks the farmer by begging to be let go. Pedro releases the monkey, and the animal repays the kindness with a promise to arrange Pedro's marriage to the daughter of a wealthy man. Through cunning, the monkey transforms Pedro into a desirable suitor. When Pedro meets the daughter, Maria, the two fall in love. But the father wants to call on Pedro at his home before agreeing to a marriage. The monkey goes to the splendid manor house of an evil giant named Burincantada and tells him that an ogre is coming his way. The giant dives into a trap door, never to be seen again, leaving the home and all of its riches up for grabs. Pedro and the monkey discover cages filled with people, whom they set free. Grateful, the captives work to get the house and land in order, and two days later, Pedro receives Maria and her father at the magnificent home. They get married and live happily ever after.

Seeds of the Gospel: This story of a poor farmer and a cunning monkey is an interesting tale that offers an opportunity to talk about the Gospel message from two different perspectives. The seeds of the Gospel evident in the story of Pedro's life are love and purity of heart—good virtues to point out and to encourage in our kids' daily lives. But a "counter-Gospel message" runs through this story that proves as tricky and pesky as the monkey itself: the monkey willingly tricks everyone into believing that Pedro is someone he is not. A careful discussion of this story could introduce kids to the notion of "the end justifying the means" and allow parents to explain the importance of acting honestly, whatever the circumstance.

Talk about the seeds of the Gospel first. Pedro has a good heart, full of love to be shared. After he traps the monkey in his cornfield, kindhearted Pedro pities the animal and sets it free. Discuss Pedro's good deed: "What else might Pedro have done with the monkey? Why do you think he set the monkey free?" The monkey chooses to repay Pedro's charity and shocks Pedro with its extraordinary cunning and insight. Talk about the monkey's cleverness: "Why do you think the monkey is so smart and able to know what Pedro wants? How do you think Pedro felt when the monkey talked to him?"

Although the monkey arranges many things for Pedro—a meeting with Don Francisco, new clothes, fancy house, land, lots of money, and, of course, the girl—Pedro's happiness stems from his love for Maria rather than the riches and comfort that the monkey provides. Love is the source of the couple's bliss. Talk about the changes in Pedro's life. "Pedro's life sure is different now," you might point out. "What are some of the things that have changed? Was Pedro happy before? Do you think he is happier now? Why?"

"Literature is news that *stays* news."

— Ezra Pound, *ABC of Reading*

Near the end of the story, Pedro and the monkey find people who have been trapped by the local giant, and they set them free. Freedom from evil is an important seed of the Gospel that can be planted within a child through this story, for Jesus came to free us from the slavery of sin, so we can live our lives in love. Discuss the presence of evil in the story: "Why did the monkey get rid of the giant? How do you think the people felt when that happened? Can you imagine how you would feel if that happened to you?" If your child is plagued by a bully, this kind of "liberation" story might offer some comfort and might call forth for you a few tidbits of information about the goings-on in your child's life.

Despite the good things that happen to Pedro in this story, something isn't quite right. The monkey sets out to repay Pedro's kindness, but he does so by tricking others. For example, the monkey knows that only riches will impress the wealthy man, so he contrives a scheme that will appeal to this value. Likewise, the monkey strokes the textile merchant's pride in gaining a "rich" client and cleverly convinces the merchant to extend him credit. You might begin talking in a general way about the monkey: "I'm not sure I like the way the monkey acts. He doesn't tell the truth. Why does the monkey make up stories about Pedro and pretend Pedro's rich?"

Talk about Pedro's reaction to the monkey's antics: "How do you think Pedro feels when he finds out about the stories the monkey makes up about him?" Then, to emphasize the deeper message of this outlandish tale, talk about the desire of Pedro's heart: "Pedro didn't ask for anything, but the monkey knew he wanted something very badly. What was it that Pedro really wanted? Why is that [love] more important than the big house and fancy clothes?"

A fun activity to share with kids is to compare and contrast various Puss 'n Boots stories, such as *Puss 'n Boots* by Marcia Brown or *Puss in Cowboy Boots* by Jan Huling and Phil Huling. Your local librarian may be able to direct you to versions of the story from other cultures as well. Talk about the ways the clever animal is different in each version of the story, and why similar stories can be so different!

—◆◆◆◆—

Luba and the Wren by Patricia Polacco

Patricia Polacco spent her early years in Michigan. When her parents divorced, she lived with her mother and maternal grandparents on a farm during the school year and with her father and his parents all summer. At age five, she moved to Florida, then to a colorful multicultural neighborhood in Oakland, California. A teacher discovered that Polacco, who still couldn't read at age fourteen, had dyslexia. When she got the help she needed, Polacco became a great student and went on to earn a Ph.D. in art history. She worked for museums, restoring ancient art, until she had children. At age forty-one, she began writing and illustrating the stories she heard growing up, producing dozens of delightful children's books.

Background: Patricia Polacco's maternal grandparents were of Ukrainian and Russian descent and shared with her many stories from their culture. This story, published in 1999, is set in the Ukraine and carries a strong Christian message, indicated in the dedication by a Scripture passage: "For where your treasure is, there will your heart be also" (Mt 6:21).

Synopsis: Luba lives with her parents, a poor farmer and his wife, in a humble dacha. Despite material poverty, Luba is joyous and free. One day, deep in the forest, Luba helps a wren escape a fowler's net. The enchanted bird speaks to Luba and grants her anything she wishes, but Luba has everything she wants—love, family, freedom to be a child. When she tells her parents about the magic bird, they beg her to request a bigger house on fertile land. Luba obeys, and their home is transformed. Luba hopes her parents will be happy, but they want still more— an estate with servants, then a palace where they can rule over the Ukraine, then a grander palace to rule as tsar and tsarina of Russia, then to rule over the whole world.

As her parents become greedier, Luba grows sadder. Finally, her parents demand she request that they become like gods. Luba, though horrified by their bombastic request, obediently braves a raging storm to find the wren. When she returns, she finds her original home, humble as ever, and her parents working on the porch. When they see her, they embrace her and call her their treasure. At long last, her parents are happy. And Luba is very happy again, too.

> Vices can be classified according to the virtues they oppose, or also be linked to the capital sins which Christian experience has distinguished, following St. John Cassian and St. Gregory the Great. They are called "capital" because they engender other sins, other vices. They are pride, avarice, envy, wrath, lust, gluttony, and sloth [...].
>
> — *Catechism of the Catholic Church,* Libreria Editrice Vaticana

Seeds of the Gospel: Luba's parents long for material wealth, but no matter how much they get, they want still more. They become meaner and more selfish with each new development, and Luba becomes more and more unhappy. Greed, or avarice, is one of "the seven capital sins," and is also mentioned in the Ten Commandments: "You shall not covet your neighbor's house; you shall not covet your neighbor's wife, or male or female slave, or ox, or donkey, or anything that belongs to your neighbor" (Ex 20:17).

Jesus addressed the problem of greed and materialism with a seed of the Gospel, saying, "Take care! Be on your guard against all kinds of greed; for one's life does not consist in the abundance of possessions" (Lk 12:15). Jesus elucidated this truth with a parable, called the Parable of the Rich Fool:

> Then he told them a parable: "The land of a rich man produced abundantly. And he thought to himself, 'What should I do, for I have no place to store my crops?' Then he said, 'I will do this: I will pull down my barns and build larger ones, and there I will store all my grain and my goods. And I will say to my soul, "Soul, you have ample goods laid up for many years; relax, eat, drink, be merry."' But God said to him, 'You fool! This very night your life is being demanded of you. And the things you have prepared, whose will they be?' So it is with those who store up treasures for themselves but are not rich toward God" (Lk 12:16–21).

Ask your child for insights into the parents' materialism: "What were Luba's parents trying to find when they asked for more and more things? Why were they still unhappy with their riches? How did they act when they became rich?"

Talk about the Gospel seed on the book's dedication page: "For where your treasure is, there will your heart be also" (Mt 6:21). Ask your child: "What did Luba's parents treasure at first? How did they change in the story?" When they become materially poor again, they become rich with contentment and joy. Talk to your child about the way they act at the end of the story and try asking: "Why do you think the parents were happier at the end? What do they treasure at the end?"

After taking over the whole world, Luba's parents ask to become like gods. What they get is not what we expect to happen in the story, yet they find happiness, the truest wealth we can receive, and learn to cherish their daughter, who is a gift to them from God. Talk about happiness coming from God and about the value of human life in God's eyes by asking: "How do Luba's parents become like God at the end of the story?"

Luba is a good and obedient child. Talk about her plight: "What made Luba sad in the story? Why was she happy at the end?" Another good conversation starter is to ask what your child would wish for if a magical bird came along. Be prepared, though, for the answer. When I asked my youngest this question during a rather hectic time in our lives, he said bluntly, "To have fun with you." It is from the mouths of babes that we often hear God's voice.

The Rainbow Fish by Marcus Pfister

Marcus Pfister has lived in Berne, Switzerland, all his life. He first worked as a graphic artist in an advertising agency. Then, in 1983, he began to write and illustrate children's books, doing most of his illustrations in watercolor. He and his wife, Kathryn, have three children.

Background: *The Rainbow Fish* is the first of Pfister's books to be sold in the United States, where it has remained a best-seller since 1992. This colorful picture book won a Christopher Award in 1993.

Synopsis: Rainbow Fish is the most beautiful fish in the ocean, with blue, green, purple, and shiny silver scales. But he is selfish and vain and ignores the other fish. One day, a little blue fish asks him to share a shiny scale, but Rainbow Fish tells him to go away. When the little fish tells the others what Rainbow Fish said, they begin to ignore the haughty fish.

Rainbow Fish soon feels lonely and pours out his heart to a starfish. Next he goes to the wise octopus to find out why no one likes him. The octopus tells the Rainbow Fish to give away his glittering scales; it will make him less beautiful, but happy. The fish thinks he can't part with any of his gorgeous scales, until the little blue fish returns and asks once more for a scale. This time, Rainbow Fish gives away a scale, and a peculiar feeling comes over him. Soon, all of the fish want one shiny scale, and Rainbow Fish begins to share. The more he gives away, the happier he becomes. With only one scale remaining, Rainbow Fish enjoys his new friends.

Seeds of the Gospel: Deep in the ocean, the mysterious octopus is like God, calling Rainbow Fish to detachment. As Christians, we are expected to become detached from possessions, willing to give them up when God desires it. The octopus knows that Rainbow Fish will only be happy when he learns to give of himself. "Why did Rainbow Fish have trouble sharing his scales?" you might begin, and perhaps: "I wonder what the octopus would ask us to share?"

The call to share what we have is a seed of the Gospel, expressed by John the Baptist: "Whoever has two coats must share with anyone who has none; and whoever has food must do likewise" (Lk 3:11). Talk about the good feeling we get from sharing, if that is appropriate for your child's stage of development. (As we parents know, kids in the early years don't particularly like sharing. It's all "mine, mine, mine"!) If it is a notion your child can handle, try asking: "Why do we feel so good when we share or do something nice for someone? Why do you think God wants us to share?"

Use this great story to talk about friendship, too. "What did Rainbow Fish do to make friends with the other fish? How do you think he felt about that?" Talk about our call to be kind to our friends: "Do good to friends before you die, and reach out and give to them as much as you can" (Sir 14:13). You might ask: "We don't have any shiny scales to give, but what are some nice things we can do for our friends?" If a good idea surfaces from your child, help your child to do the good deed, putting faith in action for a friend.

The Lotus Seed by Sherry Garland

A fifth-generation Texan, **Sherry Garland** was born in the Rio Grande Valley near the Mexican border, the youngest of nine children. Her parents worked as tenant farmers until a devastating freeze ruined their crops, forcing her father to find work as a carpenter and builder. As a result, her family struggled and moved many times during her childhood. She graduated from high school in Arlington, Texas, and from the University of Texas at Arlington, with a major in French, before her marriage. She and her husband lived in Houston for twenty-two years before moving to a house in the woods in central Texas, where they live today.

Garland has authored twenty-five books for children, teenagers, and adults, including a book on how to write. While many of her books are set in the Lone Star State, such as *The Silent Storm* and *A Line in the Sand: The Alamo Diary of Lucinda Lawrence,* seven of Garland's books, including *The Lotus Seed*, highlight Vietnamese culture and grew out of her friendships with Vietnamese war refugees who settled in Houston. The author's honors include an ALA Best Book for Young Adults Award and a Texas Institute of Letters Award.

Background: Vietnam was ruled for centuries by emperors believed to be appointed by God. In the area of Hue, one emperor built a forbidden city, much like the one in Peking, filled with lotus moats and gardens. When France colonized Vietnam in the nineteenth century, emperors lost their power. In 1925, a twelve-year-old boy, Nguyen Vinh Thuy, became the last emperor of Vietnam— *Bao Dai,* Keeper of Greatness. In 1945, the Vietnamese people wanted freedom from French rule, so Bao Dai handed over his golden seal and golden sword to Ho Chi Minh, leader of the independence movement. The Vietnamese fought in a horrible, bloody war until they defeated the French in 1954. Soon afterward, Communist forces from the north began a takeover of the newly independent nation. The United States assisted the South Vietnamese until

American public sentiment forced the United States to pull out of the conflict. In 1975, the North Vietnamese army took over the entire country, and a million Vietnamese fled their native land, mostly to America, by boat.

Synopsis: A Vietnamese narrator tells the story of her grandmother, Bá, who as a girl sees the last emperor of Vietnam crying on the day he abdicates his throne. She sneaks into the palace gardens, near the River of Perfumes, to snatch a lotus seed as a memento. She keeps the seed with her throughout the war and takes it on the boat as she flees her country to a new life in America. One day, the narrator's brother finds the seed and plants it in the mud near the grandmother's onion patch. Inconsolable, the grandmother grieves the loss of her country, until the following spring when a lotus blossom bursts forth, providing seeds for each of her grandchildren and one for herself to remember the emperor. The narrator vows to plant her seed one day, passing along this new tradition, and keeping alive her grandmother's story.

Seeds of the Gospel: Jesus often used the metaphor of seeds to explain his teachings. For example, he said, "What is the Kingdom of God like? And to what should I compare it? It is like a mustard seed that someone took and sowed in the garden; it grew and became a tree, and the birds of the air made nests in its branches" (Lk 13:18–19). Elsewhere in the Gospels he offers the parable of the sower, the parable of the seed, and the parable of the weeds. Likewise, St. Paul used the metaphor of a seed in his first letter to the Church at Corinth: "You do not sow the body that is to be, but a bare seed, perhaps of wheat or of some other grain. But God gives it a body as he has chosen, and to each kind of seed its own body" (15:37–38). Seeds are meant to represent potential, promise, and new life in Sacred Scripture as well as literature. Sometimes, Jesus used the image of seeds to represent the word of God to be planted within our hearts—full of hope and promise if properly cultivated in faith. While the seed contains new life, how that life develops depends on how it is nurtured.

Throughout Asia the lotus represents purity, beauty, and serenity. The lotus also serves as a symbol of the pure person who remains faithful to values and ideals in the midst of corruption. In Vietnam the lotus is one of the four noble plants used to represent the four seasons: the plum tree is spring; the lotus, summer; the chry-santhemum, autumn; and the bamboo, winter. Buddhist temples keep lotus blossoms present to calm the fervor of monks, or *bonzes,* and to allow worshippers to feel carried away from their cares by the flower's sweet scent. In a botanical sense, the lotus easily adapts to its surroundings, purifies the mud in which it grows, and improves the landscape with both its beauty and fragrance. Symbolically, then, the lotus represents that which can stand amidst the sordid and destroy the "stench" of evil by remaining steadfast and true. This sentiment is articulated in a Vietnamese expression that can be applied to either a person or a lotus—*Cu trần bất nhiễm trần,* meaning "Live in the society without being contaminated by its vices."

In Garland's book, the lotus seed represents the memory of an innocent girl. She clings steadfastly to the seed and to the image of what was once Vietnam, a civilization forever changed by the forced influence of other cultures and the ravages of war. In the chaos of leaving her country as one of "the boat people," the lotus seed gives her comfort and reminds her of her heritage, who she is, and where she comes from. But she keeps the seed for herself, not realizing its potential to form a special connection with her descendents.

A bit of grace allows the grandson to discover his grand-mother's treasure and to plant it in American mud, where it springs up with all the beauty and dignity of its predecessors, which once flourished in the Imperial Gardens of Hue. The seedpod produces enough seeds for each of the grandchildren—and one for the grand-mother to keep. With each seed, the grandmother passes down her heritage and her story. And the narrator plans to do the same, pass-ing on her heritage to future generations.

When Bá fled her home during a time of war, she grabbed the lotus seed rather than her beautiful combs. Talk about her decision with your kids: "Why did she choose the lotus seed?" you might ask.

Explore what might have happened if she had chosen her other option: "What would be different if she had taken the combs and not the seed? Which choice was the better one?" And don't forget the all-important: "Why?" Also, talk about what your family treasures: "What do you think we would take if we had to leave our home like that?" While ideas such as photo albums, special toys, or other items will likely come to mind, some suggested treasures may offer an element of surprise that leads to insights into a child's heart and what he or she holds dear.

Talk about the changes the grandmother endured, perhaps asking: "How do you think Bá felt to leave her country? How do you think she felt when she got to America, where people spoke a different language and lived a different way? What do you think frightened or upset her? What do you think she liked?" Try to help your child develop the compassion and understanding to which we are called as Christians by imagining what someone else feels. As we learned in John's Gospel, Jesus said: "Love one another. As I have loved you, so you also should love one another. This is how all will know that you are my disciples, if you have love for one another" (Jn 13:34).

The story of the lotus seed calls to mind a proverb from the Old Testament as well: "With closest custody, guard your heart, for in it are the sources of life" (Prov 4:23). In a biblical context, this passage refers to vigilance against evil and keeping out of trouble, but here, it also serves to underscore a truth that the heart is the wellspring of life. In Garland's story, the lotus seed is an extension of the grandmother's heart, an inextricable part of her life and all that she is. The story also calls to mind a proverb that Jesus gave us: "Where your treasure is, there your heart is also" (Mt 6:21). Through the regeneration of the seed into a lotus blossom, Bá becomes able to share a part of herself that brings her family closer together. Celebrate and share your own treasures with this wonderful story!

An important part of Vietnamese art, the lotus often appears in paintings with a duck. In literature, many poems use lotus imagery. For example:

Đố ai mà ví nhu sen?

Chung quanh cành trắng, giữa chen nhị vàng

Nhị vàng cành trắng lá xanh,

Gần bùn mà chẳng hôi tanh mùi bùn

What can be more beautiful than the lotus in the pond?

Green leaves, white flowers, yellow stamen

Gold stamen, white flowers, green leaves

Though close to the stinking mud, it does not smell its odor.

Another example offered on the back cover of Sherry Garland's book *The Lotus Seed* is:

HOA SEN

Trong đầm gì dẹp bằng sen,

Lá xanh, bông trắng, lại chen nhị vàng.

Nhị vàng, bông trắng lá xanh,

Gần bùn mà chẳng hôi tanh mùi bùn.

Nothing that grows in a pond

Surpasses the beauty of the lotus flower,

Though mired in mud, its silky yellow styles,

its milky white petals and green leaves do not smell of mud.

——◆•◈•◆——

Winnie-the-Pooh by A. A. Milne

Alan Alexander Milne was born in Scotland, but grew up in London, where his father was a schoolmaster. He was fortunate to have as teacher and mentor none other than H. G. Wells, famous author of *The Time Machine* and *The War of the Worlds*. After graduation from Trinity College, Cambridge, he worked for a humor magazine, *Punch,* until World War I began. Although Milne was a well-known pacifist, he enlisted in the Army and fought in France. His famous denunciation of the war, *Peace with Honor,* was published in 1934. Before that, Milne published a collection of verse in 1924 titled *When We Were Very Young.* His writings about Winnie-the-Pooh were published between 1926–28. Milne didn't intend to continue writing stories for children and soon moved onto other projects, including novels, plays, essays, short stories, and verse. In 1952, brain surgery left Milne an invalid. He died in 1956.

Background: A. A. Milne always said his wife, Daphne, and son, Christopher Robin, inspired the Winnie-the-Pooh stories and verse. This volume, published in 1926, is the first book Milne wrote about the funny little bear and his friends. While too long for one story session with this age group, each chapter provides a separate tale about the characters of the Hundred Acre Wood.

Note: Benjamin Hoff wrote a best seller, *The Tao of Pooh,* in which he demonstrates the Chinese philosophy of Taoism in the calm simplicity of Winnie-the-Pooh. While Hoff's argument, published in 1983, is both excellent and compelling, Milne's story also teems with seeds of the Gospel of Jesus Christ.

Synopsis: The book features anecdotes about a boy named Christopher Robin, his teddy bear, Winnie-the-Pooh, and other critters in the Hundred Acre Wood. In the first episode, Pooh asks for a balloon to float himself up to a beehive to steal honey. Pooh covers himself with mud, pretending to be a rain cloud, but still gets stung. "Silly old bear," Christopher Robin says lovingly. Next, Pooh visits Rabbit, who at first pretends he isn't home, but finally receives Pooh. On his way out of the burrow, Pooh's chubby body gets stuck in the hole, forcing him to go a week without food until his friends can yank him out. Christopher Robin calls him a silly old bear "in such a loving voice that everybody felt quite hopeful again."

Adventures continue when Piglet and Pooh go off in search of a Woozle. When Christopher Robin points out that they are following their own tracks, Pooh calls himself a "bear with no brain at all." But

Christopher Robin says he's "the best bear in the world," which soothes and cheers humble Pooh. Later, Pooh and Piglet try to catch a heffalump with Pooh's honey pot. But Pooh goes back for his treasure and gets his head stuck in the pot. Christopher Robin laughs over Pooh's predicament and brings the bear home, saying, "How I do love you."

When gloomy Eeyore comes along, Pooh notices the donkey's tail is missing and vows to help. Eeyore calls him a real friend. Pooh happens to recognize Eeyore's tail at Owl's house, where it is being used to ring the doorbell! Pooh returns Eeyore's tail, which delights them both. Later, Pooh cheers up his melancholy friend with a birthday party.

When Kanga and Roo arrive in the Hundred Acre Wood, these strangers cause suspicion because they are different—Kanga keeps her baby in a pouch. But the animals of the Hundred Acre Wood soon learn to trust and befriend the new creatures. Later, the entourage goes in search of the North Pole and learns a lesson about thoughtfulness and consideration. After a frightening flood in the forest, the story ends with Christopher Robin's party for Pooh, just because he loves his bear.

Seeds of the Gospel: Winnie-the-Pooh *is* a silly old bear who gets into difficulties because of his insatiable craving for honey. But Christopher Robin always laughs about the mishaps and tells Pooh that he loves him (chap. 2). The boy's gentleness and compassion for Pooh call to mind a description of God found in many books of the Hebrew Scriptures, such as King David's psalms: "The Lord is merciful and gracious, slow to anger and abounding in steadfast love" (103:8). "Why doesn't Christopher Robin ever get angry with Pooh?" you might ask. "How does he show him he loves him?" If the time seems appropriate, you could compare the relationship of Christopher Robin and Pooh to that of God and your child; for example: "Did you know that God loves us just like that?"

Poor Eeyore is sad most of the time. Eeyore wants friends, but he's not much fun to be around and usually refuses efforts to gladden his heart. Still, Pooh does what he can—for example, Pooh locates Eeyore's tail and returns it to him (chap. 4), which genuinely delights Eeyore; later, Pooh celebrates Eeyore's birthday (chap. 6). Meanwhile,

Christopher Robin uses a different approach with Eeyore during the "North Pole expotition" [sic] (chap. 8). When Eeyore grumbles about his tail being cold, the boy tries to help, but Eeyore continues to carp about everyone else's insensitivity to his needs. Christopher Robin simply responds, "Never mind, Eeyore." Talk about this glum character: "What makes Eeyore sad?" you could begin. "What makes him happy?" If you know a "gloomy Gus," talk about ways to help cheer up that person and why he or she may be feeling sad or blue. "What do you think of Pooh's idea to have a party for Eeyore?" you might venture. Also, talk about Christopher Robin's way of dealing with a complainer: "How does Christopher Robin help Eeyore? What does he say when Eeyore keeps complaining? How would that work with your friends?"

⟫◆⟪

"A book is not an isolated entity: it is a narration, an axis of innumerable narrations."

— Jorge Luis Borges, *In Other Inquisitions*

⟫◆⟪

As children of God, we are called to enjoy life—in *abundance*. It is an experience worth praying for with our children, asking for the gift of joy and the wisdom to recognize opportunities for joy. In the Old Testament story of Tobit, our hero prays for joy all around. "Acknowledge the Lord, for he is good," says Tobit, "and bless the King of the ages, so that his tent may be rebuilt in you in joy. May he cheer all those within you who are captives and love all those within you who are distressed to all generations forever" (Tob 13:10). Talk about bringing joy to people you meet and ways to nurture friendships with fun and camaraderie. Perhaps you could query: "Pooh makes Eeyore happy with that party, doesn't he? What are some fun things you can do with (insert name) this week?"

We are introduced to Rabbit in chapter two, when Pooh pays a visit and Rabbit pretends he isn't home! Once Rabbit realizes Pooh is at the door, he receives and welcomes him. Although parents could discuss how Rabbit lies to Pooh and tries to fool his visitor, one positive seed of the Gospel that we can unearth is Pooh's act of visiting Rabbit. Granted, Pooh admits that "Rabbit means Company...and Company means Food and Listening-to-Me-Humming, and such like," so there is some selfishness on Pooh's part. But Pooh likes Rabbit's company, and it seems to be mutual. Visiting is an act of sharing that brings grace to both parties, as we see in the example of Mary and Elizabeth in Luke's Gospel. We join the story just after Mary has found out that she is carrying the Son of God and that her older cousin, Elizabeth, is expecting for the first time as well. Mary hurries to grace Elizabeth with a visit:

> In those days Mary set out and went with haste to a Judean town in the hill country, where she entered the house of Zechariah and greeted Elizabeth. When Elizabeth heard Mary's greeting, the child leaped in her womb. And Elizabeth was filled with the Holy Spirit and exclaimed with a loud cry, "Blessed are you among women, and blessed is the fruit of your womb. And why has this happened to me, that the mother of my Lord comes to me? For as soon as I heard the sound of your greeting, the child in my womb leaped for joy. And blessed is she who believed that there would be a fulfillment of what was spoken to her by the Lord" (Lk 1:39–45).

Mary visits Elizabeth to help her prepare for motherhood. By the same token, Elizabeth surely soothes the young unwed girl who would become the Mother of the Christ by affirming her privileged role and greeting her with joy. If ever Mary worried that people would talk, the respected and holy Elizabeth made clear that Mary was truly "blessed among women." Elizabeth is a model of graciousness for receiving visits, just as Mary is a model of generosity in sharing herself by visiting. Pooh, in his own quirky little way, is also a generous giver, while Rabbit, although initially standoffish and rude, graciously welcomes his friend and breaks bread together with him. In today's fast-paced world in which visiting is becoming a lost art, this is a seed of the Gospel to plant firmly and cultivate.

Rabbit exposes his own prejudice when Kanga and Roo arrive in the Hundred Acre Wood (chap. 7). Rabbit points out that the new animals are strangers, different, Kanga carrying her baby in her pouch.

Rabbit plots to capture Roo and bribe Kanga with information of Roo's whereabouts if Kanga agrees to leave the forest. (When you really think about Rabbit, he is not the nicest character in the Wood!) Rabbit displays cunning in this episode by involving Pooh and Piglet in his plot, but he experiences a change of heart when he captures Roo and learns to love the little critter. Meanwhile, Kanga catches on to the subterfuge and plays along, pretending not to notice that Piglet is posing as Roo. In the end, everything is forgiven, and they all become friends. "Why was Rabbit suspicious of Kanga?" you might ask. "Why did he want them to leave the Hundred Acre Wood? What changed his mind?" Try to talk about tolerance and including others, even when they're different from us, remembering the words of Jesus, "Do not judge, so that you may not be judged" (Mt 7:1), for the root of *prejudice* is *to judge.*

The North Pole "expotition" offers a seed of the Gospel about thoughtfulness and consideration. When Pooh doesn't understand what "ambush" means, he asks Piglet, "What sort of bush?" Owl, "in his superior way," makes note of Pooh's ignorance, which brings on a severe reproach from Pooh's devoted friend, Piglet, who tells Owl, "Pooh's whisper was a perfectly private whisper." Later, Eeyore tells Pooh, "A little consideration, a little thought for others, makes all the difference." St. Paul explored this Gospel message in his first letter to the Corinthians: "Love is patient; love is kind; love is not envious or boastful or arrogant" (13:4–7). Owl shows no love toward Pooh with his condescending tone and the way he calls attention to Pooh's insufficient vocabulary. (In Milne's work, Owl is far from the wise, lovable bird in the Disney version of the story; on the contrary, he is supercilious and dishonest.) But Piglet stands up for his friend. Talk about Piglet's love and courage: "Piglet is really brave to stand up to Owl! Why did he speak up when Owl made fun of Pooh?"

Seeds of the Gospel abound in this story—and I could go on for several more pages unearthing them. But the rest are for you to work on. Enjoy the ideas offered here, and then venture out on your own in the many wonderful works of children's literature available today. For more ideas, check your local library as well as our list of possibilities in chapter ten.

7

Gospel Seeds Nurtured

You can't depend on your eyes when your imagination is out of focus.

— Mark Twain

In this chapter, we offer more complex stories with further opportunity for tending and watering the seeds of the Gospel to be found in popular children's literature. Some of these stories are good to read aloud to younger children, if they can deal with a story that carries over from day to day. As children become readers, you might take turns reading paragraphs, pages, or chapters together. But keep reading aloud to kids for as long as they will listen! It remains a comforting moment of family time that provides many happy memories, plus the act of listening to a story and envisioning what is happening and who is involved is a great way to encourage, enhance, and, as Mark Twain said, "focus" a child's imagination.

The Velveteen Rabbit by Margery Williams

Margery Williams Bianco was born in London, England in 1881 and came to the United States at age nine. She alternated living in both countries for the rest of her life. At age twenty-one, in 1902, Williams published her first novel for adults. In later years, she produced thirty children's books. She died in 1944.

Background: *The Velveteen Rabbit,* or *How Toys Become Real,* is the first and best known of Margery Williams' children's books. It was published in 1922.

Note: I placed this story at the beginning of this section for older children, rather than in the previous chapter, because my own kids never enjoyed it until they were at least third graders. While it seems a simple story, it is rather long and complex for very young kids to listen to and will probably take more than one reading session to complete, unless you have a really dedicated listener and a lot of time. Incidentally, it is also great for adults and formed the basis of an outstanding homily I once heard on Christmas Eve.

Synopsis: A beautiful velveteen rabbit is a boy's beloved Christmas present—for about two hours, until the boy gets other presents and forgets about him. The rabbit lives in the nursery among many toys that snub him for his insignificance. Only the Skin Horse is kind to the rabbit. The Skin Horse is an old toy, bald in patches and very wise. He knows about nursery magic and tells the rabbit about being "real," the mystical thing that happens when a child really loves a toy over a long period of time. And he tells the rabbit that sometimes it hurts being real—hair is loved off, eyes drop out, toys become worn and shabby—but that only people who don't understand think "real" is ugly. Real, though, lasts forever.

Rabbit thinks he'll never become real, but one evening the boy can't find the toy he normally sleeps with, so his Nana hands him the rabbit, who then becomes the boy's nighttime cuddle toy and eventually learns to enjoy being held so tight. The rabbit becomes shabbier and shabbier the more he is loved. In the spring, he plays outside with the boy and gets dirty. When Nana complains about the filth, the boy tells her the rabbit is real. The rabbit is overjoyed to hear this news, and the next morning Nana notices a look of wisdom and beauty on the rabbit's face.

In the summer, the rabbit encounters some bunnies in the woods, hopping around freely, that ask him to play. The velveteen rabbit feels awkward because he can't hop and doesn't even have hind legs! The bunnies ridicule him and say he isn't real. "I *am* real! The boy said so!" he cries. The boy continues to love him and he becomes even more real, misshapen and shabby. Then one day, the boy becomes very ill with scarlet fever and all his books and toys must be burned. The rabbit is tossed into a bag and taken to the garden to be thrown into a bonfire.

The gardener is too busy for burning, so that night the rabbit waits, feeling lonely. A real tear falls from his eye onto the ground and a mysterious flower springs up. The blossom opens to reveal the beautiful nursery magic fairy who cares for all playthings children have loved and makes them real. She tells the rabbit that he was real to the boy, but that now he will be real to everyone. She carries him to Rabbitland, where he will live forever with other real bunnies that hop around and play. When she kisses him, she changes him into a bunny with hind legs and fur.

Seeds of the Gospel: This story holds a message of everlasting life, of transformation and new beginnings. A boy's love makes the rabbit real, but this also means the rabbit will suffer. After the boy's scarlet fever, when all the toys must be burned, the boy's love places a seal of protection on the rabbit, which calls forth the nursery magic fairy to save him from the fire. She carries him to a new reality where he is happy, even though he can no longer live with the boy. Because of the boy's love, the rabbit is transformed into a new creature.

What a wonderful metaphor for our new life in Christ! God's love, expressed to us through the Son of God, who came to Earth as one of us, changes us. It also protects us: although once destined for "the fire" because of sin, we are saved by the love of God through the life, death, and resurrection of Christ. Talk about the love the boy has for the rabbit and how that protects him from being destroyed. You might make the connection with Christian belief that Jesus loves us as the boy loves the rabbit, and that Jesus' love can change us: "How does love change the rabbit? Why doesn't he mind getting ugly? How does love protect the rabbit at the end?"

The rabbits in the forest make fun of the Velveteen Rabbit for having no hind legs and for insisting that he's real. All of us know the sting of being teased or made fun of at some time in our lives. As parents, it's often difficult to hear about such things happening to our own children, but it's an unavoidable, unfortunate part of growing up. Just as we did, kids need to learn to handle criticism and sometimes ridicule, to learn to behave well even when others are not, and to develop compassion for others. Talk about the Velveteen Rabbit with kids and the way it feels when others make fun of us: "How do you think the rabbit felt when the forest bunnies laughed at his legs?" If stories surface about events in our own children's lives, talk about them, perhaps even sharing a story from childhood about a time when we were teased. "You know, one time a girl made fun of me because..." Reminding kids that parents were once kids encourages their imagination; at the same time it helps them to know that we are capable of understanding their problems.

In contrast, the rabbit feels wonderful when the boy says he's real. Hearing these words helps him to become even more real. Words that bring comfort and joy to others are a great gift. In the Old Testament story of Job, three friends come to soothe Job when they hear of his sufferings. Job launches into a "why was I ever even born" tirade to which his friend Eliphaz of Teman asks for a chance to respond. He reminds Job of the way his kind words have helped others in the past: "See, you have instructed many; you have strengthened the weak hands. Your words have supported those who were stumbling, and you have made firm the feeble knees" (Job 4:3–4).

Job's words, uttered long before, offered strength to others, and brought God to the listener. What we say, then, makes a difference. Even through words alone, when we show kindness and bring joy to another, we share gifts of God. Paul tells us this in his letter to the Galatians: "The fruit of the Spirit is love, joy, peace, patience, kindness, generosity, faithfulness" (6:6). God is the source of words of love and joy! Talk about the power of praise in this story of the Velveteen Rabbit: "How did the rabbit feel when the boy called him real? Why do you think Nana saw a new expression on the rabbit's face the next day?"

This story is also good to read when someone a child loves dies. In Rabbitland, the bunny can still see the boy and the boy still remembers the rabbit, although it isn't the same. The rabbit doesn't cease to exist, but begins another life—a *new* life—as a person would in heaven. If mourning is part of your life, talk about the person who died and how he or she is living a new kind of life. Affirm that the one who died still loves the child and suggest that he or she even checks in on the child once in a while. For example, "Grandpa must be happy in heaven. What do you think he's doing now?" Sometimes a shift of focus from grief about missing the person to reminding the child that the person is still "living," just in a different way, can relieve some of the heaviness of mourning.

The Big Wave by Pearl S. Buck

Nobel Laureate **Pearl Sydenstricker Buck** is best remembered for stories based on her experiences in China and Japan. Born in Hillsboro, West Virginia, the daughter of Presbyterian missionaries, she spent the first eight years of her life in Zhenjiang, where she was homeschooled in English and tutored by a local man in Chinese. Later, she attended school in Shanghai. In 1910, she enrolled in Randolph-Macon Woman's College in Lynchburg, Virginia. Graduating in 1914 with a degree in philosophy, she

returned to China and met an American agricultural econo-
mist and missionary, Dr. John Lossing Buck, whom she married in 1917. The two moved to Nanxuzhou, a poor farming
community, where she gathered material that would
become her second novel, *The Good Earth*. It became a
blockbuster best seller, winner of the 1935 Pulitzer Prize
and Howells Medal, and the basis of a 1937 motion picture
nominated for several Academy Awards (scoring a Best
Actress win for star Luise Rainer).

In 1921, the Bucks moved to Nanjing to teach at the
local university. During that year, her mother died, her
father moved in with them, the couple's first child was born
profoundly retarded, and Pearl was diagnosed with a uter-
ine tumor. In 1924, they returned to the United States to find
help for their child, who was ultimately institutionalized,
and adopted another daughter. The following year, Pearl
earned her master's degree in literature from Cornell
University. In 1927, the Bucks went back to Nanjing, but
soon fled to Japan because of a violent uprising against
westerners, returning to China a year later. In 1934, Pearl
moved permanently back to the United States. In 1935, the
Bucks were divorced, and she married her publisher,
Richard Walsh, with whom she adopted six more children.

Pearl wrote and published stories and essays throughout the 1920s. Her first novel, *East Wind, West Wind*,
appeared in 1930 and was followed by numerous works
about China and Japan. In 1938, she became the first
American woman to win the Nobel Prize for Literature. She
continued to write until her death in 1973, publishing more
than seventy books. Pearl S. Buck also became a prominent
humanitarian, founding the East and West Association to
foster understanding between the United States and Asia,
establishing the Pearl S. Buck Foundation to help
Amerasian children rejected by both cultures, and working
tirelessly on behalf of mentally retarded people.

Background: During her year in Japan, Pearl S. Buck witnessed a
tidal wave that led her to write this story. Winner of the 1948
Children's Book Award, *The Big Wave* includes beautiful pictures by

Hokusai and Hiroshige, two nineteenth-century artists known for their depictions of everyday life and landscapes in Japan.

Synopsis: Kino is a farmer's son who lives on a hillside. His playmate, Jiya, lives in a tiny fishing village below. Sometimes, when his own father doesn't need him in their rice paddy, Kino helps Jiya and his father with fishing. One day, a danger bell calls the villagers up the hill to safety as a tidal wave approaches. Reluctantly, Jiya obeys his parents and ascends the hill, where Kino's family keeps him safe as the wave washes away the fishing village, and with it, Jiya's family. Overwhelmed by his loss, Jiya faints, and Kino's father brings him to their home. Gently, Kino's family helps Jiya grieve and decides to adopt him.

One day, the Old Gentleman from the castle on the hill arrives to adopt the orphaned boy. He promises riches and the finest education for Jiya, so Kino's father tells the boy about the offer. He sends Jiya to meet the man and make his own decision. Kino accompanies him under strict orders to remind his friend of the many benefits of being the rich man's son, rather than part of a poor farming family. But, to the delight of Kino's family, Jiya chooses to turn down the Old Gentleman's offer and return to their home, where he is loved. He grows into a fine young man, marries Kino's little sister, and builds a house along the shore with a big window looking out upon the sea.

Seeds of the Gospel: Pearl S. Buck's story about living in a dangerous world and learning to face fears couldn't be more relevant to today's children. Moreover, the insights it offers into Japanese culture and tradition help kids to better understand and come to respect some differences between East and West. Often overlooked for reading with kids, this little book offers both a beautiful writing style and a touching, inspiring story that contains many seeds of the Gospel.

As fishermen, Jiya and his family live in fear of the sea. Kino's father notes that volcanoes offer something to fear on land as well. When Kino asks his father if people must always be afraid of something, the father says, "We must learn to live with danger." He tells

Kino not to be afraid of death, since it will happen at some point—
sooner or later—but to simply enjoy living. Throughout Scripture,
God tells us not to be afraid. In the Old Testament, after Moses dies,
Joshua must take the Israelites over the Jordan River into the
Promised Land. He is scared, so God says, "I hereby *command* you:
Be strong and courageous; do not be frightened or dismayed, for the
Lord your God is with you wherever you go" (Josh 1:9). In the New
Testament, Jesus tells his disciples not to be afraid in the churning
waters of the sea. This story is one of many which tell us that God is
calling us to set aside our fears.

Children develop basic normal fears, such as fear of monsters
or dogs, that parents have dealt with every day for centuries. But
children also have more profound fears, such as worrying about terrorist attacks, bombs, earthquakes, hurricanes, and strangers who
might take them away from their homes. The devastation from natural disasters in recent years, coupled with other tragedies, make it

And when he got into the boat, his disciples followed him.
A windstorm arose on the sea, so great that the boat was
being swamped by the waves; but he was asleep. And they
went and woke him up, saying, "Lord, save us! We are per-
ishing!" And he said to them, "Why are you afraid, you of
little faith?" Then he got up and rebuked the winds and the
sea; and there was a dead calm. They were amazed, saying,
"What sort of man is this, that even the winds and the sea
obey him?" (Mt 8:23–27)

When evening came, his disciples went down to the sea,
got into a boat, and started across the sea to Capernaum.
It was now dark, and Jesus had not yet come to them. The
sea became rough because a strong wind was blowing.
When they had rowed about three or four miles, they saw
Jesus walking on the sea and coming near the boat, and
they were terrified. But he said to them, "It is I; do not be
afraid" (Jn 6:16–21).

important for kids to learn healthy ways to cope. A gentle story such as *The Big Wave* may be just the balm to soothe a worried child and a gateway to dialogue among families about these difficult times.

As a fisherman, Jiya's father depends on the sea to make a living and knows the dangers lurking there. It seems he spends his life worrying about these dangers. Talk with your child about Jiya's family and their concerns about the sea, perhaps asking: "Why is Jiya's family afraid of the sea? What did Jiya's father do when one day the two boys came home late from swimming in the ocean? Why did he react that way?" Remind your child that parents worry because of their love for their children, even though worry isn't the best response to problems.

⟫◈⟪

"A compelling narrative, offering a storyteller's moral imagination vigorously at work, can enable any of us to learn by example, to take to heart what is, really, a gift of grace."

— Robert Coles

⟫◈⟪

In contrast to Jiya's father, Kino's father believes in setting aside fears in order to live well. He takes his family twenty miles from their home to see the great volcano and its rolling yellow smoke so that they might accept the fact that it could erupt and destroy them one day. He tells Kino that when we fear something, we think about it all the time, and that the way of the good Japanese is to enjoy life and not fear death. Jesus told his followers almost the same thing: "He called the crowd with his disciples and said to them, 'If any want to become my followers, let them deny themselves and take up their cross and follow me'" (Mk 8:34; Mt 16:24). We deny ourselves when we put aside our fears because human nature urges us to cling to them. Jesus is saying to embrace whatever is painful for us and get on with life. Discuss this philosophy with your child, perhaps beginning with: "What did Kino's father tell him about fears? Do you think that's a good idea? Why? Did you know that Jesus said almost the same thing?" On a more practical level, encourage your child to talk about his or her own fears and worries, and try to understand what might be causing anxiety. If big fears are weighing on your child's mind, make a point to spend more time together at bedtime so that the child can rest feeling safe and secure, perhaps sharing an extra story or chatting a little longer than usual.

Before the wave, Kino wishes his family were fishermen rather than rice farmers. But Jiya points out that the jobs complement one another: "How would fish taste without rice?" Herein is another seed of the Gospel: St. Paul tells us in his first letter to the Corinthians that "there are varieties of gifts, but the same Spirit; and there are varieties of services, but the same Lord; and there are varieties of activities, but it is the same God who activates all of them in everyone" (12:4–7). While St. Paul was writing specifically about spiritual gifts, the same principle extends to the practical level. We are called to different tasks in life because many different things need to be done to "make the world go around." Perhaps many cultures exist because God is calling us to tolerance and understanding—or more! Talk about Jiya's question, perhaps suggesting: "What Jiya said about fish and rice is interesting. What would happen if everyone did the same thing? Why do you suppose we have to do different things? What would you like to do most?"

When the bell warns the villagers to move to higher ground, Jiya doesn't want to leave his family, but his father insists. On the hillside, Kino fears for Jiya's life and waves his white girdle cloth in the air as a sign of concern. His encouragement convinces Jiya to run to Kino and his father, and they protect him as the hurricane winds begin to howl. When the sea rises up, Jiya wants to warn his family, but Kino's father holds him fast as the tidal wave sweeps away the entire fishing village. These scenes provide a beautiful metaphor for the level of involvement to which we are called as the Christian community, to be strong and helpful in times of trouble and doubt. Consider this verse from St. Paul's first letter to the Thessalonians: "Encourage one another and build up each other, as indeed you are doing" (5:11). In the original Greek, the word translated as "encouragement" is *"parakaleo,"* which means "to call alongside." Kino and his father literally call Jiya alongside them to brave the storm. When Jiya tries to descend into certain death, Kino's father sternly keeps him focused on life. Talk about the disaster scene: "Why does Kino wave the white cloth? Why does Jiya go to Kino and his father instead of the castle with the other children? How do you think Kino's father felt when he had to hold back Jiya from returning to the village? Why did he do it?"

Kino's family allows Jiya to grieve in a profoundly touching succession of scenes that may call forth a few tears. Kino's family simply communicates love to Jiya. They let him experience the numbness followed by pain that is part of grieving, and by their food and their caring he knows he is welcome and has a home. Talk about this loving family: "How did Kino's family care for Jiya after he lost his family?" Think of past experiences your family has had with death and talk about the people who came to comfort you, or people that you went to comfort, and try to remember how that felt.

When Kino's father talks about death, he offers a wonderful way to discuss the subject with kids. He calls death a "great gateway," and compares it to the "gate of life" Kino entered when he was born. He tells Kino that he cried at birth because he didn't want to be born. He desired instead to stay safe and sound in "the warm, dark house of the unborn," because he didn't know anything about life beyond that house. In the same way, the father says, Kino is afraid of death only because he doesn't know anything about it. We Christians also believe death is a gateway. Share with your child what we believe about eternal life in Christ, that we will live together with all of the angels and saints and see God face to face. To keep things positive, you might mention: "It must be fun in Heaven with all of those interesting people! Did you know that God wants us to live there when we die?"

The Old Gentleman offers Jiya material wealth and a fine education if he will be his son. But Jiya chooses to return to Kino's modest home, where he must help with farm chores. Talk about this decision:

"Why does Jiya choose to go back to Kino's house? Why didn't he want to stay with the Old Gentleman? Did he make a good choice? Why?" Also, talk about the way Kino's father insisted that Jiya go to the man's house to meet him and make his own decision—following the Chinese proverb that says, "If you love something, set it free; if it comes back to you, it is yours forever; if it flies away, it was never yours to begin with." A conversation starter might begin: "Why did Kino's dad make Jiya decide for himself where to live? Why did he send along Kino to remind Jiya of what he would gain by staying with the Old Gentleman?" Talk about Jiya's values and what is most important in learning to live well.

When Jiya grows up and tells Kino that he wants to marry his sister, Setsu, Kino is incredulous. He thinks of her as a pesky little sister who drives him crazy, but Jiya sees much more. When Kino points out that Setsu is a terrible cook because she runs off whenever she sees something interesting, Jiya says he doesn't mind burned rice and he will join Setsu to see what she sees. Discuss the differences in the way Setsu is seen by the two young men: "What does Kino think of his sister? Why? And what does Jiya think? Why? What does Jiya like about Setsu?" If sibling rivalry occurs in your household, this might be a good lead in to a discussion about it, or a subtle reminder that brothers or sisters aren't so bad, after all.

Mr. Popper's Penguins by Richard and Florence Atwater

Born in Chicago, **Richard Tupper Atwater** was a professor of classics and Greek at the University of Chicago, his alma mater, and a humor columnist for the *Chicago Evening Post*. Inspired by a film he saw about famous explorer Admiral Richard Byrd's Antarctic expedition, Atwater began writing *Mr. Popper's Penguins* in 1932, but he couldn't come up with a good ending for the story. He suffered a stroke in 1934, and his wife, Florence Hasseltine Atwater, finished the novel, which was published in 1938 and became an instant hit for children and their parents. The book won the 1939 Newbery Award.

Background: The Atwaters never intended to collaborate on a book. When Richard fell seriously ill and could no longer write, Florence completed this novel for him. Together, they made some memorable, witty moments in story.

Synopsis: Mr. Popper is a house painter in Stillwater who loves his wife and children, yet dreams of adventure. Excited by newsreels of Admiral Drake's expedition to the South Pole, Mr. Popper writes to the famous explorer about how much he enjoys penguins. On the radio from Antarctica, Drake announces that Mr. Popper will receive a surprise. The next day, a penguin arrives at the Popper house, bringing with him shockers at every turn as the penguin tries to fit into small town American life. The new pet, named Captain Cook, even brings about a change in the usually unkempt Mr. Popper, who begins to slick his hair and dress in tails in penguin style! After a journalist covers the story, the Poppers become famous.

When Captain Cook becomes ill, Mr. Popper writes to the head of an aquarium, who diagnoses Captain Cook's illness as loneliness and sends the Poppers another lonely penguin, named Greta. Captain Cook normally nests in the refrigerator, but the Poppers' fridge isn't big enough for *two* penguins, so the Poppers open their windows and make the entire house frigid! With snowdrifts and ice in the living room, the children and the penguins have a grand time at play. Poor Mrs. Popper, who likes everything tidy, is distressed, but goes along sportingly—even when Mr. Popper moves the furnace into the living room to make room for an ice plant in the cellar! These modifications are expensive, and Mr. Popper, who never works in winter, begins to amass considerable debt.

Greta lays eggs in the cellar, and soon ten penguin chicks hatch. Mr. Popper sinks a diving pool in the cellar, creates an ice rink, and begins to feed the penguins fresh fish, running up even bigger bills for the family. Nevertheless, the Poppers are happy with the situation because Mr. Popper delights in his pets and stays out of Mrs. Popper's hair all winter. Soon, however, she begins to worry about money. Mr. Popper suggests they train the penguins and create a show. He moves the family piano onto the ice rink, and Mrs. Popper accompanies the penguins' three tricks: a march, a sliding exhibition, and a fight, with music. Popper's Performing Penguins are a sensation, packing theaters from coast to coast and earning thousands from product endorsements. After a terrible misunderstanding, Mr. Popper and the penguins land in jail. Admiral Drake posts bail and asks Mr. Popper to send the penguins to the North Pole to start a breed. Momentarily, Hollywood offers to make the penguins movie stars and make the Poppers rich. Mrs. Popper whispers, "I don't want to live on Easy Street. I want to go back to Proudfoot Avenue."

After a difficult decision, pale, haggard Mr. Popper announces that he will refuse Hollywood's millions and send the penguins to the North Pole. Although he is heartbroken to send them away, Mr. Popper knows it's best for his pets. However, Drake wants Mr. Popper to join the expedition, so Mrs. Popper, with enough money for several years, cheerfully sends him on his way to fulfill his dream of adventure.

Seeds of the Gospel: Although wonderfully absurd, the Poppers' story includes Christian messages that parents can help kids understand. Mr. Popper's untidiness and his seasonal work clearly annoy Mrs. Popper, but she never points out his shortcomings unkindly. Rather, Mrs. Popper gently approaches Mr. Popper as his equal (chap. 13) to discuss family matters; in turn, her husband responds to her with the utmost respect and consideration. Such behavior is rooted in the Gospel; Peter tells us in one of his letters to "speak gently and respectfully" (1 Pt 3:16), while Paul, with a refreshing frankness, asks, "What would you prefer? Am I to come to you with a stick, or with love in a spirit of gentleness?" (1 Cor 4:21). Talk to kids about the way Mrs. Popper handles this stressful penguin situation: "How does Mrs. Popper feel about having the penguins in the house? How does she tell Mr. Popper about the things that trouble her? How does he talk to her about her worries?"

When Hollywood offers the Poppers a chance to live on "Easy Street" (chap. 19) with an opportunity for tremendous fame and fortune, Mrs. Popper says she wants to go home to Proudfoot Avenue, where they were happy. Mrs. Popper worries about money problems, but she doesn't value money in itself. She values a simple life as well as her service work with the Ladies Aid and Mission Society, where she undoubtedly has friends. "Why did Mrs. Popper want to go back to their old house in Stillwater?" you could ask. "What does she miss on the road with the penguins? What do you think she likes about the Ladies Aid and Mission Society?" If the opportunity arises, talk about our call to put our faith in action through service, as Mrs. Popper does.

Upon rereading this book as an adult, the ending (chap. 20) initially left me with a feeling of ambivalence. In one sense, Mrs. Popper seems to want the money and freedom to do her own thing with her friends, while Mr. Popper goes off for a few years to establish the penguin colony at the North Pole. But Mrs. Popper truly loves Mr. Popper and knows that this experience will fulfill his long-held dream of adventure. Moreover, he will be with Admiral Drake, whom he holds in the highest regard. He will get something she knows he needs, while she and the children will get what they need—a return to a "normal" way of life. Ask kids: "Why didn't Mrs. Popper complain when Mr. Popper went away? Do you think she'll miss him? What about the children; won't they miss their dad?" For kids with a mom or dad who travels for business or is in the military, this is a good conversation starter about things that may weigh on their minds.

In chapter nineteen, Admiral Drake compliments Mr. Popper on his penguins' abilities, saying, "I've seen a lot of penguins in my time, but never such educated ones as these. It certainly shows what patience and training can do." This is a seed of the Gospel for us parents, for God is the source of all patience and encouragement, as we learn from Paul's letter to the Romans (15:5). As we strive to train our children in the way they should go, let's pray for the kind of patience Mr. Popper has with his birds. If kids are old enough to talk about the concept of patience, ask them: "Why is patience important? Why did Mr. Popper need patience to work with the penguins? Did you ever work on something that took a lot of patience? How did you do it?"

Most of all, relax and enjoy the silliness of this story and, perhaps, imagine: "I wonder what it would be like if we had penguins in our house..."

———————◆◆◆◆◆———————

Abel's Island by William Steig

William Steig is probably best known nowadays for writing *Shrek*, the ogre tale that became a hit movie in 2001, featuring the voices of Mike Meyers, Eddie Murphy, and Cameron Diaz. Steig, author of many wonderful children's books, was once dubbed by *Newsweek* magazine as "the King of Cartoons." In 1930, he began as an illustrator for *The New Yorker* magazine, producing 1,600 drawings and 117 covers for the publication. In 1968, at age sixty-one, Steig launched a second career in children's literature. His third book, *Sylvester and the Magic Pebble,* won the Caldecott Medal and is considered by many critics and scholars to be his masterpiece. He later won several Newbery Honors and a Christopher Award for his 1972 novel, *Dominic.*

Steig, born in Brooklyn, New York in 1907, was the son of an Austrian immigrant who painted houses. Both of Steig's parents dabbled in fine arts in their spare time, and his brother, Irwin, who taught him to paint, became a professional artist. The family fed the children's imaginations regularly with story, especially Grimms' fairy tales, Carlo Collodi's *Pinocchio,* Howard Pyle's *Robin Hood,* and other classic works of fiction.

After college, during the Great Depression, he supported his parents and younger brother by cartooning. He was father to three artists as well—a musician, a painter, and an actress. Steig died in 2003, at age ninety-six.

Background: *Abel's Island* won a Newbery Honor when it was published in 1976. Critic M. Hobbs called the story a fable for our times. Steig considered it a spoof on the Victorian novel.

Synopsis: Abelard Hassam di Chirico Flint, of the Mossville Flints, is a privileged Edwardian mouse. In 1907, he and his beloved wife, Amanda, are picnicking when a hurricane hits. Amanda's scarf is torn from her neck by the wind, and gentlemanly Abel rushes to rescue it. Swept away by rushing water, Abel becomes stranded on an island, where he must abandon his genteel ways to fend for himself. He makes several attempts to escape from the island, first by fashioning a boat, then a catamaran, and later by weaving a rope bridge, building a path of steppingstones across the river, catapulting himself, and gliding across the river with a catalpa leaf. But Abel remains stranded, missing Amanda terribly. In his loneliness, he notices a star rising in the sky, one his nanny said was his own personal star, one he once talked to, "but only when he was his most serious, real self, and not being any sort of a show-off or clown." The star seems to notice Abel, so he asks what he should do. The star seems to answer, "You will do what you will do."

Abel gains strength from the star's encouragement and begins to wonder if his ordeal is a test. He wonders why Amanda loves him, since he's not handsome or particularly accomplished. He remembers that once during an argument she called him frivolous, a snob and a fop, and that he acted silly during their wedding. He contemplates what sort of mouse he is. Abel prepares for a long stay on the island, but thinks constantly of his loved ones and feels sorry that they must grieve for him. In his solitude, he begins to appreciate nature, sculpt, keep busy, and spend time in wonder. When an owl discovers and terrorizes Abel, he kneels in prayer to ask why "God makes owls, snakes, cats, foxes, fleas, and other such loathsome, abominable creatures. He felt there had to be a reason."

Abel endures a long winter and delights in a beautiful spring. One day, Gower, an elderly frog, arrives, and the two become friends. After a long stay, Gower swims away, promising to send help. Abel cries, knowing the poor frog will forget him. In August, a drought allows Abel to cross the river. Although a cat snatches him on the other side, Abel escapes and continues toward home and Amanda. At last, he sees Amanda sitting on a park bench, so he quietly goes home to prepare for their reunion. Everything is the same at home and Amanda is thrilled to see him, but his elegant clothes feel uncomfortable. Abel has changed.

Seeds of the Gospel: Besides offering a love story, *Abel's Island* demonstrates the strength we gain through suffering and through reflection. A year of isolation and hardship teaches Abel to be creative, self-sufficient, and resilient. He returns to Amanda a far better mouse and husband than he was before the hurricane. "How does Abel change during his year on the island?" you might ask. Talk about the things Abel learns to do and how that makes him feel about himself and his place in the world.

Talk about Abel's time to think and reflect (chaps. 8–10): "Abel was able to do a lot of thinking on that island...and he came up with a lot of good ideas for ways to spend his time. What do you like to think and wonder about?" Discuss the importance of wonder and reflection and how it is a good use of time, rather than a waste. Since creativity comes from being created in the image of God, perhaps you will want to encourage your kids to create a special "thinking time" or "thinking place" for dreaming and being creative. Also, talk about how we use the time we have: "If you were stranded on a desert island, what would you like to teach yourself to do? Why?"

Abel remembers how to pray on the island. Talk about how praying helps him deal with his loneliness, sadness, and fear, and how prayer helps us in our everyday lives. "How does Abel feel after praying?" you could begin. "Do you ever feel like that when you pray?" Also, talk about Abel's humorous prayer in chapter eleven, asking why God created things that scare him. "What do you think God thought about Abel's prayer?" you might ask. "What about mice? Abel is a mouse, and some people are scared of mice. Do you think Abel could imagine himself on a list of horrible creatures?" You can use this opportunity to talk about things your kids find "loathsome" or scary. Invite them to talk to God about their feelings—and maybe to realize that some things that seem scary might not be so scary after all.

Abel never loses hope of getting home, although it certainly seems hopeless at times. Talk about the enduring love he feels for Amanda and his family and friends and how that love sustains him. "What kept Abel going all that time?" you might begin. "Why did he keep on trying to get home?" And when Abel finally did get home, Amanda and her abundant love awaited him, reminding us of Paul's words in first Corinthians, "Love never fails" (13:8). Talk about Amanda's steadfast devotion to her husband: "How do you think Amanda felt while Abel was gone? How do you think she felt when he came back? Why do you think she was so happy to see him?"

The frog tells Abel that he should become a sculptor (chap. 14). Talk to your child about his or her own gifts and celebrate them in conversation. "You know, you're a really good painter (or pianist or flautist or jump-roper or whatever). Do you enjoy doing that? What do you think you might do with that when you're grown up?" Remind your child that all of his or her gifts come from God and that, like Abel, we are happier when we learn what to do with them.

Island of the Blue Dolphins by Scott O'Dell

Odell Gabriel Scott was born in Los Angeles, California, in 1898. As a child, he moved throughout Southern California. Later, he also moved through four colleges—Occidental College, University of Wisconsin-Madison, Stanford University, and University of Rome—only taking classes that interested him. In 1925, he began work in Hollywood as a cameraman for Metro-Goldwyn-Mayer, then as a technical director for Paramount. In 1934, he began writing books. During the 1940s and 1950s, he also wrote a book column for the *Los Angeles Mirror* and worked as the book editor for the *Los Angeles Daily News*. When a typesetter accidentally set his byline as "Scott O'Dell," he liked it so much he made it his legal name!

In the late 1950s, he began writing children's books, publishing twenty-five titles in all. *Island of the Blue*

Dolphins (1960) was followed by *The King's Fifth* (1966), *The Black Pearl* (1967), and *Sing Down the Moon* (1970), all Newbery Honor books. In 1972, he received the Hans Christian Andersen Award for lifetime achievement in children's literature. In 1981, he established the Scott O'Dell Historical Fiction Award to recognize outstanding works for children. The author died in 1989, asking his wife of twenty-three years, author Elizabeth Hall, to finish his manuscript for *Thunder Rolling in the Mountains,* which she published for him in 1991. When O'Dell's ashes were scattered over the Pacific Ocean off La Jolla, California, and the mourners turned back toward shore, a pod of dolphins burst from the water and escorted the boat into the harbor—just like the scene in *Island of the Blue Dolphins.*

Background: Scott O'Dell came across the story of a Native American woman who lived alone for eighteen years on San Nicolas Island, California. Her story moved him to anger. He began to write about it, but didn't know he had written a children's book until a friend convinced him. The novel won the 1960 Newbery Medal, the 1961 Lewis Carroll Shelf Award, and numerous other honors.

Synopsis: On an island off the California coast, Native Americans live in the Ghalas-at village. Aleut hunters led by a Russian fur trader, Captain Orlov, arrive to hunt sea otters. Chief Chowig agrees to let them camp on the island in exchange for half the catch. When the party prepares to leave without giving the chief his share, Chowig confronts Orlov, and the captain orders his hunters to board ship. The bloody skirmish that follows leaves twenty-seven Ghalas-at men dead, including Chowig, and a number of Aleuts.

Village women must now break with tradition and assume the men's roles in the community. Chowig's daughters, Karana and Ulape, gather abalone and take care of their little brother, Ramo. The new chief, Kimki, searches for a better place for them. He sends a ship to fetch the villagers when he finds one. Aboard ship, Karana sees Ramo still on the island and swims back to him. Ramo is soon killed by wild dogs, and Karana is left alone, awaiting the ship's return.

Karana tries to leave the island by canoe, but turns back, accompanied by a pod of blue dolphins. She realizes she is happy to be home and builds a comfortable house with a fence and a second shelter in a cave. To minimize the threat from the wild dogs, she decides to kill the leader of the dog pack. She lures him to her with fire, and then shoots him and two others with bow and arrow. The leader survives, so Karana takes him home and cares for him, naming him Rontu.

Karana crafts a skirt of yucca fibers and wears flowers in her hair. She also builds a canoe and creates a hiding place from the Aleuts, who return after a few years, bringing along a girl who discovers Karana. Named Tutok, she compliments Karana's skirt. Karana is proud of her work, but doesn't trust the Aleut. Later, Karana finds a beautiful necklace from Tutok and begins to communicate with her. In friendship, Karana makes Tutok a wreath for her hair. When the Aleuts leave, Karana misses her new friend. They leave behind many wounded sea otters that Karana humanely spears, except one which Karana nurses back to health and befriends. She makes friends with birds and a fox as well. Years pass and Rontu dies, so Karana catches the dog's son and names him Rontu-Aru. Together, they survive an earthquake and many long years until, one day, a ship from her people arrives. Karana dresses according to their custom, with a blue streak painted across her face, and boards the boat to Mission Santa Barbara, reflecting on the Island of Blue Dolphins and her happiness there.

Seeds of the Gospel: Karana's awe-inspiring courage and perseverance in the face of adversity emerge as the most obvious seeds of the Gospel in this story. Despite the tremendous hardships she faces, she carries on, just as we are called to do when we meet suffering in our own lives. As Christians, we can apply the call to perseverance found in Paul's first letter to the Corinthians: "Therefore, my beloved, be steadfast, immovable, always excelling in the work of the Lord, because you know that in the Lord your labor is not in vain" (15:58). Another great passage about perseverance comes from the letter of James: "But those who look into the perfect law, the law of liberty, and persevere, being not hearers who forget but doers who act—they will be blessed in their doing" (1:25). We are called to keep on going in our lives and our faith no matter what happens to us along the way—just as Karana keeps on going all alone on her island—living without complaint and finding joy wherever we can. Talk about the virtue of perseverance: "How does Karana deal with living alone on the Island of Blue Dolphins for so many years? What are some of the things she does to stay alive?"

Karana's courage is admirable as well. As Christians, we are called to heroic virtue. Talk about her bravery, perhaps asking: "Why does Karana go back to the island? How do you think she felt when she saw Ramo still standing on the shore as the boat was leaving? (chap. 7) Do you think you would jump into the water and swim back like that? Why?" Karana's courage continues throughout the story, too. You might discuss the way she handles the wild dog problem (chap. 15) or how she prepares for the return of the Aleuts (chap. 20). Another true sign of her courage is the dignity with which she greets the white men who arrive on the island at the end of the story (chap. 28). Ask: "How do you think Karana felt when other people came to the island? What did she do about it?"

Don Bosco and Grigio

Don Bosco, patron saint of children, was befriended and protected by a ferocious grey shepherd dog named Grigio at a time when Waldensian heretics were trying to stop his good works. In his memoirs, Don Bosco said he felt frightened in a desolate area when Grigio showed up to escort him. Later, an assassin missed his shot, but Grigio bit the gunman. In 1854, thugs attacked Don Bosco—until Grigio scared them away. Once, the dog refused to let Don Bosco out of his house; minutes later, a neighbor raced to tell the saint of a plot against him that night. And when Don Bosco was lost in a terrible storm, Grigio showed him the way home.

Another important theme tucked into *Island of the Blue Dolphins* is that of waiting. Karana waits for years for her people to return for her. Amazingly, she never responds to her predicament with anger or resentment, so we come to know Karana as a patient, steadfast, hopeful person. She has deep faith that someone will come for her, as well as an apparent belief that she is loved and wanted by her people. Waiting is part of the biblical experience as well. The Chosen People waited for the coming of a savior who would bring them new life. King David expressed this sentiment in the psalms: "Be strong, and let your heart take courage, all you who wait for the LORD" (31:24). A passage from the book of the prophet Isaiah expresses this anticipation as well: "It will be said on that day, 'Lo, this is our God; we have waited for him, so that he might save us. This is the LORD for whom we have waited; let us be glad and rejoice in his salvation'" (25:9).

⫸·◇·⫷

"Make it a rule never to give a child a book you would not read yourself."

— George Bernard Shaw

⫸·◇·⫷

When Jesus ascended into heaven, the disciples waited for the promised Holy Spirit, who descended at Pentecost. Now that Jesus sits at the right hand of the Father, we wait for his return in glory at the coming of the Kingdom. We are always waiting for that day when we shall see God face to face. Meanwhile, we are called to go about our daily lives finding God among us even now.

Karana makes a home for herself, gathers food, stays busy. Talk about the way Karana spends her time: "What does Karana do each day? Why does she do it? What if you were alone on an island? What do you think you would do? How can you use your imagination when you are waiting for something or someone?"

One of the most charming scenes in the book shows Karana making herself new clothes and putting flowers in her hair (chap. 18). Even though she is all alone on the island, Karana preserves her human dignity by caring for herself and accepting the small pleasures afforded by the island. For example, she makes a skirt from yucca fibers and a sealskin belt and sandals "just to be dressed up." She makes wreaths of flowers for herself and for her dog, Rontu. Later, when the Aleut girl gives her a necklace, Karana fashions matching earrings (chap. 23). Talk about the marvelous self-esteem evidenced in these actions, perhaps asking: "Why did Karana put flowers in her hair? How do you think that made her feel? Do you like to get dressed up? Why? How does that make you feel?"

Clearly, Karana loves herself in the way we are called to love ourselves, an important seed of the Gospel expressed by Jesus in Matthew's Gospel: "...A lawyer, asked [Jesus] a question to test him: 'Teacher, which commandment in the law is the greatest?' He said to him, '*You shall love the Lord your God with all your heart, and with all your soul, and with all your mind.* This is the greatest and first commandment. And a second is like it: *You shall love your neighbor as yourself.* On these two commandments hang all the law and the prophets'" (Mt 22:35–40). All of our teaching hangs within these words, but "as yourself" are often overlooked. Karana models self-respect that families can point to and celebrate.

Karana, putting flowers in her hair amidst a backdrop of hardship, provides a wonderful metaphor for Christians: that we are called to enjoy all that God has provided for us, in spite of the suffering we endure or the adversity we face. A seed of the Gospel worth nurturing is found in the first letter of Paul to Timothy, in which we learn that "God...richly provides us with everything for our enjoyment" (6:17). Our *enjoyment!* That's good news worth celebrating and enjoying! Talk about things you like to do together, ways you can enjoy one another's company or the good things God provides, such as favorite meals, or flowers, or birds. "What's your favorite..." you might begin.

When the white men come to take Karana to Mission Santa Barbara, she goes willingly, expectantly, in hopes of seeing her people. She wears her best clothes to greet them and paints her face in the tradition of her culture, but the first thing they do is take away her beautiful cormorant skirt and otter cape and give her an ugly blue dress that covers her from throat to feet. The dress is scratchy and hot to wear, so Karana doesn't like it, although she doesn't complain. Without knowing anything about this strong, vibrant, courageous woman, the white men have taken away an important part of her—the signs of her culture. Talk about this change for Karana: "How do you think Karana felt when they gave her the dress? What about the skirt that she had worked so hard to make—how do you think she felt to have that taken away?"

Today, the Church desires that missionaries go about spreading the Gospel with greater respect for indigenous cultures. In the example of Christ, who became flesh and lived among us, we are called to bring Christ to others without taking away the culture with which God has gifted them. Instead, we are called to *inculturate* the Gospel, to make it understood within various cultures and to celebrate how these cultures uphold the Gospel message. In the words of Pope John Paul II: "While it demands of all who hear it the adherence of faith, the proclamation of the Gospel in different cultures allows people to preserve their own identity...to foster whatever is implicit in them to the point where it will be fully explicit in the light of truth" (*Fides et Ratio*, no. 71). Talk about how the white people could have

Saints and Animals

Animals are an important part of Creation—and some saints are associated with certain critters.

St. Francis of Assisi tamed a wolf that terrorized the town of Gubbio, Italy, and the wolf gave Francis his paw in agreement.

St. Clare of Assisi, St. Francis' best friend, talked to animals and nursed them back to health.

Blessed Jordan of Saxony tamed a weasel.

St. Martin de Porres set up a pet hospital in Lima, Peru.

St. Roch, stricken with plague, was restored to health by a dog that brought him bread and licked his wounds.

Blessed Julian of Norwich befriended a cat that she cuddled and prayed with daily.

approached Karana's culture in a way that she deserved: "What would you have said to Karana when you saw her in her outfit? Do you think she was happy where she went? Why?"

This wonderful story provides ample seeds of the Gospel to seek out and cultivate with kids. Other themes include friendship, generosity, kindness to animals, and self-reliance. No matter which way this story takes you in conversation with a child, remember to enjoy it and celebrate it together!

Charlotte's Web by E. B. White

Elwyn Brooks White was known as the greatest essayist and literary stylist of his day with a healthy following for his articles in *The New Yorker* magazine. Almost every high school and college student has encountered his famous book, *The Elements of Style,* in a composition class, but he'll be forever remembered for his children's books. He wrote *Stuart Little* to amuse his niece, launching a career that would also produce *Trumpet of the Swan* and *Charlotte's Web.* While many children are very young when they encounter Charlotte and Wilbur, the experience might be better if saved until they are ten or so, when kids can better appreciate the depth of this story's themes.

Background: In the summer of 1933, E. B. White and his wife were anchored off the coast of Maine and noticed a beautiful farm ashore. The next day they bought it, and the place inspired White's wonderful animal stories. One day he was trying to figure out a way to save his pig from slaughter when he noticed a large gray spider near the barn. His imagination transformed that experience into a literary masterpiece, *Charlotte's Web.*

Synopsis: A litter of pigs is born, and Farmer Arable decides to slaughter the runt. Fern, the farmer's daughter, valiantly saves the piglet from her father's ax and names him Wilbur. She loves him more than anything. When Wilbur grows bigger, he is sent to the farm that belongs to Fern's uncle, Homer Zuckerman. Wilbur is miserable in his new home. None of the other animals will play with him. Despondent and lonely, Wilbur sobs into his manure heap. In the still of night, a voice calls him by name and asks to befriend him. The voice affirms him and gives him joy.

His new friend is an impressive gray spider named Charlotte A. Cavatica, who lives in the doorway of Wilbur's pen. At first, he is put off by her "rather bold and cruel exterior" and the way she devours unsuspecting prey, but Charlotte has a kind heart and proves to be loyal and true to the end.

When the animals inform Wilbur that Homer is fattening him up for Christmas dinner, Wilbur panics. Charlotte gets to work to save him, spinning mysterious words into her web. People flock to see "Zuckerman's Famous Pig," read the messages, and call the words miraculous. All agree that Wilbur is indeed special, definitely not meant to be bacon.

Fern, meanwhile, visits Wilbur nearly every day. Quietly she sits and listens to the animals—and she understands what they are saying to one another. When she reports the daily barn goings-on to her mother, Mrs. Arable worries about Fern. She confides her concerns to an elderly physician, who tells her, "Children pay better attention than grown-ups. If Fern says that the animals in Zuckerman's barn talk, I'm quite ready to believe her."

At the county fair, Charlotte produces another miracle—the word "humble" appears in her web above Wilbur's stall. Charlotte is sure he is now safe from harm and begins her masterpiece: an egg sac containing 514 eggs, an event that heralds the end of her natural life. Sadly, Charlotte dies, but her friendship with Wilbur endures beyond death, for Wilbur honors their bond with an act of loyalty and devotion sure to touch your children's hearts.

Seeds of the Gospel: *Charlotte's Web* carries a wonderful theme of respect for life. From the beginning, vulnerable lives are defended. When Wilbur is about to be slaughtered, Fern rushes to his rescue.

Her father tells her that a weakling is trouble, but Fern valiantly pleads for the runt's life, calling his slaughter a terrible injustice (chap. 1). Consider beginning a conversation in this way: "Fern was brave to protect Wilbur, wasn't she?" or "It's a good thing Wilbur had Fern looking out for him, wasn't it?" Or you might create opportunities to talk about social justice: "Wow, Fern really stands up for what she believes in! That takes a lot of courage...." This could lead to examples of other courageous acts in real life or in other stories.

⟾⊶⟸

"...Literature is my Utopia. Here I am not disfranchised. No barrier of the senses shuts me out from the sweet, gracious discourse of my book-friends. They talk to me without embarrassment or awkwardness."

— Helen Keller, *The Story of My Life*

⟾⊶⟸

Charlotte, in her small voice, speaks to Wilbur in his darkest moment and offers to be his friend (chap. 4). She has been watching him from above his pen, and she likes what she sees. Charlotte teaches Wilbur about life, offers him wise counsel, and invites him to discover joy. When he needs help, she gives it freely and creatively (chap.11). "I would like to have a friend like Charlotte," we might suggest, or "I hope I can *be* a friend like Charlotte when someone needs me." Talk about Charlotte's loyalty and her willingness to help her friend Wilbur. Ask about special friends in your child's life and what he or she likes most about those friends.

By setting aside her own need to lay her eggs in order to help Wilbur, Charlotte displays genuine love for him. Her example recalls the words of Jesus: "No one has greater love than this, to lay down one's life for one's friends" (Jn 15:13). With your kids, think of ways we can "lay down our lives" for others—putting aside our own desires for the good of someone else, doing something we don't want to do to help another, letting another person go before us, etc.

In chapter eleven, Lurvy, a farmhand, drops to his knees in prayer after he sees the words "some pig" in Charlotte's web; when Mr. Zuckerman arrives, he trembles in awe. They call it a miracle and declare that Wilbur is special. Mrs. Zuckerman points out that the *spider* must be special, but no one agrees with her because the message points to Wilbur (chap. 11). Sometimes miracles come through the hands of other people, like the healing that takes place through a doctor's skill. Charlotte shows us that we are God's hands on Earth, and she also demonstrates an important part of that job: she waits quietly and patiently for inspiration, but when it arrives she gets right to the task. This aspect of the story can lead us in many directions— prayer, wonder, waiting hopefully, listening to our inspirations and acting on them. The root word of *inspiration* is spirit, so let the Spirit guide you in conversation about Charlotte!

Another important theme in this passage is the power of media to influence people. Mr. Zuckerman and Lurvy believe Wilbur

Ad Industry Spends Billions to Target Kids

Marion Nestle, chair of the Department of Nutrition and Food Studies at New York University, estimates that $13 billion a year is spent marketing to American children—by food and drink industries alone. Food advertising makes up about half of all advertising aimed at kids.

— Marion Nestle and Margo Wootan as quoted in "Spending on Marketing to Kids Up $5 Billion In Last Decade," *The Food Institute Report*, April 15, 2002.

Channel One's twelve-minute in-classroom broadcast, featuring two minutes of commercials for every ten minutes of news, is compulsory on 90 percent of the school days in 80 percent of the classrooms in 40 percent of U.S. middle and high schools. Companies pay up to $195,000 for a 30-second ad, knowing that they have a captive audience of 8 million students in 12,000 classrooms across the country.

— Center for Commercial-Free Public Education, "Channel One." www.commercialfree.org/channelone.html

From the website of The Center for a New American Dream: www.new-dream.org/campaign/kids/facts.html

is "some pig" just because Charlotte's web says so. And Charlotte has an uncanny knack for advertising! How often do we believe what we read or view with no knowledge of the source? Nowadays, ironically, we have our own Web as well as other media that we need to learn to consume judiciously. Perhaps as an experienced reporter and essayist, E. B. White already saw this need coming in 1952, when he published *Charlotte's Web.*

This theme in *Charlotte's Web* is a great opportunity to bring up the important subject of media education; for example: "I saw a website with a funny picture of a man with frog legs; do you think that's real or do you think somebody created that with a computer?" Or: "What is the best drink (or shoe or hamburger...)?" After they respond, ask the all-important "why?" Sometimes kids have their own opinion about a product based on experience, but often they surprise us by reciting the words of a TV ad! If so, take a moment to explain advertising goals: the purpose of advertisements, why companies want us to buy certain things, how ads target various audiences by appealing to that particular group in the ad, and how advertising claims are sometimes exaggerated to capture our attention.

Charlotte's Web is so rich with Christian themes, we could continue tilling for seeds of the Gospel for many pages! You and your children will enjoy uncovering them together.

❖•❖•❖

The Borrowers by Mary Norton

Mary Spenser Norton was born in London in 1903 and grew up in a Georgian manor house in Bedfordshire, the setting of *The Borrowers.* After completing her education and spending a year with the Old Vic Theatre Company, she married shipping magnate Robert Charles Norton in 1927. The couple lived in Portugal until 1939, becoming the parents of four children. When they returned to England in 1940, Mary took a job with the BBC and the War Office until the family moved briefly to New York City, where Mary worked for the British Purchasing Commission and began writing to supplement the family income. After the war, she returned to England and became a full-time actress and writer, authoring six books about the Borrowers, two *Bedknobs and Broomsticks* books, and a novel about retired fairy tale characters called *Are All the Giants Dead?* She died of a stroke in 1992.

Background: *The Borrowers* was published in 1952 to great critical acclaim. The novel won the Carnegie Medal, the Lewis Carroll Shelf Award Book, and was named an ALA Distinguished Book. It became the first volume in a delightful series of *Borrowers* books, including *The Borrowers Afield* (1955), *The Borrowers Afloat* (1959), *The Borrowers Aloft* (1961), *Poor Stainless: A New Story About the Borrowers* (1971), and *The Borrowers Avenged* (1982). In the last book, the Borrowers finally live safe and sound in a home, the Old Rectory. The story became a British television series and a Hollywood movie.

Synopsis: Mrs. May is an old lady who lives with Kate's family. When Kate loses a crochet hook, Mrs. May tells her about the Borrowers, tiny people who take things from all over the house, such as safety pins, pencils, and match boxes. Borrowers believe humans were created to provide for Borrowers' needs; but it's all a secret, for their greatest fear is Being Seen. Mrs. May says the Borrowers in Kate's house are Pod, Homily, and Arrietty, and she tells Kate about a time long ago when her brother got to know them...

As a boy, her brother discovered Pod on a mission to "borrow." Pod and Homily reveal to their daughter, Arrietty, that another world exists beyond her Borrowers' existence, and tell cautionary tales about relatives who were Seen. Nevertheless, Homily suggests Pod take their daughter with him on his next trip to borrow. Pod is distressed over the danger and because no *girl* has ever borrowed, but he finally brings Arrietty "upstairs," where she is Seen by the boy, who is as afraid of her as she is of him.

Arrietty bravely keeps the location of her home a secret from the boy, but tells him all about borrowing! She keeps her encounter a secret from her parents, and later sneaks away to the boy's room.

Angry, Pod appears in the doorway and silently escorts Arrietty home to tell Homily what has happened. Arrietty defends humans to her disbelieving parents.

During the night, the boy brings the family furniture from a dollhouse, and the parents stand frozen in terror. Arrietty agrees to read to the boy in exchange for many gifts from the doll house, and soon the Borrowers' home is luxuriously appointed. Arrietty shows no interest in the material wealth, but she craves the knowledge she gains from her conversations with the boy. Homily, however, begins to take on airs and demand more finery. When the boy's maid discovers the Borrowers' home, she thinks they are vermin and calls in a rat catcher. The boy tries to carry the Borrowers to safety, but the distraught Homily goes berserk. He opens an escape route for them, and the Borrowers "emigrate" to a new "rural" home in a badger set.

Seeds of the Gospel: On one level this story is a simple fantasy about the kind of little people we find in stories from many cultures. Sown between the lines, though, are seeds of the Gospel ready to germinate. The Borrowers are ethnocentric; they think they are the center of the universe and that "human beans" exist to serve their needs. Arrietty is shocked to discover that humans and Borrowers coexist in the world and that Borrowers are but a tiny part of creation. "Why does Arrietty think she's better than the boy?" you might say to start a conversation on this topic. "How does she feel at the end of the story? How did her attitudes change? What caused the changes?" Talk about the events that altered her worldview: getting to know the boy, venturing out of her small home, reading and gaining knowledge and new ideas. If your child has experienced other cultures, talk about that and what was learned. "What surprised you when you learned about that?" you might ask.

Another aspect of Arrietty's revelation is that another world exists around her of which she hasn't been aware. As Christians, we believe that the Kingdom of God is at hand, that God is working among us, that saints and angels are helping us and interacting in our lives, and that we are part of the mystical body of Christ. All around us things are happening of which we are not always aware—unless they are somehow revealed to us. Plant this seed of the Gospel through a discussion about Arrietty: "How do you think Arrietty felt at first when Pod and Homily told her about the world upstairs? How did she feel when she got up there and met the boy? What goes on around us that we might not know about?"

Also, talk about Arrietty's interaction with this new world: "What did Arrietty want from the boy? How was that different from what Homily wanted?" Point out Arrietty's love of learning and her open-mindedness toward the human world. Discuss the gift Arrietty had to give the boy—her ability to read and to share stories with him. "The boy loved stories, didn't he?" you might say. "Why do you think so? Did you know that Jesus was a good storyteller? Can you think of why he told stories when he was teaching people? Can you think of one of the stories Jesus told?"

Homily really causes the demise of the family's existence in the house. Her craving for more and more material wealth leads Pod to start borrowing larger, more valuable items from Great Aunt Sophy. An important seed of the Gospel seen through Homily's behavior relates to the words of Jesus, who told his disciples that "it is easier for a camel to go through the eye of a needle than for someone who is rich to enter the Kingdom of God" (Mk 10:25). Wealth won't prevent a person from entering eternal life, but it will make it much more difficult if the rich person values material possessions over a relationship with Christ. Talk about Homily's behavior, perhaps asking: "Why wasn't Homily satisfied with what she had? What does Arrietty value most?" Discuss Pod's response to Homily's wishes: "Why does Pod grumble when Homily asks him to borrow more? Why does he keep borrowing to satisfy her desires?" Also, talk about the end result of Homily's greed, asking: "How does her desire for more things cause the family's problems in the end? What do you think Jesus would say about that?"

Use the opportunity proffered by the story to talk about the difference between wants and needs. One day, in a big department store, I was genuinely stunned by something my then-eight-year-old said. Moving toward a standard underwear section, past a colorful lingerie area next to the jewelry counter, Peter said, "Oh, look what they did: they put the wants in front of the needs." And indeed they had. At the front of the store were fabulous nighties and slippers and jewelry that a shopper had to pass by en route to the plain old necessary underwear and socks. Recovering from my momentary shock from his insight, and resisting the urge to shout out in motherly pride, I pursued the thread: "That's right! So how do you get to what you need in here?"

"You go past what you want," he said. "But it would be hard to go past it, I think." From the mouths of babes...

Talk with your child about what we really need—food, shelter, clothing, and someone to love us. Compare that to what we want: the latest and greatest video game or toy, cool clothes, the "right" shoes... Jesus called us to contemplate the true value of worldy possessions, asking: "For what will it profit them if they gain the whole world but forfeit their life? Or what will they give in return for their life?" (Mt 16:26). Explore the underlying causes of materialism and this seed of the Gospel that addresses it: "Why do you suppose we want so many things that we really don't need? How can we do things differently in our house?"

Another topic that this book brings up is "borrowing." Talk about the discussion in chapter ten between Arrietty and the boy, who tells her that "borrowing" is really stealing. "Do you agree with the boy or with Arrietty about what 'borrowing' is? What do we do when we want to borrow something?" The principle of respect for other people's property is part of the Jewish heritage that comes to us in the Decalogue, the Ten Commandments. The seventh commandment states: "You shall not steal." The law commands justice and charity in caring for the fruits of others' labors (CCC, no. 2401) and connotes an attitude of respect for life in the way another's property is respected.

Another good topic for parents and kids to discuss is keeping secrets. Arrietty doesn't tell her parents that she has met the boy at first. But Pod finds her in his room, talking to him. Bring up the reasons that Pod was angry about Arrietty's secretiveness, namely that he was worried for her safety. In a culture affected by blind internet communications and news of crimes against children, parents have some reason for concern. Perhaps most fruitful would be pointing out what happened to Arrietty after Pod discovered her: "Pod was angry with his daughter, wasn't he? But what happened to her after that?" She went home, of course, where she was scolded but, most of all, loved. Use this window of opportunity to reiterate something you've already undoubtedly said—that you love your child and that, *because* of that love, you get angry when a child is disobedient. That is a seed of the Gospel we all need to remember, for the Gospel, in a word, is love.

8

Gospel Seeds Growing

> If you want to build a ship, don't herd people together to collect wood and don't assign them tasks and work, but rather teach them to long for the endless immensity of the sea.
>
> — Antoine de Saint-Exupèry,
> author of *The Little Prince*

By this stage in a child's life, from middle school to junior high school age, Gospel seeds have been tilled and nurtured and are ready for the adventure of growth. Children old enough to read the books covered in this chapter will be able to make connections and participate in conversations that can lead to real faith sharing. Prepare to walk through a secret garden, escape from Mexico to California, visit the Deep American South, and journey with a fuzzy-footed fellow from Hobbiton. But first, we'll go to a place where Gospel seeds flourish— the land of Narnia!

The Chronicles of Narnia by C. S. Lewis

Clive Staples Lewis intended that his readers find Christian messages in his work. He had written many scholarly books on literature and religion when a moment of grace encouraged him to create a fantasy. During the World War II air raids on London, when children were evacuated into the English countryside and assigned to various homes for care, four children arrived at his house. The Oxford professor was surprised at how few imaginative stories these children knew, so he decided to write one for them. And the rest is...well...*his story*.

Having a rich background in story—ancient myths, legends, and fairy tales, as well as stories written by Beatrix Potter, E. Nesbit, and Hans Christian Andersen, C. S. Lewis mixed a concoction of fantasy and Christian belief to create something entirely new[34]—a seven-part series of books filled with important Gospel themes. We'll take a look at the first two books.

The Magician's Nephew

Background: *The Chronicles of Narnia* begin with this "prequel" that describes Narnia's creation and explains how people began traveling there. This book was not written first, but Lewis wanted it read first to set the stage for the adventures to come.

Synopsis: *The Magician's Nephew* tells the story of Digory Kirke and Polly Plummer, next-door neighbors in London who discover a secret room that belongs to Digory's uncle, a magician. In this room, several rings gleam and hum. Looking like a madman, Uncle Andrew appears through a trapdoor and locks them all inside. He gives Polly a ring, and she disappears. Digory demands that Uncle Andrew go after her, but he replies, "You don't understand. I am the great scholar, the magician, the adept who is *doing* the experiment.... Supposing I got killed, what would become of my life's work?" (chap. 2)

Digory valiantly goes to her rescue with another ring. After he finds Polly, they encounter the fierce Empress Jadis, a power-hungry witch whom they bring back to Uncle Andrew's study. The witch enslaves Andrew and sets out to take over the world, first by wreaking havoc upon London. Using the magic ring, Digory zaps Jadis, Andrew, Polly, and himself back out of this world to a place called Nothing.

In dark and empty Nothing, a voice begins to sing and light suddenly bursts forth. A Lion, Aslan, is singing a new world into existence, his warm breath moving his creation as fire flashes in the sky. Then, "the deepest, wildest voice they had ever heard was saying: 'Narnia, Narnia, Narnia, awake. Love. Think. Speak. Be walking trees. Be talking beasts. Be divine waters'"(chap. 9).

In this new creation a tree of life grows, like the one in the Garden of Eden. The witch devours one of its apples and tempts Digory to take one for his dying mother. Digory, however, offers the apple to Aslan, who gives him another apple in return. When the boy feeds Aslan's apple to his mother, she is fully restored. Digory buries the core in his back yard, and another apple tree grows.

Seeds of the Gospel: Consider the description of creation in the prologue of John's Gospel: "In the beginning was the Word, and the Word was with God, and the Word was God. He was in the beginning with God. All things came into being through him, and without him not one thing came into being. What has come into being in him was life, and the life was the light of all people. The light shines in the darkness, and the darkness did not overcome it" (Jn 1:1–5).

Through Jesus, all things came to be. Likewise, through Aslan, the Christ-figure in the story, Narnia comes to be (chap. 9). Knowing that Aslan represents Jesus, we can recognize the deeper meaning Lewis intended in the story. The lion, king of beasts, is like Christ, our King of kings, the Word made flesh through whom the universe was created in love.

Kids usually enjoy imagining the events described in Narnia's creation. If they are familiar with the biblical story of creation (Gen

1–2), their reaction is much stronger, especially when they make the connections themselves. "Oh, that's just like what God (the Father) did," one of my kids said when he first read chapter nine.

"That's right," I replied. "So, in the story, who is Aslan like?"

"Jesus, of course!" he exclaimed.

Patrick made the connection fairly easily. At this age, children may not be able to articulate "creation through the Word," but they will be able to grasp the creation allegory that Lewis offers in *The Magician's Nephew*.

The story also carries a strong message about the importance of respect for life. Uncle Andrew shows that he has little regard for the welfare of Polly or Digory by sending them off into the Other Place with no concern for what they might encounter (chap. 2). Digory, on the other hand, is willing to lay down his life for Polly, going to parts unknown to rescue her (chap. 3). "That uncle is so mean!" my daughter, then nine, exclaimed when we read this book. This led us to talk about how people should act for others' welfare, and how God wants us to care for and love one another. With my teenager, who listened as I read aloud to Diana, the story later led to a conversation on issues of justice involved in human experimentation, and whether the quest for knowledge can ever surpass the call of the Gospel to respect life and afford people the dignity they deserve.

Another overarching topic suggested by Uncle Andrew's character is self-respect. Jesus said to love our neighbors *as ourselves* (cf. Mt 19:19). The magician shows love for neither neighbor nor self, willingly accepting degradation from Jadis out of a sense of his own worthlessness (chap. 6). He makes so many poor choices that, in the end, he becomes a pathetic creature who cannot even hear Aslan's voice (chap. 10). Yet he is so full of pride at the beginning of the story! You might ask kids: "When mean people, like bullies, pretend they're cool, do you think they believe they're cool? Do you think they're covering up anything by acting that way?" Such questions could lead to an interesting conversation about school life, friends, "enemies," and peer pressure.

Pay attention to details in this book because they'll help you understand the next volume in the series. One important tidbit concerns the identity of the professor in *The Lion, the Witch, and the Wardrobe;* another explains the origins of the door into the land of Narnia and how it came to be a piece of furniture in the professor's house.

The Lion, the Witch, and the Wardrobe

Background: C. S. Lewis wrote this fantasy for children who were curious about an old wardrobe in his home. He developed a story, as it came to him in his imagination, in which four children enter another world through its doors. Although this is the second book in the Narnia series, it was written first.

Synopsis: Digory has grown up and become a professor by the time four children—Peter, Susan, Edmund, and Lucy—arrive at his country home and discover Narnia through the back panel of an old wardrobe. Lucy is the first to find Narnia, but a talking faun, who is a spy for the evil White Witch, likes Lucy and sends her back to the wardrobe to protect her from the witch. When Lucy returns to the professor's house, no earthly time has passed, so her siblings refuse to believe her story. After a few miserable days, Lucy returns to Narnia—this time secretly followed by Edmund, who meets the witch and tells her all about his family. Tempting him with the promise of a delectable Turkish delight, the witch sends him home with instructions to return with his siblings.

Edmund, "becoming a nastier person every minute" (chap. 5), pretends Lucy is lying about Narnia. Only the professor (Digory, the magician's nephew) believes her, until all four children suddenly find themselves in the snow-covered land where it is always winter but never Christmas because of the witch. All soon realize that Edmund lied about going there before. Ashamed and alienated by his own choices—and corrupted by the witch's Turkish delight—Edmund decides to deliver his siblings over to the witch.

The children discover that the faun was imprisoned for helping Lucy, and they go off to save him. On the way, they learn that Aslan has returned to Narnia and that they themselves fulfill a prophecy about four humans who will end the witch's reign. At that, Edmund sneaks off to betray them to the witch.

But the witch's grip on Narnia is loosening already: Father Christmas (Santa Claus) returns, and new life bursts forth from the melting snow. Edmund finally realizes that the witch is evil, but, like Uncle Andrew in the first Narnia book, he is already enslaved by his own poor choices. Peter, Susan, and Lucy find Aslan at the great Stone Table and tell him that Edmund has joined the White Witch. Peter, however, assumes some of the blame: "I was angry with him and I think that helped him to go wrong" (chap. 12).

As the witch prepares to kill Edmund, Aslan's creatures rescue him. But the White Witch appeals to Aslan on grounds of Deep Magic, which gives her the right to take a traitor's life. Aslan offers his own life in exchange for Edmund's. The great lion is humiliated and slain on the Stone Table, but, through a deeper magic, is resurrected. All whom the witch had cursed are restored to life, just in time for a massive battle in which Aslan kills the witch. The four children are crowned kings and queens of Narnia.

Seeds of the Gospel: For Christians the allegory is obvious: Aslan represents Christ, who offered his life in place of ours; whose death and resurrection won our freedom and redemption. In Aslan's loneliness and sorrow, we recognize Jesus' agony in the garden; in his humiliation and shearing, Jesus' passion; and, of course, in Alsan's resurrection, the Easter story (chap. 15). While it would be easy to point out the way Lewis constructed this story around the central Gospel message, children benefit most by finding the connections themselves. So, a brief but "leading" comment might best facilitate deeper understanding: "Oh, he rose from the dead!" If your children are familiar with the story of Jesus, they will get it.

In chapter six, Edmund accidentally reveals that he lied about going to Narnia, and the children, especially Peter, become angry with him. Edmund vows revenge, making excuses for his bad behavior. A good conversation-starter with kids might be: "I wonder if Edmund is embarrassed. Do you think he knows he's doing something wrong?" or "I wonder why people make excuses when they've done something wrong, like Edmund did."

Deeper into the morality theme at the end of chapter six, Edmund questions whether the fauns are right about the witch being the villain, and says, "We don't really know anything about either" (chap. 6). Kids, especially those who are older, may have a lot to say—and perhaps ask—about this passage. How *do* we know right from wrong? If we can't tell the difference, how can we figure out what to do? Parents might talk about times when we they struggled to figure out the right thing to do and reassure kids that the struggle is normal—as well as hard! We might suggest to kids who seem perplexed about situations in their own lives that God is always there for us and that we can pray for guidance in our struggles, or ask for help...something that might have helped Edmund better understand and respond to his dilemma!

Peter acknowledges that his own anger caused Edmund's betrayal (chap. 12). Because sin alienates or excludes us from others, Jesus not only forgave sin, but also reintegrated sinners into the community.[35] Think of the prodigal son: the son is forgiven—and welcomed home with a party! You might initiate a dialogue on this theme by saying: "I wonder what would have happened if Peter had forgiven Edmund right away?"

Aslan makes the children kings and queens of Narnia and the adventure continues. Do they make it back to the wardrobe? It's worth more than a peek to find out!

The Rest of the Series

The *Chronicles* continue in five more volumes, entitled:
> *The Horse and His Boy*
> *Prince Caspian*
> *The Voyage of the Dawn Treader*
> *The Silver Chair*
> *The Last Battle*

Each contains Gospel themes woven within captivating adventure. At the end of *The Voyage of the Dawn Treader,* in chapter sixteen, Aslan reveals that he called the children to Narnia so that they could more clearly recognize him under a different name in their own world: "by knowing me here for a little, you may know me better there." May a better understanding also be true for all who venture into C. S. Lewis's fantastic world!

———◦•••◦———

Esperanza Rising by Pam Muñoz Ryan

Pam Muñoz Ryan has written over twenty-five books for young people; several works have garnered awards, including *Esperanza Rising, Riding Freedom, Amelia and Eleanor Go for a Ride,* and *When Marian Sang.* Born and raised in Bakersfield, California, the author grew up in a large, close-knit family, the oldest of three sisters and twenty-three cousins on her mother's side. She calls her cultural background an ethnic smorgasbord: Spanish, Mexican, Basque, Italian, and Oklahoman. As a child, she spent most of her time in the local library because, she says, it was air-conditioned! After graduation from San Diego State University, she married, had children, became a teacher, a school administrator, returned to San Diego State for a master's degree, and then began her first book at the encouragement of a friend who believed she could write. She and her husband, Jim Ryan, and their four children now live in North San Diego County, California. Her writing awards include the national Willa Cather Award and the California Young Reader Medal for *Riding Freedom;* the ALA Sibert Honor and NCTE's Orbis Pictus Award for *When Marian Sang;* and numerous awards for *Esperanza Rising.*

Background: An acclaimed young adult novel, *Esperanza Rising* was awarded the Pura Belpre Medal, the Jane Addams Peace Award, an American Library Association (ALA) Top Ten Best Book for Young Adults, and the Americas Award Honor Book. The fictional story is based on the immigration experiences of the author's grandmother,

Esperanza Ortega. The real Esperanza was already married when she arrived in California, but the author chose to make the fictional Esperanza a young teenager to help young readers identify more closely with her protagonist. The author's note at the end of the book includes historical details about the story's time period: the Great Depression.

Note: The chapters are not numbered in *Esperanza Rising*. The author uses a clever device that mirrors the way farm workers think and talk about time—by the fruit or vegetable they are harvesting. Chapters are titled "Peaches," "Almonds," "Avocados," and so on.

Synopsis: Esperanza is the only child of a wealthy rancher in Mexico. When she is six years old, in 1924, her father teaches her how to feel the heartbeat of the earth in their vineyard. Six years later, Esperanza ceremoniously begins the harvest of the ranch grapes, an honor normally afforded to males, but granted to her because she is her father's pride and joy. Esperanza is a girl of privilege—well to do, schooled, preparing to debut into society, expecting marriage to a wealthy young man. On the eve of her thirteenth birthday fiesta, bandits murder her father. When his will is read to Esperanza and her mother, Ramona, the lawyer explains that mother and daughter have inherited the house and furnishings, but, since Mexican land could not be passed down to women, her father's brother has inherited the ranch. The uncle offers to buy the house at a very low price, and Ramona refuses. He responds with a marriage proposal. When she refuses that, too, he vows to make life difficult for them. He is as good as his word: the house burns to the ground. The cruel uncle proposes again. This time, Ramona accepts, but begins to hatch a plan to escape to California, along with their most trusted former servants: the housekeeper, Hortensia; the boss of the ranch hands, Alfonso; and their son, Miguel.

Grandmother, Abuelita, arranges for her two sisters, who are nuns, to help them escape. The sisters provide a trunk of clothes and travel documents for Ramona and Esperanza. Abuelita tells Esperanza not to be afraid of starting a new life, that she did it when she immigrated to Mexico from Spain. She says that they are both like the phoenix that rises up from the ashes. Later, Esperanza, Ramona, and Hortensia climb into the secret compartment of a fruit wagon and, with Miguel and Alfonso at the reins, flee their home in the dead of night. Two days later, they board a northbound train to the United States.

Esperanza notices a change on the train ride as Ramona confides in a peasant woman, but Esperanza still thinks herself in a higher social class. In California, Alfonso's relatives take them to a company farm camp, where they have arranged jobs and living quarters for them all. They share a cabin with Alfonso's family, and Esperanza tends the home while the adults work in the fields. Gratitude for everything she has eventually replaces Esperanza's anger over what she has lost. A violent dust storm causes Ramona to contract Valley Fever, an infection caused by agricultural dust in the lungs, and she becomes gravely ill. Esperanza stays by her side, asking Our Lady of Guadalupe for guidance. When Ramona is hospitalized, Esperanza pretends to be older and works to earn money to pay the medical bills and to bring Abuelita to California. On a grocery shopping trip, she sees a migrant workers' camp and becomes hypnotized by the squalor. She and Miguel learn that a farm labor strike is brewing. The strike provides Miguel a chance to work as a railroad mechanic, and it unleashes compassion and social concern in Esperanza. At last, Ramona returns home and Abuelita arrives, both finding in Esperanza a diligent, responsible, loving young woman, where once stood a spoiled princess.

Seeds of the Gospel: This wonderful book, a personal favorite, provides insights into the life of Mexican farm laborers and migrant workers in a way that pierces the heart at the same time that it charms the reader. While John Steinbeck's masterpiece *The Grapes of Wrath* (another personal favorite) tells the story of a migrant family in a way that can cause readers to feel depressed, this novel, written for a younger audience, builds a feeling of hope and promise as we struggle with Esperanza as she makes a new life in a world of injustices. Moreover, Roman Catholic families will appreciate the way in which Esperanza's faith develops as she matures. Her faith is woven into the fabric of her character, rather than included as a detail in the story. If ever there was a piece of popular culture that portrays Catholicism in a positive light, this is it.

⟾⬦⟽

"Literature adds to reality, it does not simply describe it."
— C. S. Lewis

⟾⬦⟽

Esperanza Rising is about starting over, rising up from the ashes like the mythical phoenix into a new life. While an inspiring tale of the immigrant experience in the United States, the story also serves as a metaphor for our own new life in Christ. The phoenix is a symbol of Christ (see page 221). Its rising from the ashes mirrors the resurrection of Jesus. Esperanza, who has everything a girl could want at the beginning of the story—parents who adore her, wealth, luxury, comfort, friends, no sibling rivalry, a carefree existence—must learn to rise up when her idyll is destroyed by death and her home is burned to ash. Esperanza emerges from the tragedy, but she only rises after she takes on, along with her new lifestyle, the attitude of Christ in truly loving and caring for her neighbor. Talk about the two settings for the story, the luxurious ranch in Mexico and the meager cabin in the farm camp, perhaps asking: "What was Esperanza's life like at the beginning of the story? When she moved to California, what was different? What was the same?"

Although Esperanza seems to have everything at the ranch, she comes to realize she is lacking life skills, patience, humility, and love. Esperanza changes when she begins to notice her neighbor, in the way Jesus taught us through the story of the Good Samaritan (Lk 10:29–37). Discuss the things Esperanza learns in her new life: "How does Esperanza change when she gets to the farm camp? What are some of the things she does that help her become different?" A few examples are her giving up her doll to Isabel ("Peaches" chapter), after she had refused to let another little girl on the train even *touch* it, and her generosity with the migrant workers ("Potatoes" chapter); another is the way she begins to help Hortensia rather than expecting to be served by her former maid ("Almonds" chapter).

Being part of the privileged class in Mexico, Esperanza's worldview is based on a stratified society—with her family on the top layer. In "a moment of self-importance," she tells Miguel, the house-keeper's son and her childhood playmate, that they come from oppo-site sides of a deep river (first "Grapes" chapter). Miguel stops speaking to Esperanza and begins to call her *"mi reina,"* Spanish for "my queen." Things change in California when the two live equally as family, but when Miguel refuses to speak out at his demotion at work, Esperanza tells him he remains on the other side of the river ("Peaches" chapter). He points out her unchanged pride, and Esperanza feels the weight of her lingering conceit. These scenes are rife with seeds of the Gospel! Consider the following Old Testament proverb: "When pride comes, then comes disgrace; but wisdom is with the humble" (Prov 11:2). Also, consider Peter's statement when he realizes that the Gospel is not reserved for the Jews, but is for everyone: "I truly understand that God shows no partiality" (Acts 10:35). Talk about Esperanza's haughtiness: "Why does Esperanza think she's better than Miguel at the beginning? What happens in the end that shows us that she has finally changed? Which way does God want us to act? Why?" Also talk about Esperanza's different views of "rising": at first, she thinks only of rising in prominence in society; later, she is rising up above problems that keep her down, rising to new life. Ask: "How do Esperanza's expectations change? How does she learn to find happiness in her new way of life?"

This story offers great insights into another seed of the Gospel, from the Beatitudes: "Blessed are the poor in spirit, for theirs is the kingdom of heaven" (Mt 5:3). When Esperanza encounters Carmen, a peasant woman on the train, she cannot understand why the woman seems happy in her poverty ("Guavas" chapter). Later, in

Catholic Social Teaching

Pope Leo XIII issued the first comprehensive ecclesial document on social justice, *Rerum Novarum,* which stressed the rights and responsibilities of both employers and employees to promote human dignity and equality and called the Church to speak out on social issues. In 1931, Pope Pius XI issued *Quadragesimo Anno,* warning against Communism for its abolition of private property and calling for a just wage for all workers.

Pope John XXIII enumerated economic, scientific, social, and political developments since *Rerum Novarum* in his 1961 encyclical *Mater et Magistra,* pointing out disparities between rich and poor nations and calling on lay people to "see, judge, act" in society. In 1963, following the erection of the Berlin Wall and the Cuban Missile Crisis, he issued *Pacem in Terris,* calling for social rights and responsibilities throughout the world to ensure peace. The same year, the Vatican II document *Gaudium et Spes* called us to scrutinize technological and social changes and how they affect families as well as society in general. In 1967, Pope Paul VI issued *Populorum Progressio* to express urgency about the growing disparity among nations and its inherent temptation to use violence and revolution as a resolution.

the farm camp, Esperanza desires Isabel's uncomplicated happiness that allows her to delight in the smallest pleasure ("Potatoes" chapter). Discuss the reasons why Esperanza finds it so hard to adjust to poverty: "What does Esperanza value at the beginning of the story? Why is she unhappy in California? What changes to help her become happy in the end?"

In the first "Grapes" chapter, Abuelita teaches Esperanza to crochet. The grandmother unravels the girl's messy stitches and tells her not to be afraid of starting over. Later, in the "Figs" chapter,

Abuelita tries to encourage Esperanza by recounting how she started over as a girl when she immigrated to Mexico from Spain. Talk about the differences that Abuelita experienced: "What did Abuelita like about the changes? How did she cope with her disappointments? Why is she telling the story to Esperanza?" When Ramona is gravely ill, Esperanza pulls out a blanket Abuelita had been working on and continues the work because in it are all her grandmother's love and good wishes. As Ramona grows more and more pale, the blanket grows more colorful because women in the camp contribute whatever yarn they have to the project. Talk about blankets and how they make us feel. If your child has a special blanket, talk about that. As for Esperanza's effort, suggest: "How do Esperanza's neighbors show her they care when she is tending to Mama? How does that affect the blanket? Why is she working on the blanket?"

Prayer and worship is an important part of Esperanza's life, especially as she matures. When Ramona is sick and cannot mother Esperanza, the girl turns to Our Lady of Guadalupe for help ("Onions" chapter). She visits a grotto of Our Lady, fashioned out of an old washtub, behind the cabin and finds comfort in praying with Mary. Talk about Esperanza's faith and her growing relationship with the Blessed Mother: "Why does Esperanza talk to Mary? What does she ask? Can you imagine what Our Lady of Guadalupe might say to Esperanza? Why? What would you like to tell Mary?"

Part of Esperanza's growing faith and love is her burgeoning social concern as she interacts with her neighbors. While this story is told from the point of view of farm workers who preferred not to strike to get higher wages and better living conditions, the fact that both improvements were needed is evident. Through Esperanza's struggles of conscience, we are invited to think about the needs of the poor. As Catholic Christians, such social concern is an important aspect of our call to build the Kingdom of God. Talk about Esperanza's visit to the migrant workers' camp: "How does Esperanza react to the conditions in the migrant camp? How is the camp different from where she lives? How does her attitude begin to change?" Also talk about Esperanza's feelings toward Marta, a

Our Lady of Guadalupe

Our Lady of Guadalupe appeared in 1531 to a poor Aztec Indian at Tepeyac hill, northwest of Mexico City, the site of an ancient Aztec temple. She instructed Juan Diégo, who was on his way to Mass, to tell the bishop to build a church in her honor there. The basilica is now one of the most popular Marian shrines in the world, receiving ten million visitors yearly.

The story of Juan Diégo's encounter is described in a six-teenth-century document written in the native Nahuatl language and includes wondrous miracles as well. Our Lady of Guadalupe, surrounded by heavenly music and dazzling light, appeared and spoke to Juan Diégo, a convert to Christianity six years before. She caused roses to spring from the frozen earth and, with her own hands, arranged a bouquet for him to give to the bishop. She miraculously imprinted her image on Juan Diégo's *tilma,* a poor quality, cactus-cloth wrap that today, nearly five centuries later, shows no signs of decay and defies all scientific explanations.

Our Lady of Guadalupe, patroness of the Americas and protector of the unborn, offered a message of love and compassion, promising help and protection to all her children. Less than twenty years after her visit, nine million Aztecs converted to Christianity. Over the centuries, scores of miracles have been attributed to her.

The feast of Our Lady of Guadalupe is celebrated on December 12.

migrant worker and activist: "How does Esperanza feel about Marta at first? How does that change in the story? Why?"

This story is brimming with possibilities for discussion. Other talks might focus on the value of work in helping Esperanza learn to belong in the camp or her relationship with Miguel and how he expresses his love to her patiently and with respect despite her behavior. Explore the changing roles of Hortensia and Alfonso and how they minister to Esperanza throughout her life. Above all, enjoy this well crafted story, a lovely piece of genuine American art.

———◆·•◆·•◆———

Sounder by William H. Armstrong

Born in 1914, **William H. Armstrong** grew up on a farm in Lexington, Virginia. A man of faith, he claims to have asked bothersome questions as a boy; for example, in Sunday school when he learned how Jesus cast demons out of a person and into a herd of swine that consequently drowned, Armstrong asked: "What about the poor man who owned the swine? Who paid for his loss?" The inquisitive youth became a scholar, graduating from Hampden-Sydney College in 1936 and doing graduate work at the University of Virginia. In 1942, he married Martha Williams. Together they had three children, but Martha died when they were very young. Armstrong raised his children alone, or as he says, father and kids "grew up together." In 1945, he became a history master at Kent School in Kent, Connecticut, where he taught for fifty-two years. Also handy with tools, he cleared land on his small sheep farm overlooking the Housatonic River and built a house with his own hands, becoming a skilled carpenter and stonemason in the process. He published several non-fiction books before publishing *Sounder.* He also wrote several books on historical and biblical characters.

Background: Armstrong's notes indicate that this story comes from an old African-American man who taught the author to read. Set in the late nineteenth century, *Sounder* is Armstrong's first novel and most acclaimed work, winner of the 1970 Newbery Medal. Its sequel is *Sour Land.*

Synopsis: This story features nameless African-American characters—the boy, his mother, father, and schoolmaster. Only the dog has a name, Sounder, for his powerful bark. The family ekes out a living sharecropping. Among the boy's simple pleasures are listening to his mother singing and telling stories, and being with Sounder. One morning, after days of eating only corn mush, the boy wakes to the smell of ham and sausages. Three days later, the sheriff arrests the father for stealing the meat and leads him away. Sounder follows, but a deputy shoots the dog, who limps under the porch to die. The next morning, when the mother goes to town, the boy crawls under the house to look for Sounder's body. Nothing is there. When the mother returns, she tells the boy that dogs sometimes heal their wounds in oak leaves, and that Sounder may be alive. On Christmas Day, the mother bakes a cake that the boy carries across town to the jail. A guard crumbles the cake to see if it contains an escape tool before allowing the boy to visit his father, who tells him not to come again. The next morning, a one-eyed, one-eared Sounder returns home; but the dog no longer barks. Soon, the mother learns that the father has been sentenced to hard labor for his crime.

The mother takes on more work, and the boy starts working the fields and weeding to help support the family. In the winter, the boy journeys to prison camps in search of his father, picking up discarded newspapers and magazines to practice reading. Years go by; the family works, the boy searches. As he stands outside a prison camp one day, peering through the fence for his father, a guard smashes his hand with a jagged piece of iron and laughs. On the way home, the boy finds a discarded book, too hard for him to read, but he takes it along. He notices a schoolhouse and meets the schoolmaster, who washes his wound, tells him the book was written by Montaigne, and reads from it to him. The boy goes home to ask his mother if he can live with the teacher and go to school in exchange for chores. She says it is God's will and sends him off. Years go by, and the boy goes to school each winter and returns home to work the fields each summer. When he reads to his siblings, his mother says the Lord has come to him.

One hot day, a lone figure walks toward the cabin. Sounder barks and races to the father, who has come home, limping and withered. In the fall, the father and Sounder go hunting. The boy, home to help gather walnuts and wood, watches them hobble into the darkness. Sounder returns and leads the boy to his father, who is dead. Knowing Sounder will die, too, the boy digs a grave before he leaves for school; Sounder is resting there when he returns for Christmas. The boy reflects on the words of Montaigne from his battered old book: "Only the unwise think that what has changed is dead."

Seeds of the Gospel: As a story of love, *Sounder* is brimming with seeds of the Gospel. The dog, the boy, the father, and the mother are all bound in a circle of love that gives them hope, fosters loyalty, and provides strength to carry on throughout their tragic circumstances. In contrast to their abundant love for one another is the immense hatred they face from others because of the color of their skin. The family doesn't talk about their love for one another, they show it—the way Scripture calls us to do: "Little children, let us love, not in word or speech, but in truth and action" (1 John 3:18). Talk about the way the family shows love in action, perhaps asking: "How do the mother and father support their family? What does the boy do to contribute to the family? When the boy goes to school, how does he continue to help? Why do they do it?"

A big part of Armstrong's message in *Sounder* is the power of story. The boy likes to hear his mother's stories, especially those from the Bible. In the first chapter, she tells him about Noah and the Great Flood, from Genesis 6–9, and his imagination finds a positive note in the tale of destruction—he wouldn't be lonely if all of the houses floated together! At the end of the chapter, he wishes he could read so that he would never be lonely. In chapter four, when his father is in jail, he imagines the jail is warm because of a story his mother told him about Shadrach, Meshach, and Abednego, who are cast into a jail stove by a king. In chapter six, the boy talks about journeys described in the Scripture and remembers stories about King David. On one of his own journeys, he finds a book that leads to an opportunity for education, much of it through the power of story. In chapter eight, when it's his turn to tell stories, he recounts over and over again the story of Joseph, who was sold into slavery and rose to prominence. The boy has turned the stories over in his imagination, and they have become part of him, informing his decisions. Armstrong is saying that the boy is moved and guided by story; as a result, his existence will be different from that of his father's.

Armstrong had reasons for the specific biblical references woven into the story of *Sounder*. Each Bible story involves characters who rose above adversity. Shadrach, Meshach, and Abednego literally rise up from the flames into a place of honor in a foreign land. Young David slays a giant with a slingshot and becomes king of Israel. And Joseph, sold by his own brothers into slavery, rises to a position of importance in Egypt and eventually stands in judgment of his kin. As an African-American sharecropper's son during Reconstruction, the boy lives with disenfranchisement. Although slavery was officially over, African Americans remained oppressed and bound by prejudice and hatred at the time of this novel's setting. The boy dreams of a better future and continues on in search of it. When education changes his life, Armstrong sends a message for all of the world's marginalized people that the route out of poverty is paved with literacy and learning. Talk about the way school changes the boy's life: "Why did the schoolmaster offer the boy a chance to go to school? Why did he take it? How did it change his life? How did it help his family?" If your child is familiar with Bible stories, talk about favorites in your household—or start learning a few. Besides the spiritual nourishment it offers, knowledge of Bible stories provides a door to deeper meanings tucked into fiction.

Sounder is named for his big bark, a voice that carries through the night. After he is shot and maimed by the cruel deputy, he returns to his home and merely whimpers. Yet when his master returns, Sounder barks again. Talk about this lovable coon dog: "How did the boy feel when Sounder came home? Why had he stopped barking? Why does he start barking again near the end of the story?" If you have pets, talk about what they mean to the

The story of Shadrach, Meshach, and Abednego comes from the Old Testament Book of Daniel. The three handsome young men were companions of Daniel, appointed by King Nebuchadnezzar to oversee matters in Babylon. When the king erected a golden statue in the plains of Dura, they refused to worship this false idol. Some Chaldeans tattled on the three men. The king became enraged and cast them into a fiery furnace. They avowed their faith in Yahweh, who sent an angel to protect them. When the king heard them singing and saw the angel escorting them out of the inferno without the slightest singe or scorch, King Nebuchadnezzar decreed that no one should blaspheme the God who saves (Dan 3:1–30).

The Book of Daniel is one of the early pieces of apocalyptic writing found in the Bible, written to express the experience of Jewish exiles in Babylon and demonstrate that Yahweh has the power to save. The stories of Daniel in the lion's den and Shadrach and company in the furnace foreshadow resurrection and tell us that God is in control and everything will work out in the end. William Armstrong's mention of the story aims to underscore the need for hope in the character of the boy in *Sounder* as he navigates through the heat of injustice and hatred.

members of the family. This aspect of the story demonstrates Sounder's loyalty to the father, yet it also serves as a metaphor for the way African Americans were silenced and marginalized before the Civil Rights movement. Just for speaking out or sometimes simply for being themselves, blacks were victims of unspeakable brutality, such as beatings and lynching, just as Sounder was shot for no apparent reason other than to torment the family. Talk about the way Sounder is treated: "How do you think the family felt when Sounder was shot? How would you feel if someone did that to your pet? Why did the deputy do that? What would Jesus say about that?"

The prison guards' treatment of the prisoners and the boy (when the one guard smashes his hand) is abominable. Brutality, racial slurs, injustice, and inhumanity are expressed in the story through the behavior of the white guards. Talk about the way their prejudice and hatred make the boy and his family feel: "How does the boy feel when he walks through town? What does the boy think about when the guard smashes his hand? How would you feel if that happened to you? What about the mother: how does she feel about the way people act toward them? What does she say when the boy comes home with the book? Why does she react that way?"

Armstrong, a master of ancient history, uses a reference to the French Renaissance philosopher Michel de Montaigne (1533–1592) to add layers of meaning in one small passage. When the schoolmaster peruses the book the boy has picked out of a trash bin, he chooses to share a story that Montaigne borrowed from Xenophon's *Cyropedia*. In the tale, King Cyrus desires a prize horse owned by one of his soldiers and offers his kingdom for it. The soldier refuses the kingdom, but says he would trade his horse for a friend. (Shakespeare referred to the story as well when Richard III utters the famous line, "A horse! A horse! My kingdom for a horse!" *Richard III*, act V, scene IV.) The schoolmaster befriends the boy by sharing story. The story from Montaigne's book indicates that this friendship will bring with it wisdom and knowledge through history, philosophy, literature, and observation. By choosing to include mention of Cyrus in *Sounder*, I believe Armstrong is teasing us to think a little more about this king and what he means to the boy and his people.

Cyrus is important in the history of the Jews. King Nebuchadnezzar (whom we meet in the story of Daniel, Shadrach, Meshach, and Abednego) destroyed Jerusalem in 586 B.C. and exiled many Jews to Mesopotamia, the beginning of a period known as the Babylonian Captivity. When King Cyrus ruled the region, this changed. In 538 B.C., he sent a group of Jews to Jerusalem to rebuild the Temple and resume their lives there, ending the captivity. Through the schoolmaster's choice of story, Armstrong is saying that education will end the boy's "captivity" in the rural South and foster a new attitude. Moreover, it sends a message to all oppressed people that it is time for change, for a new attitude.

The reference to Montaigne layers even more meaning into the story. Montaigne searched for truth by reflecting on his readings, travels, and experiences. He was a great proponent of fideism, a philosophy affirming that the fundamental act of human knowledge consists in an act of faith, that humans cannot reach wisdom through their own brain power but through divine revelation. In the story, the schoolmaster points out some similarities between the boy and Montaigne and tells him, "People should read his writings. But few do." Through this reference, Armstrong is calling the boy out of the Dark Ages of the American South into a renaissance, a time of expanding horizons through knowledge—but with the humility of faithful believers, who know that all wisdom comes from God.

Perhaps you are thinking: "All that in this novel for kids?" Indeed. Rich with literary, biblical, and historical references as well as a wonderful, moving story, *Sounder* provides nourishing food for thought for children and adults alike. It offers opportunities for long conversations with kids about life's deeper meanings.

The Secret Garden by Frances Hodgson Burnett

Frances Hodgson was fifteen years old when she emigrated with her family from Manchester, England, to Tennessee at the end of the Civil War. She brought with her a healthy appetite for story, especially fairy tales, and began writing short stories for magazines to help her widowed mother pay the bills. She was a published author by the age of eighteen.

Later married to Dr. Swan Burnett, Frances supported her family by writing until her husband's medical practice was established in 1877 in Washington, D.C. She became a well-known author, critically acclaimed for her novels and plays. In 1886, she published the classic *Little Lord Fauntleroy*, which became a runaway best-seller and inspired a line of products related to the story—toys, candy, playing cards, even blue velvet suits.[36]

Frances Hodgson Burnett wrote more than forty books before her death in 1924, including *A Little Princess* (1905) and *A Secret Garden* (1911).

Background: Frances Hodgson Burnett loved gardening. As a literary celebrity, she bought a manor house in Kent, England, and transformed an old, walled orchard into a rose garden. She often wrote in the garden and, there, got her first ideas for *The Secret Garden*. She later wrote the book in another garden at her home in Long Island, New York. The character of Colin is based in part upon her own son, Lionel, who was bedridden and died of tuberculosis when he was sixteen.[37]

Synopsis: Mary Lennox is orphaned in Colonial India and sent to live with her rich uncle in Yorkshire, England. His enormous manor house is dark and creepy, with strange noises occurring at night. Martha, a maid there, looks after Mary. Cheerful and honest, Martha uses straightforward charm to unmask Mary, unloved and bitter beneath her affectations. The forthright maid unabashedly points out Mary's wastefulness and haughtiness, but she also encourages Mary to discover her own inner resources.

Ben Weatherstaff, the groundskeeper, also speaks plain truth to Mary about her nasty temper and dreadful disposition, admitting that he has the same flaws. Mary has never heard the truth about herself before. Martha and Ben encourage her to stay outdoors all day, walking the grounds, jumping rope, and playing, which improves her disposition tremendously and brings Mary a healthy appetite and, at last, sleepful nights.

Mary's uncle, the grieving Archibald Craven, is a hunchbacked widower. His beloved wife died from a fall in a beautiful garden on the grounds, so he sealed it off and won't allow anyone to talk about it. He won't even see Mary when she first arrives, so self-absorbed is he in his own pain. Meanwhile, his son, Colin, is bedridden. Mary isn't told about Colin, but she hears horrible cries in the house.

One day she finds an old key buried outside; another day, she finds the door to the secret garden, and her key opens the lock. Inside, shoots of new life are bursting through the earth, so Mary begins to weed. The garden leads Mary to Dickon, Martha's brother, a redheaded boy with a funny face who smells of fresh heather and grass. Mary shares with him her secret garden, and he shows her how to plant and tend seeds.

Mr. Craven finally sees Mary, and she asks him for "a bit of earth." He tells her she can have whatever she wants and to make things come alive. Later, exploring the house, Mary discovers and befriends her cousin Colin and, secretly, shares with him her garden, which transforms his life and his father's as it has hers.

Seeds of the Gospel: The metaphor of a secret garden is filled with spiritual themes. A garden is the source of life in our Judeo-Christian tradition; from the Earth we were fashioned in God's image (cf. Gen 1). Moreover, Jesus went into a garden before his passion began, speaking intimately there with God and accepting his role in the salvation of the world. Each of us has within us, metaphorically, a secret garden to be cultivated—weeds of sin and neglect to be extracted, soil turned, seeds of new life to be planted and to flourish with water and light. In that garden, we are fashioned by God, and there we can speak to God and accept the call to do God's will.

Mary learns to love in the garden. Throughout the story, her willfulness is transformed into determination, and her anger and bitterness into high-spirited energy and empathy for others. She

In *The Secret Garden*, Mary is transformed from a tree of self-defeat into a tree of self-realization. She finds charity, friendship, love, gratitude, trust, kindness, and warmth in the story. In the way she enjoys and works the garden and shares it with Colin, Mary bears all of the fruits Mother Teresa lists.

Mother Teresa of Calcutta once wrote about two "trees"—a tree of self-defeat and a tree of self-realization. See how well these images apply to the story of *The Secret Garden:*

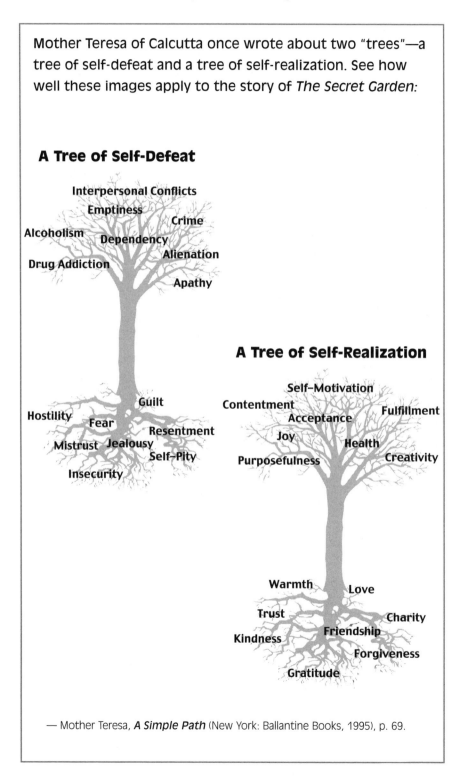

A Tree of Self-Defeat

Interpersonal Conflicts
Emptiness
Crime
Alcoholism Dependency
Alienation
Drug Addiction
Apathy

Guilt
Hostility Fear
Resentment
Mistrust Jealousy
Self–Pity
Insecurity

A Tree of Self-Realization

Self–Motivation
Contentment
Acceptance Fulfillment
Joy
Purposefulness Health
Creativity

Warmth Love
Trust Charity
Friendship
Kindness
Forgiveness
Gratitude

— Mother Teresa, *A Simple Path* (New York: Ballantine Books, 1995), p. 69.

imparts these lessons to Colin, who is very much like herself, and he is transformed by life-giving mercy and love (chap. 24).

Mary makes a difference because she discovers meaning in life. Rude and spoiled at the beginning, she learns to use her forthrightness to help Colin, by being honest with him and challenging him (chap. 14). "I wonder what would have happened if Mary hadn't been strong enough to talk to Colin the way she did," you might muse aloud. An ensuing conversation may lead to a discussion on when it is the appropriate time to speak up, and how love can lead us to confront others.

Another great conversation-starter is Martha's pointed question to Mary: "How does tha' like thysel'?" Mary replies, "Not at all—really...but I never thought of that before" (chap. 7). Mary is a difficult person because she suffers from what is now called "low self-esteem." This is certainly a seed of the Gospel sown in *The Secret Garden*, because Jesus commanded us "to love our neighbors *as ourselves*" (cf. Mt 22:39). The first step in becoming Christ-like, then, is to love *ourselves*, to see ourselves as children of God. Find out what your kids think by asking them the same question Martha asked Mary: "How do you like yourself?" Or begin by saying: "When Mary starts to like herself, she accomplishes wonderful things, doesn't she?" This could become an inroad to a wonderful sharing experience with children about self-image as well as their hopes and dreams for their own lives.

The Lord of the Rings by J. R. R. Tolkien

Unlike his friend, C. S. Lewis, **John Ronald Reuel Tolkien** disliked allegory and said he did not intend a specific Christian connection in his work when he began his story. But that hasn't stopped leagues of devotees to his books and to Peter Jackson's outstanding film series based on *The Lord of the Rings* from drawing Gospel parallels.

Tolkien never denied that his story of a great journey to destroy evil had "applicability" to Christian motives and themes, especially in the battle of good and evil; the need for courage, perseverance, mercy, and self-sacrifice in carrying out a vocation; and the selfless choices made by various characters. His background as a devout Roman Catholic colored his tales of Middle Earth: *The Hobbit, The Lord of the Rings,* and *The Simarillion.* (Tolkien's son, Christopher, completed *Simarillion* after the author's death.) Years into his writing, he told a priest friend that the fundamentally religious and Catholic nature of *The Lord of the Rings* emerged unconsciously in the story, but that he later developed the parallels consciously in his revisions.[38]

Tolkien's personal faith was strong. In fact, he encouraged C. S. Lewis on his way to becoming a Christian believer. In return, Lewis encouraged his Oxford colleague to write. The two helped to form a writers' group, called The Inklings, to discuss and critique literature, including their own stories.

Tolkien aimed to create— *"faerie"* in his fantasy, meaning a feeling he called *heart's desire,* in which we yearn for another world. Lewis called the feeling *joy,* not in the sense of mere happiness, but of overwhelming desire. Swept up in Tolkien's saga of Middle Earth, we feel *faerie* and *joy* as we yearn along with Frodo and company for freedom from evil and the redemption of the world. Here, we will examine the first part of the story—*The Hobbit*—and delve into the first volume of *The Lord of the Rings,* titled *The Fellowship of the Ring.*

The Hobbit

Background: Tolkien wrote *The Hobbit* to amuse his own four children—three sons and a daughter. His fun-loving family valued story, so in the evenings the author found himself delivering the latest installment at the foot of one of the youngsters' beds. It all began one day while Professor Tolkien was grading papers and, in a moment of boredom, scrawled, "In a hole in the ground there lived a hobbit." As he followed the yarn his imagination was spinning, Tolkien developed a story that not only his children, but also millions around the world, would come to know and love.

Synopsis: *The Hobbit* sets the stage for a grand epic to come. While *The Lord of the Rings* focuses mainly on Frodo Baggins, this volume concerns Frodo's older cousin, Bilbo Baggins, a hobbit—a small, human-like creature with furry feet—who stands but three and a half feet tall.

Before Bilbo's adventure began, Bagginses never did anything unexpected. The wizard Gandalf, on the other hand, brings adventures wherever he goes. He convinces Bilbo to set off with thirteen dwarves to reclaim a fortune stolen by a dragon. They travel through Rivendell, home of the elves, and into the Misty Mountains, where a terrible storm drives them into a dank cave—only to be captured by goblins! Escaping, Bilbo is trapped in a tunnel, where he finds a golden ring and meets a small, slimy creature named Gollum.

Gollum lives on a rock in an underground lake and plans to eat Bilbo. But Bilbo bargains for his life in a game of riddles with the creature. When Bilbo wins, Gollum plots to double-cross him and realizes that Bilbo has found his "precious"—a magic ring of power. Bilbo slips the ring on his own finger to safeguard it, and discovers that it makes him invisible! Unseen, he has the opportunity to destroy Gollum, but, moved with pity for the miserable creature, he leaves with his new treasure.

Challenges continue along the journey—wolves attack, eagles rescue, giant spiders ensnare, and wood-elves imprison the brave group. Using the ring's power to make him invisible, Bilbo organizes their escape. When at last they reach the dragon's lair, Bilbo slips in and takes some of the treasure. Furious, the dragon attacks a nearby town, where a bowman, Bard, kills him. Bard requests the treasure that was stolen from his own people, but the dwarf king Thorin, now in possession of it, wants it all.

To avert war, Bilbo snatches the most valuable gem—the Arkenstone—and delivers it to Bard to negotiate peace. War ensues nonetheless when goblins and wolves come after the treasure. Mortally wounded in battle, Thorin learns the value of friendship over earthly riches and says goodbye to Bilbo, adding, "If more of us valued food and cheer and song above hoarded gold, it would be a merrier world" (chap. 18).

Seeds of the Gospel: The most obvious lessons of *The Hobbit* concern the consequences of greed and materialism. Consider this passage from Scripture: "One is tempted by one's desire, being lured and enticed by it; then, when that desire has conceived, it gives birth to sin, and that sin, when it is fully grown, gives birth to death" (Jas 1:14–15).

In chapter five, Bilbo meets Gollum, an essential character, especially in *The Lord of the Rings*. It is his ring—his "precious"—that Bilbo finds. But what good is the ring of power to Gollum? He is a slimy and hideous creature, living on a clammy rock in the underground darkness. The power of the ring first tired him, then galled him, and now possesses him. His rage and despair over losing the ring make his eyes glow green! Gollum, creepy though he is, is sure to elicit good conversation. "That ring really made him horrible, didn't it?" you might ask. "What did it do to him? Why do you think that happened?"

⟫◈⟪

"Reading gives us someplace to go when we have to stay where we are."

— Mason Cooley, *City Aphorisms*

⟫◈⟪

When Bilbo finds the treasure in chapter twelve, he is so consumed with desire that he almost forgets a dragon is guarding it! Of course, "It does not do to leave a dragon out of your calculations" (chap. 12). After Bard kills the dragon, Thorin's desire for riches clouds his judgment; he refuses Bard's request for a portion of the wealth and prepares to defend it in battle. However, he ultimately recognizes his errors and remembers to treasure friendship over gold (chap. 18). A lesson in friendship is a lesson in Christianity, for at its root is love. In conversation with kids, talk about what Thorin learned, suggesting: "It was good that Thorin wanted to make up with Bilbo, wasn't it?"

Bilbo proves himself peace-loving and strong when he snatches the Arkenstone and delivers it to Bard as a bargaining chip (chap. 16). "I thought Bilbo was going to leave with that stone," you might point out, or: "Gosh, did you think he would give up the stone like that? Why would he do such a thing?" This scene offers an excellent opportunity to talk about ways to encourage peace, even when it involves great personal sacrifice.

When Bilbo returns to the Shire, he is forever changed. How is he different? Well, that's for you story-adventurers to talk about!

The Fellowship of the Ring

Background: Tolkien wrote *The Hobbit* as a children's story, but his publisher as well as The Inklings encouraged him to keep writing about hobbits. He had already begun constructing a history of Middle Earth, but he set that aside and resumed the story of the ring, which took him years to publish. The result is an intriguing tale best appreciated in the teen years or beyond. *The Lord of the Rings* is often called a trilogy, but Tolkien intended it to be one novel in six books, with appendices.[39] Usually published in three volumes, the first one is *The Fellowship of the Ring*. Its story begins fifty years after the adventures found in *The Hobbit*.

Synopsis: Bilbo has invited everyone to a birthday party he has organized for himself and his cousin, Frodo. The young hobbit shares Bilbo's birthday and is turning thirty-three—coming of age for a hobbit. Bilbo adopted Frodo and plans to officially name him his heir before departing from the Shire forever. He wants to leave Frodo the ring of power—now his "precious"—but finds the prospect daunting. At Gandalf's insistence, Bilbo finally gives it up and leaves.

Twenty years later, Gandalf returns to share what he has learned about the ring and throws it into the fire. Flaming letters appear on the gold band in the language of Mordor, a place so evil that Gandalf refuses to pronounce the words in their original tongue. Translated, the inscription reads: *One ring to bring them all and in the darkness bind them.* Gandalf knows about a set of rings: three were made for elven-kings, seven for dwarf lords, nine for mortals, and one master ring to rule them all—the ring Frodo now possesses.

Gandalf says that Sauron, the Dark Lord, who forged the ring, has returned and plans to take over the world, but to do so he needs the one ring. Frodo and all of Middle Earth are in danger. Valiantly, Frodo decides to protect the Shire by fleeing with the ring. He takes along his gardener, Sam Gamgee, his two cousins, Pippin Took and Merry Brandybuck—and the epic journey begins.

Pursued by Sauron's Black Riders, the hobbits enter the Old Forest and meet Tom Bombadil (a character omitted from the film version of *The Fellowship*). Master of the forest, Tom helps the hobbits get safely to the town of Bree. Tom is the embodiment of happiness and unadulterated goodness in a world succumbing to evil. When he tries on the ring, he doesn't vanish, and, in time, that makes sense.

In Bree, Frodo notices a strange-looking, weather-beaten man seated in the shadows. Strider, whose true name is Aragorn, joins their party. Soon, evil forces find them, and, in his terror, Frodo puts on the ring. While invisible to the others, Frodo is still seen by his attackers—ghostly men with merciless eyes who pierce him with a cursed dagger. The elf Glorfindel rushes Frodo to an elven dwelling called Rivendell to save his life. (In the film version, the gorgeous Arwen performs this task.)

Frodo is healed and finds Bilbo, whose greed for the ring resurfaces. Bilbo sadly realizes the burden he has placed upon his young cousin. Elrond, lord of Rivendell, calls a council of elves, dwarfs, Strider, Gandalf, Frodo, and another man named Boromir. The council reveals that Strider is a king whose royal ancestor failed to destroy the ring when he had the chance. Someone must now complete the task by casting the ring into the fires of Mt. Doom, where it was forged. Frodo volunteers for the quest, and Sam is assigned as his companion. Others offer to protect and guide them: Pippin, Merry,

Strider, Boromir, Gandalf, the elf Legolas, and the dwarf Gimli. The fellowship of the ring is off to save the world.

Other important characters to anticipate in this volume include Galadriel, the beautiful elf queen, and Saruman, a wizard gone bad.

Seeds of the Gospel: This story's nuances and complexities would be largely missed if introduced prematurely to children. Also, a younger child might be turned off to a wonderful vehicle for thinking about morality, suffering, sin, deceptive appearances, and a host of other topics by the long and steady pace of Tolkien's yarn. However, for kids thirteen and up, this is a great story to share.

———⊰⬥⬦⊱———

"If I have something that is too difficult for adults to swallow, then I will write it in a book for children."

— Madeleine L'Engle

———⊰⬥⬦⊱———

The Lord of the Rings is not an allegory, nor does it offer a definitive Christ-figure. Several characters exhibit Christ-like qualities, such as a pure heart. For example, Gandalf's reverence for the truth leads him to help Frodo because it is what needs to be done (book I, chap. 2). Frodo reveals self-sacrificing love when he chooses, despite his abhorrence for the task, to carry the ring to protect others from its temptation and harm (book II, chap. 2). Strider displays sensitivity to justice when he joins Gandalf and commits to the fellowship (book II, chap. 2). They "bear one another's burdens" (cf. Gal 6:2) in a quest for good. With your kids, try comparing the motives of Gollum, Saruman, and Boromir to those of Frodo, Gandalf, and Strider. Why does the ring corrupt some and not others?

In Book One, when Frodo says he wishes the ring hadn't resurfaced in his lifetime, Gandalf replies: "So do I...and so do all who live to see such times. But that is not for them to decide. All we have to decide is what to do with the time that is given us" (chap. 2). Talk about ways we choose to spend our time. Ask your kids to consider how they freely choose to use the gifts of time and talents they have been given.

"Why did it come to me? Why was I chosen?" laments poor Frodo (chap. 2). Indeed, a hobbit seems least likely to save the world—but then, "God chose what is foolish in the world to shame the wise; God chose what is weak in the world to shame the strong; God chose what is low and despised in the world, things that are not, to reduce to nothing things that are..." (1 Cor 1:27–29). Frodo does seem an odd choice for ring bearer, but what necessary traits does he possess? Consider why Gandalf, Strider, Elrond, or Galadriel were not chosen instead.

Strider's deceptive appearance is worth a chat (chaps. 9–10). Does he seem like a king, the rightful heir to his father's throne? Why or why not? If the timing seems right with your young reader, compare the "deceptive" appearance of our Lord, an infant born in a squalid manger who was the Son of God, a humble carpenter who was King and Savior of the world. Many in his day couldn't accept that a Nazarean was God's Son.

Many other themes arise from this story. Enjoying it on the surface alone is fun, but deeper meanings await those willing to till such rich soil.

9

Hope with Harry

What wisdom can there be to choose, what conti-
nence to forbear, without the knowledge of evil?
— John Milton from the *Areopagitica* (1644)

Having reviewed several nuggets of twentieth-century story and
demonstrated how such fictional works can create openings to dialogue with our children, it's time to talk about *Harry Potter,* the most
celebrated, controversial, beloved, hated, thrilling, feared, and,
breathlessly anticipated story of our day. J. K. Rowling's tale of a
young wizard's coming of age, told in a series of books, has enchanted millions of children and adults throughout the world, igniting
excitement and near-pandemonium at the release of each episode.

The books have set publishing records, and the movies have
attracted millions of viewers. According to Scholastic Corporation,
the U.S. publishers of the *Harry Potter* series, the number of *Harry
Potter* books in print in the United States total just under 100 million
copies. The hardcover edition of *Harry Potter and the Order of the*

Phoenix, the fifth book in the series, released at midnight on June 21, 2003, sold five million copies in the first twenty-four hours in the United States alone, making it the fastest-selling book in publishing history. The previous publishing records were held by Rowling's fourth book, *Harry Potter and the Goblet of Fire.*[40]

Before the release of the first film in the series, *Harry Potter and the Sorcerer's Stone,* advance tickets sales, mainly over the Internet, smashed all previous box office records—a phenomenon attributed to the fierce loyalty of Rowling's book audience. One ticket web site, Fandango.com, estimates that at any given time on the first movie's opening day, 2,000 people simultaneously tried to buy tickets online.[41] Even in Israel, according to *The Jerusalem Post,* ticket sales for the first movie's opening exceeded 50,000 advance purchases—an unprecedented number in that small country.[42] Advance ticket sales boosted box office takes for each debut weekend of the *Harry Potter* movies, mainly because of the loyal following among readers. During its first weekend in 2001, *Sorcerer's Stone* ticket sales totaled $90.2 million at the box office. The second film in the series, *Harry Potter and the Chamber of Secrets,* released in 2002, brought in slightly less than its predecessor during opening weekend: $88.3 million. The third installment, *Harry Potter and the Prisoner of Azkaban,* opened June 4, 2004, and topped both previous movies with a box office take of $93.6 million during its first weekend alone.[43] Clearly, *Harry Potter* is a cultural icon that will influence the global generation coming of age in the early twenty-first century. And that's not such a bad thing.

A Message of Hope

Despite the vehement debate in certain circles concerning the appropriateness of a story set in a wizarding world, the *Harry Potter* books can be an entryway to dialogue between our faith and the culture in which we live. The books bear seeds of the Gospel aplenty: love, self-sacrifice, discipline, friendship, and freedom are just some of the themes woven into the series. When approached from a Christian perspective, Rowling's story portrays a message of hope that affirms

Potter-ed Plants

Harry Potter's cultural influence extends into the scientific world—a rare new jungle plant species takes its name from a term in J. K. Rowling's popular books. The term is "apparate." Rowling uses it as a verb to describe a wizard's ability to disappear and reappear elsewhere. The newly discovered flower is called *Macrocarpaea apparata* because it seemed to "apparate" in front of the scientists who discovered it.

Plant taxonomist Lena Struwe is a *Harry Potter* fan. She and colleague Jason Grant, both experts in rainforest flora, were exploring the tropical, mountainous region of southern Ecuador when they noticed strange plants along the side of the road. They recognized them as genus *Macrocarpae,* from the gentian family found around the world, but this species was a kind never before seen. To confirm their discovery, they searched for a specimen with flowers. Rain-soaked in encroaching darkness, the scientists were about to give up when, suddenly, at the last minute, the tall nocturnal flowering tree with yellowish-white, bell-shaped blossoms "almost magically" appeared. Struwe and Grant agreed that it had *apparated,* like a wizard in a *Harry Potter* story, and quickly dubbed it the *"apparata."*

Struwe and Grant, combined, have named over thirty newly identified species of flora. The *apparata* is the first Potter-ed plant in the world.

— *This story has been adapted from a June 24, 2003 news release issued by Rutgers, the State University of New Jersey.*

the principles of our faith. In an increasingly scary and confusing world, Harry speaks to the mystery that kids experience in their own lives, such as the presence of evil and the fear it causes, the joy in good friendships, and the love we feel, which we can neither explain nor understand. Most of all, Harry's story encourages all of us to make good choices.

Although Rowling's story unfolds in a magical world, Harry and his friends are very much like the kids who love them—full of jumbled emotions, desires, needs, gifts, hormones, abilities, virtues, and vices that they are learning to discipline and manage. Harry is not perfect, but neither are kids today (and neither are we, I might add). He is delightfully flawed, a character learning to discern right from wrong, which makes him as lovable and believable as a real kid.

Harry's virtues are realistic, too. His courage prompts him to strive to make heroic choices that build character—and this valor appeals to our children's innermost yearnings. Kids want to believe that they can face the challenges of their future, that they can choose good when faced with the not-so-good. In her marvelous story, J. K. Rowling, the Scottish mother and teacher who heeded a powerful inspiration to write these books, in turn inspires hope that, in the words of another writer from Great Britain, the mystic Julian of Norwich, "All will be well, and all will be well, and all manner of thing will be well."

Over the past several years, I have written extensively about Harry Potter and the phenomenon surrounding his story. In the process, I have been privileged to converse about Harry with children and parents from many countries around the world. In my observations, those who love the story share one thing in common, no matter what their race, creed, or cultural heritage: their eyes light up when they talk about it. Never has a child brought up the subject of real witchcraft in speaking of Harry's story. Instead, children talk about the characters. They genuinely love Harry and his friends, and enjoy spending time with them, because they can relate to the Hogwarts gang so well. They are thrilled by the mysteries presented in each volume and look forward to getting to know the characters a little better each time. Their imaginations are stimulated, and they relish the experience. I sincerely believe that the phenomenon is as simple as that.

Love, Truth, and Freedom

The *Harry Potter* story includes basic Christian principles within a setting of magic. Whether Rowling's intention was explicitly

Christian makes little or no difference to a reader's ability to discern these themes—the seeds of the Gospel are there! In Rowling's wizarding world and in the world we share today, love and truth remain at the heart of what it means to be human.[44] As in C. S. Lewis's *Chronicles of Narnia,* love is the deeper magic that protects and frees Harry from the dark forces of Lord Voldemort—a magic that Voldemort will never understand.

Like the elusive snitch in Rowling's game of Quidditch, truth swirls in a maelstrom of activity and confusion at Hogwarts, just as in our world. The chaos of illusion and falsehood ends only when a focused seeker recognizes and grasps this truth. Harry is such a seeker—on the Quidditch field as well as in his battle against evil. He struggles to ignore warnings and predictions that suggest his fate is sealed by a destiny he cannot control, and he learns to base his choices upon truth and morality. These choices create intrigue and drama in the story because Harry's life and the lives of other characters hinge upon what Harry chooses to do or not to do under the pressure of being pursued by evil.

Through Harry Potter's story, Rowling intended to demonstrate how our choices can facilitate evil or good in the world. In an interview with Catholic News Service, Rowling said:

> Evil will be the result of very poor choices and possibly insufficient bravery to take the right path. And that's what I'm attempting to show with my villain [Lord Voldemort]. Here is someone who had choices—he had a great deal of natural talent, which he's abusing. He's totally self-serving, but he could have gone a different way. That's supposed to be contrasted quite strongly with Harry, who has come from an equally difficult start in life, but who consistently tries to make the right choices. Sometimes he fails. I want to show that [he's human]; I want him to sometimes make mistakes... But he is generally acting with the best of intentions.[45]

Through his choices, as he comes of age, Harry develops character and a strong conscience, and moves toward becoming the wizard he is called to be. This relationship between truth and choices is a seed of the Gospel that also echoes Pope John Paul II in *Evangelium Vitae (The Gospel of Life),* who said that our conscience is formed by "the recovery of the necessary link between freedom and truth."[46] Harry, like all of his classmates at Hogwarts, is called to become a great and noble wizard, but Rowling makes clear that Harry is not destined to any certain fate. Like all of us, Harry is free to make choices; he sometimes makes poor choices but in the things that really matter, Harry chooses the honorable and the virtuous path.

Character and Virtue

The word "character" comes from a Greek word that means mark or brand. Harry's "character," the lightning bolt scar on his forehead, is an outward sign that he possesses something that defeats evil.[47] We learn that Harry is protected by sacrificial love because his mother died to save him. In Harry's world, as in our own, love conquers even the most powerful force of evil. Love stays with Harry, right upon his head, and shapes his inner character by reminding him of his mother's sacrifice and helping him to recognize the presence of evil.

Two professors at the University of St. Thomas in St. Paul, Minnesota, Catherine Jack Deavel and David Paul Deavel, who are also a married couple, note that magic in Harry's wizarding world is a talent that can be used for good or evil purposes. This raises the moral stakes in the stories as the characters explore the complexities of free will through sound philosophical observation.[48] We see this in the way conflict arises between good and evil without assuming that witches and wizards are always good, and non-magical people are always bad. Both magical and non-magical people are free to choose the good or the bad. The difference lies in how the characters use their magic.

Another important consideration is that no matter how great their powers, the characters in Harry Potter's story do not defeat evil with their own magical skills, but through virtues such as courage and self-sacrifice. In the second volume, when Harry is about to die in the Chamber of Secrets, a phoenix comes to his rescue, not because of Harry's conjuring powers, but because he refuses to choose evil and remains loyal to Dumbledore. Harry and his friends are becoming better human beings at the same time that they are becoming more accomplished wizards. Again, it's a matter of making good choices or poor choices, a conversation well worth having with our children—and having many times!

※·◇·※

"Just as M. Night Shyamalan's movie, *The Sixth Sense*, was not really about ghosts, but instead about parenting, Harry Potter is not really about magic, but about character."

— Catherine Jack Deavel and David Paul Deavel

※·◇·※

Although supremely entertaining and filled with perched-on-the-edge-of-your-seat excitement, the adventures of *Harry Potter* offer more than a fantasy about a lovable boy wizard. In its portrayal of character and virtue, love and redemption, the story offers a model of living in community that is consistent with Christian teaching and that demonstrates how our choices impact our world. In the words of the Professors Deavel: "The kind of character Rowling portrays as good [is] strongly consonant with what Paul VI called a 'civilization of love' and what John Paul II has called a culture of life."[49]

The Occult, Authority, and Moral Relativism

Some critics of *Harry Potter* claim the story poses a serious threat to the spiritual lives of children—namely, that the books and movies introduce kids to the occult or promote moral relativism. A Vatican spokesperson offered another view in a statement made on February 3, 2003 at a press conference concerning the release of *Jesus Christ: The Bearer of the Water of Life*, an official Church document on New Age spirituality and the occult. According to Reverend Peter Fleetwood, "*Harry Potter* does not represent a problem"—a statement that made headlines around the globe.[50] A former member of the Pontifical Council for Culture, Fr. Fleetwood placed *Harry Potter* in the context of other childhood fantasy tales and added that "in each one's childhood there have been fairy godmothers, magicians, angels, and witches, which are not bad things, but a help for children to understand the conflict between good and evil."[51]

As a parent, I don't worry about moral relativism being a problem connected with *Harry Potter* because the strong moral code promoted and lauded within the wizarding world immediately nullifies such a claim. I was concerned at one point, however, that the books piqued interest in the occult. After prayer, reflection, and a little investigative reporting into witchcraft, I concluded that the magic Rowling employs in Harry's story is nothing more than a literary device that adds flavor and spice to a story that is really about moral development and making choices.

In fact, while writing an article for a religious publication about pre-teen reactions to *Harry Potter,* I happened to meet an editor of another publication who told me that she practices Wicca, the pagan religion associated with witchcraft. An answer to prayer, I thought! I asked her about *Harry Potter,* expecting her glee over *Harry's* having brought attention to something she holds dear. Instead, she was exasperated and told me that *Harry Potter's* brand of magic is more the sleight-of-hand variety, not what she called the "disciplined and involved religion" she practices. She said *Harry Potter* ultimately pokes fun at her pagan beliefs because of the humorous incantations and happenings in the story—not to mention the inclusion of Christmas celebrations at Hogwarts. Frankly, I breathed a sigh of relief. Parents have no need to worry about fascination with real occult practices when our kids enjoy *Harry Potter.*

For most parents, perhaps the most important and troublesome critique of *Harry Potter's* story concerns Harry's rebellion against authority. Harry sneaks off to places he shouldn't, lies occasionally, and disobeys rules and teachers' commands. The happy endings to various escapades often hinge upon disregard for school policies, for which Harry is ultimately forgiven.

This rebelliousness is one of the flaws J. K. Rowling has woven into the character of her protagonist. On one hand, it seems unsettling, especially from an adult/parental point of view, that this kid—the story's hero—gets away with bucking the system. On the other hand, that habit of bending rules sits at the very crux of Harry's greatest gift—discerning evil and possessing the courage to fight it. If rules prevent him from serving the greater good, he never lets them stand in his way. And Dumbledore recognizes and appreciates this quality.

However, children don't use the highest levels of moral reasoning in making decisions. They normally can't discern the ultimate good and rarely can they see value in certain rules parents impose. While the occasional critic points to Harry's disregard for rules as a dangerous problem for families, I have never experienced it, nor have any of my peers. So what can a parent do if a kid begins to think he can bend the rules a little, just like Harry? I'm not sure there are any definitive answers, but if rebelliousness becomes a problem because of *Harry Potter,* it makes sense to use the story to address the subject. Bring up a time when Harry bends the rules and ask your child what he or she thinks about it. This is a good opportunity to not only reinforce your parental expectations, but to find out what may be going on below the surface in his or her life, and to introduce the reality that there are always consequences when rules are broken.

In fact, Harry himself faces consequences for bending the rules at Hogwarts. He causes Gryffindor House to lose points for various missteps and his housemates are penalized along with him. The horrible headmistress in volume five, *Harry Potter and the Order of the Phoenix,* subjects him to dreadful punishments for breaking rules and talking back. Perhaps the most effective chastisement he receives comes from someone he respects, Remus Lupin,[52] his deceased father's dear friend. After Harry sneaks out to Hogsmeade village for some fun, Lupin covers for Harry but then reprimands him, reminding him that his risk-taking behavior is a poor way to repay his parents' sacrifice for him (*Prisoner of Azkaban,* chap. 14).

The Deavels make an excellent point concerning Harry's questionable behavior and supposed disdain for authority in saying that Dumbledore "commands Harry's respect and loyalty because he is virtuous. He is virtuous precisely because he acts according to a 'higher law' of moral standards."[53] Despite his adolescent antics, Harry knows, deep down, where virtue lies. At the same time, the Deavels also note that Harry routinely forms flawed theories about whom he can trust—Snape, for example, whom Dumbledore trusts completely—showing that young wizards (and young people!) are fallible and make mistakes. They need moral guidance and it's up to us parents to provide it.

One very important distinction made by the Deavels is that Rowling's work demonstrates confidence in the importance of freedom and truth:

> ...The *Harry Potter* books consistently present a world in which the moral worth of a choice depends upon the moral worth of what is chosen. Choice itself is not what Dumbledore promotes, but rather the choice of the *good*. Of course, what the good *is*, is the question. One central indication of a commitment to objective moral criteria is the emphasis on truth, a truth which unfailingly serves as a litmus test for characters' actions and judgments. The *Harry Potter* stories make clear that the first criterion for making the right choice in any situation is that it conform to Truth—with a capital "T." There is no postmodern subjectivizing but instead a confidence that the Truth is out there and that it is knowable.[54]

Because Harry's tale is a multivolume coming-of-age story that follows his character development from childhood into adulthood—passing inevitably through adolescence and its usual testing of limits—we can understand why making mistakes is part of his story. Making value-based decisions in extenuating circumstances helps form the moral fiber of Harry's character.

Another literary boy hero faced similar criticism—Tom Sawyer, the protagonist of a story written by Samuel Clemens (a.k.a. Mark Twain) between 1872–75. Tom plays hooky from school, convinces his friends to fulfill the obligations of a punishment for him, runs off with Huckleberry Finn and Joe Harper, and has the whole town dragging the river for their bodies. When they return gloriously to their own funerals, they become local heroes. Like Harry Potter, Tom Sawyer has problems with authority and rules, but proves to be brave and altogether lovable in the end.

Finding the Right Time

Rowling herself issues a word of caution on sharing *Harry Potter* with kids who are not ready for its themes. In a conversation with *Time* magazine in 2000, Rowling said: "I consciously wanted the first book to be fairly gentle—Harry is very protected when he enters the world. After the publication of *Sorcerer's Stone*, I've had parents saying to me, 'My six-year-old loves it,' and I've always had qualms about saying, 'Oh, that's great,' because I've always known what's coming. So I have never said these books are for very young children."[55]

And they really aren't. As with some of the popular tales explored in the previous chapter, story makes the deepest impression when the reader or listener is ready to receive and appreciate the themes presented. When I see precocious first graders carrying around *Harry Potter and the Goblet of Fire* (volume four in the series) or *Harry Potter and the Order of the Phoenix* (volume five), I think, "Too bad!" And not because I think Harry's story is spiritually subversive or morally bankrupt. On the contrary, I love the books and the movies! Rather, it disappoints me to think such young kids—bright, good readers that they are—will miss much of the humor, clever nuances, and themes because they're not developmentally ready for them. They'll also be introduced to scenes that are too scary for them—something like riding a roller coaster for the big kids before reaching the minimum height requirement!

For those who are ready to delve into *Harry Potter's* fantastic adventures, however, entering his world is a delight. Talk about a roller coaster! This story takes us high into excitement and hilarity, only to bring us down into profound sadness and desperate fear as we journey with Harry and his friends through their encounters with wild and mysterious creatures and characters in addition to pure evil.

Once I've started reading them, I cannot put the books down without grieving momentarily. They provide wonderful entertainment while making us think, feel, and reflect upon our lives: *Could we be as brave as Harry, placed in his situation? Do we, like Harry and his friends, make heroic, virtuous choices in our lives, or do we, like Slytherins and Death Eaters, make choices that give wrongdoing the upper hand? And what does that say about us?*

Why Parents Can Thank *Harry Potter*

Throughout this book, I have suggested that sharing story is a great way to listen to kids through their reactions, to learn what's on their minds and find common ground for communication, and to nourish their spiritual development. Given the popularity of the *Harry Potter* series—books and movies—sharing J. K. Rowling's story is an opportunity not to be missed. In the words of Pope John Paul II, the Spirit "speaks to us through the very events of history."[56] "*Harry Potter* mania" is an event of cultural history, and by listening to that voice, we parents can learn many things about our children—their hopes, dreams, fears, attitudes, and what they think about themselves as individuals and as a generation. If encouraged to explore the seeds of the Gospel scattered within the story, kids will also find spiritual nourishment to help them on their journey to communion with God.

So, let's begin probing J. K. Rowling's work for some of the seeds of the Gospel to be found there. The books are all long and complex, so the suggested topics are only offered as a starting point for discussions. With time and practice, you'll be able to come up with your own questions and make new connections within the story.

Harry Potter by J. K. Rowling

Joanne Kathleen Rowling holds a degree in French from Exeter University. She worked briefly as a bilingual secretary before venturing to Portugal for three years to teach English as a foreign language. Teaching afternoons and evenings, Rowling used her mornings to write a story, about a boy wizard, that had popped into her head years before.[57] When she returned to Scotland, the Scottish Arts Council recognized the story's potential and gave Rowling a grant to complete *Harry Potter and the Philosopher's Stone,* which was released in the United States as *Harry Potter and the Sorcerer's Stone.* By the time the book was published, Rowling was working as a French teacher in Edinburgh. *Harry Potter's* success has allowed Rowling to pursue writing fulltime.

Background: The story of Rowling's inspiration to write the series is as enchanting as the books themselves. Rowling said the idea came into her head, along with a huge rush of adrenaline, while stuck on a train between Manchester and London and staring at a field of cows.[58] Four hours later, when she got off the train at King's Cross station, many of her characters had been invented. Rowling says the trip was "the most interesting train journey I've ever taken."[59]

Harry Potter and the Sorcerer's Stone

Synopsis: The first volume of the seven-part story introduces Harry Potter, an orphaned infant with a mysterious lightning-bolt-shaped scar on his forehead. He is taken to live in the home of his Aunt Petunia and Uncle Vernon Dursley and their spoiled son, Dudley. For a bedroom, Harry is given the closet under the stairs. On his eleventh birthday, he receives an invitation to attend Hogwarts School of Witchcraft and Wizardry and learns that he is not only a wizard, but also the most famous boy in the wizarding world. Hagrid, the gigantic creature-keeper at Hogwarts, delivers the letter of acceptance into the school, and tells Harry that his scar came from the evil Lord Voldemort, who killed Harry's parents but couldn't kill him. Harry's survival made him famous. Harry accepts Hagrid's invitation and sets off with him to begin a new life.

Their first stop is Diagon Alley, a London street seen only by wizarding folk, where Harry discovers that he has a mountain of inherited gold stashed in Gringott's Bank. Harry gets his books, school uniform, broom, and a wand—one with a phoenix feather inside. Then he's off to King's Cross station to catch the Hogwarts

Express from Platform 9 3/4—another location hidden from the view of Muggles, or non-magical people.

At Hogwarts, a magical Sorting Hat divides the incoming class among four houses: Gryffindor, Ravenclaw, Hufflepuff, and Slytherin. Lord Voldemort once belonged to Slytherin, where Harry's nemesis, Draco Malfoy, is assigned. Harry and his new friends, Ron Weasley and Hermione Granger, are sorted into Gryffindor House, known for bravery and headed by Professor Minerva McGonagall, the transfiguration teacher.

Harry discovers he is naturally gifted at broomstick riding. So, when Malfoy torments classmate Neville Longbottom (an important part of Harry's story in later volumes), Harry soars into the air to defend him. Professor McGonagall notices Harry's flying prowess and immediately places him on the house Quidditch team. (Quidditch is a ball game played on broomsticks, with a fanatical following in the wizarding world.) Harry becomes a specialized player called the Seeker, and then someone mysteriously sends him the latest and greatest broomstick model, the Nimbus 2000.

Mystery continues when Harry, Ron, and Hermione find a three-headed dog guarding something...*but what?* Later, when Harry and Ron rescue Hermione from a gargantuan mountain troll, the three become inseparable friends. During Christmas break, Harry remains at Hogwarts rather than go back to the Dursleys. Harry has never received a Christmas present until, at Hogwarts, the Weasleys give him a hand-knitted sweater, and someone anony- mously bequeaths him his late father's invisibility cloak. Harry uses the cloak to explore the school in secret and comes upon the Mirror of Erised, a looking glass that reflects the deepest, most desperate desires of the heart. Harry looks into the glass and sees himself with a loving family.

The three friends try to help Hagrid out of a sticky situation, but end up breaking rules and getting caught. They serve detention in the Forbidden Forest looking for a unicorn! After Harry sees a strange creature drinking unicorn blood, a centaur tells him it is Voldemort. The friends deduce that the evil lord has come to

Hogwarts to take something being guarded by the three-headed dog—the Sorcerer's Stone, which grants its bearer everlasting life.

Harry, Ron, and Hermione race to retrieve the stone before Voldemort can get to it. Through a series of circumstances, Harry ends up alone, face to face with his enemy. Good conquers evil, and Harry learns that it was his mother's love that saved him from death as a baby and again in this second face-off with Voldemort.

Seeds of the Gospel: The most obvious Gospel message expressed in *Sorcerer's Stone* is that love conquers evil. At the end of the book, in chapter seventeen, Harry learns that his mother's love will protect him forever. Just as God's love is always available to us, love protects Harry unto his darkest hours. Moreover, Harry learns (also in this chapter) that Voldemort, the embodiment of evil, cannot understand love. He can't bear to touch Harry because of the love that surrounds him.

The parallel for Christians is clear—Jesus, out of love, offered himself to save us from death, and that love protects us. Talk about Harry's mother and address the theme of love in this story. "Isn't it amazing," you might begin, "how Harry's mother died to save him and how that protects him from Voldemort?" If your child recognizes the message of Christ in that, give a shout! If not, you might consider asking: "Do you know anyone who died to save us?" and use the moment to share the central tenet of our Christian faith. The message that love is the most powerful force in the universe is conveyed in the sacrifice of Harry's mother, a reflection of the infinite love expressed in the passion, death, and resurrection of Christ. In time, kids will learn that God *is* love and that Jesus is the ultimate expression of that love.

The Dursleys, in contrast, seem to have no real love in their hearts. They treat Harry as sub-human, keeping him under the staircase until they fear they may be punished for it (chaps. 2–3). Moreover, they indulge Dudley's every material whim, which parents know is often much easier than loving a child enough to set limits. As a result, they create a "monster" just as horrible as any Harry will encounter in the wizarding world (chap. 3). Begin a conversation about these dreadful characters, perhaps by saying: "The Dursleys treat Harry and Dudley so differently, don't they?" On another thread, you may ask: "The Dursleys don't seem to want Harry around. So why didn't they want him to leave to attend Hogwarts?" When my nine-year-old and I began reading this story, he said, "Mom, I have a question. Why are the Dursleys so mean to Harry? He is such a nice boy." Rather than answer, I asked, "Well, what does Harry have that they don't?" Peter thought for a moment and said, "Oh, magic! Do you think they're jealous of Harry?" And we ended our day with a delightful conversation about envy, gratitude, and humility.

Harry's invitation to the school is a wonderful metaphor for the universal call to holiness.[60] Although his mean-spirited relatives prevent him from receiving it on a number of occasions, the invitation at last is hand-delivered to Harry by Hagrid (chap. 4). Harry discovers that he is not a loser who lives under the stairs, but a wizard with magical gifts to be developed. He is called to a new life of mystery and wonder, just as we are called to new life in the mystical body of Christ. "Harry never dreamed something so good was waiting for him, did he?" you could begin. "I wonder what gifts you'll find you have!"

Harry's call remains an invitation, not an order, underscoring our freedom to choose—in religious terms, the gift of free will. Harry, like all of us, is free to make choices. He chooses a life that will radically change his perspective and his future.

The Philosopher's Stone

One topic parents may want to crack open for its food for thought is the *original* title of this book. U.S. publishers changed J. K. Rowling's title, *Harry Potter and the **Philosopher's** Stone,* used throughout the world, to *Harry Potter and the **Sorcerer's** Stone,* because they claimed "sorcerer" would attract more American readers than "philosopher." As a result, they jettisoned an important clue to deeper meanings in the book.

The "philosopher's stone" is a mythical substance that alchemists believed could turn ordinary metal into gold and produce an elixir that would grant eternal life. In fact, the English word "elixir" comes from the Arabic word for "philosopher's stone," *al iksir.* Many works of literature long before Rowling's book contain references to the "philosopher's stone," including Mary Shelley's *Frankenstein,* Charles Dickens' *The Cricket on the Hearth,* and Charlotte Brontë's *The Professor.* Hans Christian Andersen wrote a story called "The Philosopher's Stone," and Mozart composed part of an opera by the same title. In contrast, "sorcerer's stone" has no literary, mythical, or historical reference; it is merely a name created by American publishers.

In the Middle Ages, when alchemy emerged as a pseudo-science, Geoffrey Chaucer used references to the "philosopher's stone" to satirize the disreputable practice. Nearly three-hundred years later, seventeenth-century poet-playwright Ben Jonson followed suit. But his contemporaries, poets George Herbert and John Donne, recognized and exploited the Christological significance of the "philosopher's stone" as an analogy to spiritual growth and change, purification, and regeneration.[61]

In its transmutation of ordinary metal into gold, the stone represents the conversion of ordinary human beings into saints. The elixir of life produced by the "philosopher's stone" evokes the "living water" Jesus spoke of, and his promise of eternal life. In his poem, "The Elixir," written in 1633, Herbert went further still—"that famous stone," the "philosopher's stone" is Christ. If our lowly, mundane actions, our "drudgerie," are God's will, Herbert is saying, they are transformed by Christ into glorious, meritorious deeds.[62]

Just as Harry Potter works to keep the "philosopher's stone" from Voldemort, we, too, must work at the "drudgerie," in our daily lives. But our actions can be transformed into heroic virtue through grace. Harry wasn't trying to be a hero when he wished to have the "philosopher's stone," he simply wanted to keep it from Voldemort. That action, that wish, was transformed by Dumbledore's magic into genuine heroism, for only that person could obtain the stone, through Dumbledore's enchantment.

The Elixir

Teach me, my God and King,
In all things Thee to see,
And what I do in anything,
To do it as for Thee.

Not rudely, as a beast,
To run into action;
But still to make Thee prepossest,
And give it his perfection.

A man that looks on glass,
On it may stay his eye,
Or, if he pleaseth, through it pass,
And then the heav'n espy.

All may of Thee partake;
Nothing can be so mean
Which with his tincture (for Thy sake)
Will not grow bright and clean.

A servant with this clause
Makes drudgery divine:
Who sweeps a room as for Thy laws,
Makes that and th' action fine.

This is the famous stone
That turneth all to gold;
For that which God doth touch and own
Cannot for less be told.

Herbert, George. *The Works of George Herbert in Prose and Verse* (New York: John Wurtele Lovell, 1881), 288–289.

Harry Potter and the Chamber of Secrets

Synopsis: During summer break, the Dursleys lock up all things magical—including Harry's books, supplies, and his owl. An elf named Dobby, enslaved by a wizard family, appears and warns Harry not to go back to school. Harry refuses to make such a promise, so Dobby wreaks havoc upon the Dursleys, who then imprison Harry in his room. To the rescue come the Weasleys—Ron and his twin brothers, Fred and George—who take Harry away in a flying car to their wonderful, wacky home.

⋙·◆·⋘

"Some friends play at friendship, but a true friend sticks closer than one's nearest kin."
— Proverbs 18:24

⋙·◆·⋘

When they get to the train station, Harry and Ron can't enter Platform 9 3/4, so they take the flying car to Hogwarts and crash into the ancient Whomping Willow. Inside Hogwarts, Harry hears a voice that no one else hears. A mysterious message that says the Chamber of Secrets has been opened is scrawled across a wall. As proof, a petrified cat hangs ominously next to the message. Legend claims that in the Chamber lurks a monster that can be controlled only by the heir of Salazar Slytherin.

One day, Harry unconsciously speaks "parseltongue," the language of snakes. Because Sytherin was a "parselmouth," the whole school thinks Harry is his heir apparent. When a student is petrified, Harry, Ron, and Hermione suspect Malfoy is the heir, so they concoct a potion to transform themselves into Malfoy's cronies in order to talk to him about the mystery. They discover Malfoy is not the heir, but learn that a student died when the Chamber opened fifty years before.

Harry finds a diary from that period and writes in it. The book, which belonged to a former student, Tom Riddle, responds to Harry's words! Harry is swept back in time to a confrontation between Riddle and Hagrid, who is protecting a spider that Riddle claims killed the student. Harry believes Hagrid was expelled from Hogwarts for opening the Chamber and releasing that spider.

When Hermione is petrified, Harry and Ron, hidden in the invisibility cloak, visit Hagrid—just as he is being taken to wizard prison and Dumbledore is suspended from his job as Hogwarts headmaster. Hagrid sends the boys into the Forbidden Forest to find the spider he once protected. They discover that Hagrid never opened the Chamber of Secrets and that the monster lurking there is not the spider, but a giant serpent, a basilisk, which captures Ron's younger sister, Ginny.

Ron and Harry go to rescue Ginny, who is barely alive inside the Chamber. There Harry meets Tom Riddle and discovers that Riddle is the young Lord Voldemort, whom Harry must confront once more. When all seems lost, Dumbledore's phoenix arrives with help, and good triumphs over evil for a happy ending.

Seeds of the Gospel: Wonderful themes of dignity and freedom are ready to be unearthed in this second volume of Harry Potter's story. For starters, talk about Harry's unjust treatment by the Dursleys in the first two chapters. As we learned in the first book, Harry's magic is a gift he must develop through education and discipline in order to become the wizard he is meant to be. He didn't seek his magic; the magic came to him. Yet, the Dursleys despise him for it. Even if you've already discussed this point after the first book, talk about the way the Dursleys respond to magic, perhaps asking: "Why do you suppose the Dursleys are so cruel to Harry?"

Another important lesson comes from the dreadful Malfoys. They are snobs who look down on those with less money than they or those who have less than pure wizarding blood (chap. 4). They afford Dobby no dignity and punish him cruelly (chap. 10). They call people who are part-muggle "mudbloods" (chap. 7), a foul term in wizard lingo. The Malfoys live the antithesis of the Golden Rule, which Jesus teaches in Luke's Gospel: "Do to others as you would have them do to you" (cf. 6:31). Talk about this seed of the Gospel by discussing its absence among the Malfoys, asking: "Why do the Malfoys think they're better than everyone else? Is anyone really better than anyone else? How should we treat people who are different from us?"

Another justice issue that can be addressed in this story is false accusation. When he speaks in "parseltongue," Harry is accused of being the heir of Slytherin and of telling a snake to attack another student (chap. 11). Hagrid is unjustly accused of opening the Chamber of Secrets twice (chap. 13). Begin a conversation to plant the Gospel seed of social concern with this or a similar question: "It must be terrible to be accused of doing something you didn't do. How do you think that would feel?"

Throughout the book, Harry must make many choices. Dumbledore, wise headmaster of the school, tells him that his choices, not his abilities, prove who he truly is (chap. 18). "I wonder what Dumbledore means by that?" you could ask. "How do our choices reveal things about us? How do we go about making good choices?"

Mysterious Mandrakes

J. K. Rowling's inclusion of mandrakes in *Harry Potter and the Chamber of Secrets* has been criticized, both because mandrakes are associated with fertility and because the plants in the story seem almost human. While Rowling's mandrakes resemble babies, real mandrakes' roots do not. Here's a bit of background on the age-old *mandragora*.

Mandrakes have been celebrated since Biblical times. In Genesis, Jacob, the son of Isaac, who "steals" his brother's birthright (cf. Gen 27), falls in love with Rachel and asks to marry her. But her father tricks Jacob into marrying Leah, the older daughter. After a week, Jacob negotiates to marry Rachel, too. Leah desperately hopes Jacob will love her as she bears child after child. Meanwhile, Rachel remains barren.

One day, Leah's oldest son, Reuben, finds some mandrakes in the field and brings them to his mother (cf. Gen 30:14–24). Rachel begs Leah for them, and Leah replies, "Was it not enough for you to take away my husband, that you must now take my son's mandrakes, too?" Nevertheless, Leah agrees to hand over the mandrakes in exchange for a night with Jacob—and she conceives Jacob's fifth son. Leah goes on to bear two other children, while Rachel, despite the mandrakes, remains barren. When Rachel finally bears Joseph and Benjamin, no mandrakes are mentioned; God's life-giving power prevails over hocus-pocus and old wives' tales.

Symbols of Christ in *Harry Potter*

Throughout the story of *Harry Potter,* author J. K. Rowling has included significant Christian symbolism. Here are three of the most obvious.

Phoenix: A symbol of resurrection, the mythical bird burns and rises up from the ashes. Dumbledore keeps Fawkes the Phoenix in his office at Hogwarts. Harry witnesses Fawkes bursting into flames; the bird later saves Harry from the basilisk (a serpent, symbol of evil) in the Chamber of Secrets. The Order of the Phoenix (formed in the fifth *Harry Potter* book) is a group committed to fighting evil in the wizarding world.

Unicorn: In medieval times, the unicorn became a symbol of Christ, with the horn symbolizing the unity of God and Christ. It was also meant to symbolize the Trinity and to represent purity and strength.

Stag: Another symbol of Christ from the Middle Ages, a cross is often portrayed in the prongs of its antlers. When Harry is about to have his soul sucked out by a dementor, he produces a *patronus* in the form of a stag that scares them away—a stag that initially seems to be a unicorn and walks on water! His *patronus* is extremely relevant in *Harry Potter and the Order of the Phoenix*—not to mention the spell Harry uses to call it up: *Expecto Patronum,* or, "I wait and watch for a savior!"

In ancient and medieval times, mandrakes were used to make all sorts of potions, especially for sleep. In Shakespeare, Cleopatra quaffs a draught to sleep off her agonizing separation from Antony (*Antony and Cleopatra,* act I, scene V), and Iago refers to their narcotic power in *Othello* (act III, scene III). *Harry Potter's* mandrakes recall the later superstition that their roots would scream when yanked out of the ground, also mentioned in Shakespeare. In *Romeo and Juliet,* before Juliet drinks the friar's potion, she wonders whether she might wake up in the crypt and hear ghosts with "shrieks like mandrakes torn out of the earth that living mortals, hearing them, run mad" (act IV, scene III); in *Henry VI,* after he is banished from the kingdom for murdering Gloucester, Suffolk wishes that he could think up a curse to "kill, as doth the mandrake's groan" (act III, scene II). It is interesting to note that in the same scene of *Henry VI,* the king recognizes Suffolk's evil and calls him a basilisk— the same monster lurking in the Chamber of Secrets.

Harry Potter's mandrake scenes provide parents with another opportunity to talk to kids about story themes. Kids today generally know nothing about mandrakes' ancient association with fertility, and probably won't read anything into it, or to connect it to a possible innuendo that hormones are beginning to stir in Harry's class at Hogwarts. Yet, valuable lessons exist in these mandrake passages because the students must care for the plants carefully and with extreme caution—and only under strict adult supervision. Harry's amusing difficulties demonstrate the prudence required in circumstances fraught with potential danger. Harry isn't at all mischievous with his mandrakes, but acts conscientiously and obediently. He trusts his teacher's advice, follows it, and, amidst chaos and stress, acts sensibly. Use your imagination to consider ways this lesson can underscore important life lessons in your own household.

Harry Potter and the Prisoner of Azkaban

Synopsis: Harry's friends remember his thirteenth birthday with presents, but Uncle Vernon's sister, Marge, arrives and insults Harry and his deceased parents. Infuriated, Harry inflates Aunt Marge like a balloon and runs away into the night. Just before the magical Knight Bus rescues Harry, he notices a black dog staring at him. On the bus he learns that a dangerous wizard named Sirius Black has escaped from Azkaban prison, where many prisoners go insane.

Harry spends the rest of his summer vacation in Diagon Alley. Ron and Hermione arrive to do their annual school shopping, and Harry overhears the Weasleys talking about Sirius Black—and that he's looking for Harry! To protect students from Black, the Ministry of Magic assigns Azkaban guards aboard the Hogwarts Express. Called dementors, these soulless creatures suck out the souls of their prey with a kiss. Harry seems especially sensitive to their presence and faints when they are near.

At school, Professor Lupin replaces Gilderoy Lockhart in defense against the dark arts class (Lockhart had replaced Quirrell in the last book); Professor Trelawney teaches divination; and Hagrid teaches the care of magical creatures. This year is not a great one for Harry. Professor Trelawney divines that a black dog—representing death—lurks in his future; a hippogriff attacks Malfoy in Hagrid's class, and Malfoy demands the creature be executed; Harry is left behind during a field trip to Hogsmeade wizarding village; and he faints during a Quidditch match, losing his fallen broomstick to the Whomping Willow.

Fred and George Weasley cheer up Harry with the gift of the magical Marauder's Map, which he uses to sneak into Hogsmeade. Harry discovers that Sirius Black was not only his father's best friend, but also his own godfather, and that Black betrayed Harry's parents by revealing their hiding place to Voldemort.

Harry gets a new broomstick for Christmas and resumes Quidditch playing, helping Gryffindor win the Quidditch Cup against Slytherin. But Harry is soon in the doghouse when he's caught in Hogsmeade, and Professor Lupin takes away his Marauder's Map. Even more crises ensue: the hippogriff is executed; Trelawney predicts Voldemort is on the move; Sirius Black drags Ron under the Whomping Willow, and Harry must fight the infamous Black to save his friend.

In their encounter, Harry learns that Professor Lupin is a werewolf and that Scabbers—Ron's pet rat—is really a wizard named Peter Pettigrew. Even more shocking, Lupin says that Pettigrew, Black, and Harry's father, James Potter, were his best friends at Hogwarts and that they learned to transform themselves into animals to keep him company when he was in wolf form. Black reveals that he was not the Potters' betrayer, but that it was Pettigrew (now Scabbers).

Chaos erupts as the story concludes—Lupin turns into a werewolf, Pettigrew escapes, and the dementors arrive to suck out Harry's soul. Harry produces a *patronus* that scares the dementors away—and loyal, brave Hermione engineers a surprising happy ending for everyone.

Seeds of the Gospel: Betrayal is an important theme in this volume, as Sirius is unjustly thought to have betrayed the Potters' location to Voldemort (chaps. 4, 10, 11), while the real rat is Scabbers/Pettigrew (chap. 17), who worked for the evil lord. Betrayal is an important theme in all four Gospels, too. Judas Iscariot betrayed Jesus' location in the Garden of Gethsemane (Mt 26:47–50; Mk 14:43–46; Lk 22:47–48; Jn 18:1–3). On the surface, Judas betrayed Jesus for money, but it may be worth contemplating the deeper motivations that may have led Judas to hand over his redeemer and friend—and, in doing so, his dignity and hope.

By the same token, it is interesting to think about what might have prompted Pettigrew to betray the Potters (chap. 19). Talk about betrayal with kids: "Why would someone turn on a friend? Why did Pettigrew do that? Why do you think he helped Voldemort? What do you think Pettigrew got out of it?" By talking about the absence of virtue in acts like betrayal we help cultivate seeds of the Gospel that bloom into virtues such as loyalty, trustworthiness, and honor.

Friendship is an important theme in this volume as Harry's own friendships deepen and old friendships are revealed among Lupin, Black, and James Potter. Harry proves to be a devoted friend to Ron when he is dragged under the Whomping Willow (chap. 17), and Harry, Ron, and Hermione try to help Hagrid during his troubles with the hippogriff (chap. 6). Explore with kids what it means to be a good friend—even to those who are marginalized, like Lupin.

Lupin brings up another form of betrayal when he talks about his student days at Hogwarts in chapter eighteen. Dumbledore admitted Lupin into Hogwarts when no other school would have accepted a werewolf. A champion of outsiders, Dumbledore gave him a chance and trusted him to do whatever necessary to prevent any bloodshed. Lupin tells Harry that Black, Pettigrew, and Harry's father learned to transform themselves into animals to keep him company (chap. 18), but in so doing broke rules Dumbledore had established for everyone's safety. He tells Harry that he felt guilty for betraying Dumbledore's trust. Talk about this form of betrayal with questions such as: "Why does Lupin say he betrayed Dumbledore's trust? What did Dumbledore do for him? Why do you think Dumbledore accepted Lupin? When someone places trust in us, like Dumbledore did in Lupin, why do we need to honor that?"

Lupin's friends betrayed Dumbledore's trust for a noble purpose. In contrast, Pettigrew betrayed the trust of Sirius and the Potters for self-serving, evil reasons (chap. 19). The sad truth is that not everyone we encounter is trustworthy. Rowling introduces this concept in chapter one with Ron's birthday present to Harry: a "Pocket Sneakoscope," which lights up and spins when someone untrustworthy is around. Scripture accounts for this reality of unsavory characters by telling us to choose our friends wisely:

> When you gain friends, gain them through testing,
> and do not trust them hastily.
> For, there are friends who are such when it suits them,
> but they will not stand by you in time of trouble.
> And there are friends who change into enemies,
> and tell of the quarrel to your disgrace.
> And there are friends who sit at your table,
> but they will not stand by you in time of trouble.
> When you are prosperous, they become your second
> self,

and lord it over your servants;

but if you are brought low, they turn against you,

and hide themselves from you.

Keep away from your enemies,

and be on guard with your friends.

Faithful friends are a sturdy shelter:

whoever finds one has found a treasure.

Faithful friends are beyond price;

no amount can balance their worth.

Faithful friends are life-saving medicine;

and those who fear the LORD will find them.

Those who fear the LORD direct their friendship aright,

for as they are, so are their neighbors also (Sir 6:7–17).

These words of wisdom are sobering because they suggest that it's hard to know whom to trust. Talk about ways we can know if our friends are true, and how to know with whom to share our time and our lives. You might ask: "How do you think Ron felt when he found out about Scabbers? (chap. 18) What about Sirius Black—how do you think he felt when he realized that Peter Pettigrew betrayed the Potters? I wonder how I would feel if I had a friend like Pettigrew who betrayed me?" If the time seems right, you might even venture to wonder how Jesus felt when Judas betrayed him: "Do you remember that story about the night Jesus was betrayed?"

The Weasleys are a wonderful family with lots of children. When they win some much-needed prize money, they use it to visit Ron's brother in Egypt (chap. 1). They choose to spend their windfall by enjoying a family vacation together, which tells us a lot about their family values. "What do the Weasleys value?" you might ask. "They could have bought stuff with that money. Why did they go to Egypt? What would you do if you got a lot of money? Why?"

Compare and contrast the families we've met throughout the *Harry Potter* series—the Weasleys, Malfoys, Dursleys, Grangers—to explore their values with your kids. Ask: "Which family do you like best? Which one do you like least?" And never forget the all-important: "Why?"

Harry Potter and the Goblet of Fire

Synopsis: Peter Pettigrew, the wizard who betrayed Harry's parents to Voldemort and took the form of a rat (Ron's pet, Scabbers) is reintroduced in this volume as Wormtail. Now personal servant to Lord Voldemort, he lives with the villain at the Riddle homestead, scheming a way to defeat Harry Potter. When Voldemort kills his house caretaker, Harry feels the evil searing through his lightning-bolt scar. Later, when the Weasleys take Harry and Hermione to the Quidditch World Cup, Voldemort's Death Eaters emerge and torture muggles.

At Hogwarts, another new defense against the dark arts teacher has arrived—Mad-Eye Moody, who replaces Lupin and takes a special interest in Harry. The school year begins with preparations for the Triwizard Tournament, a competition involving representatives of three wizard schools—Hogwarts, Beauxbatons (France), and Durmstrang (Germany). Hopefuls are asked to place their names in the Goblet of Fire, which will select one competitor from each school. The goblet selects Bulgarian Quidditch star Viktor Krum of Durmstrang, beautiful Fleur Delacour of Beauxbatons, and Cedric Diggory, a Hufflepuff from Hogwarts. Mysteriously, the goblet sparks a fourth time and produces another name: Harry Potter. Although underage, Harry is required by wizard rules to compete. He insists that he did not submit his own name, but only Hermione and Dumbledore believe him; Harry and Ron have a falling out.

In the first tournament event, competitors retrieve a golden egg guarded by a dragon, and Harry ties Viktor for first place. Harry and Ron make up before getting some dreadful news: they must go to the Yule Ball, and Harry, as a champion, must *dance!* Harry first asks Ravenclaw's Cho Chang to go with him, but she is going with Cedric Diggory. So Harry and Ron invite the Patil twins, and Viktor takes Hermione, who looks spectacular at the ball. During the event, the boys learn that Hagrid is part giant—a race known for cruelty and generally shunned in the wizarding world. An annoying news reporter disguised as a bee, Rita Skeeter, gets the scoop and publishes a scandalous story about Hagrid.

The next triwizard event involves rescues. Cho, Hermione, Ron, and Fleur's sister are magically held captive at the bottom of a lake. Cedric rescues Cho, Viktor gets Hermione, and Harry gets Ron. But Fleur is late in reaching her sister, so Harry steadfastly waits underwater, unwilling to leave the girl to die, and finally rescues both. Harry exceeds the challenge time limit, but stays in first place because of his courage.

⟹◈⟸

"Do not weep, for I shall be more useful to you after my death, and I shall help you then more effectively than during my life."

— St. Dominic, to his brothers

⟹◈⟸

Meanwhile, Sirius Black, disguised as a dog, hides nearby. He gives Harry, Ron, and Hermione some details about the ministry of magic. Later, Harry has a disturbing dream that causes his scar to burn, and Sirius insists he tell Dumbledore. In the headmaster's office, Harry looks into the *pensieve*, Dumbledore's thought-catcher, and learns more about the Death Eaters, notably that Snape is a spy.

In the last triwizard event, they must master a maze to capture the winner's cup. Harry and Cedric work together and take the cup, which zaps them into a trap where Voldemort awaits. Wormtail kills Cedric and performs an ancient ritual to restore Voldemort to human form, using the bones of Voldemort's father and a vial of Harry's blood. Voldemort returns to bodily form, calls a meeting of the Death Eaters, and challenges Harry to a wizard's duel.

Harry seems doomed, but both wizards carry a wand with a feather from the same phoenix—Fawkes. Their magic combines to create a powerful force that restores Harry's hope. Harry hears the song of the phoenix, followed by the echoes of Voldemort's victims. Their ghosts emerge from Voldemort's wand to encourage Harry to stay the course and fight the evil lord. They protect Harry and help him return to Hogwarts, carrying Cedric's body. The Ministry of Magic refuses to believe Voldemort is back, but Dumbledore begins to forge an alliance of witches and wizards—and outcasts such as werewolves and giants—to fight the Death Eaters.

Seeds of the Gospel: A dark tone colors this volume as Rowling explores the depths of sin and evil. One of the darkest images is Voldemort in his reduced form—a helpless, thoroughly inhuman organism that cannot live on its own (chap. 32). When Wormtail removes this diminished Voldemort from his wrappings, he could have chosen to walk away and let him die. But instead, Wormtail chooses to cooperate with evil and performs the ritual that allows Voldemort to regain his strength and power (chap. 32).

Wormtail must work hard throughout this volume to accomplish his task, choosing to cooperate with evil at each step. His journey proves an arresting metaphor for sin—at each point along *our* way, *we* can choose to say no to evil; the more we choose sin, the greater its hold on us and the more devastating its results. By the same token, we can choose whether to cooperate with grace. Explore Wormtail's motivation for helping Voldemort: "Why would Wormtail go to so much trouble to help Voldemort? What does he want from it?" And explore the alternative: "If Wormtail had turned his back on Voldemort and asked for Harry's forgiveness, what would have happened?"

A more positive Gospel parallel is Dumbledore's call for alliances to fight Voldemort (chap. 36). The characters he wants to call together are not pureblooded wizards, but fringe members of their society—giants, werewolves, part-muggles. For Dumbledore, all that matters is that they are united against evil. In his ministry, Jesus reached out to people considered less respectable in his society—tax collectors, prostitutes, Samaritans, lepers, the poor. For Jesus, what matters is that believers turn from evil to build God's Kingdom on

Fawkes the Phoenix

Rowling's name for Dumbledore's phoenix is Fawkes—an intriguing choice worth thinking about. Guy Fawkes was an English Roman Catholic who participated in "the Gunpowder Conspiracy" (1605) to blow up Parliament and King James I. Catholics and Puritans had hoped for tolerance after Queen Elizabeth I's persecutions, but James, who succeeded her in 1603, re-instituted harsh penalties for recusancy (refusal to join the Church of England). Catholics went underground and practiced their faith in secret. Guy Fawkes was executed for treason, and the violent plot led to harsher penalties for Catholics.

Each November 5, Guy Fawkes Day, effigies of Fawkes burn in bonfires across England to recall the treason. While Fawkes, then, is a humorous name for a bird that bursts into flames, Fawkes the Phoenix is not a villain in Rowling's story. Rather, he is a lovable character whose feather rests in Harry's wand. He arrives in the Chamber of Secrets because of Harry's loyalty to Dumbledore, blinds the basilisk, and heals Harry with his tears. Since Dumbledore embraces the outcast and marginalized, perhaps Rowling is sounding a call to unity in naming this phoenix, a symbol of Christ, "Fawkes."

Earth. "What sort of people is Dumbledore calling to help him?" you might ask. "What would Fudge or Malfoy say about these people? Is that the way we are called to think about people? Why?"

In chapter four, the Weasleys come to the Dursleys' home to take Harry to the Quidditch World Cup. The contrast between the two families is conspicuously funny. The Weasleys arrive through the fireplace, which is boarded up with a fake fire in front of it. They blast themselves out into the living room and Aunt Petunia faints. Mr. Weasley, in his delightful childlike manner, exults over muggle items such as the TV and VCR, and tries valiantly to start a conversation. When Harry says good-bye, Uncle Vernon says nothing in return. Mr. Weasley pauses and makes a point of reminding Vernon that Harry is his nephew and that he is leaving for a long time; surely he wants to say something. Vernon grudgingly responds, proving arrogant and stingy. Compare the behaviors of these two adults. Enjoy a conversation about the delightful Weasleys, beginning with the father. "Mr. Weasley is nice to everyone, isn't he?" you could say. "He even points out faults nicely! Why do you think he reminded Uncle Vernon that Harry was leaving?"

A deeply moving scene occurs when Harry and Cedric Diggory are transported to an encounter with Voldemort, and Voldemort orders Wormtail to "kill the spare," meaning Cedric (chap. 32). We are saddened by the tragic death of such an honorable young man—dedicated to fair play, affable, hardworking, and good looking to boot. His death is senseless; he simply happens to be in the wrong place at the wrong time. Perhaps that's what makes his death so poignant. Every day in the real world innocent lives are caught in the crossfire of someone's cooperation with evil; people are forced to suffer for the choices of others. Dumbledore tells the students to remember Cedric Diggory whenever they must make choices between doing what is right and what is easy (chap. 39). "What does Dumbledore mean by choosing between the right thing and the easy thing?" you might say to launch a conversation about the topics brought up by Cedric's death. "Why do you think Dumbledore asked the students to remember Cedric when they had to make choices? What happens in the long run when people don't do the right thing every time?"

One facet of this book disturbed my oldest son and me terribly, and anything upsetting is a "must" for conversation. When Harry realizes that he was duped by Barty Crouch posing as Professor Mad-Eye Moody (chap. 35), we were crushed for Harry and for every child who loves him. Of course, the sad reality that our children can't trust everyone sometimes makes life in our world difficult. But how do we know whom we can trust? You can use this opportunity to talk about how appearances can be deceiving, how people with evil intentions sometimes want to harm us, and what to do when we've been tricked. A good opener might be something about Crouch: "Weren't you surprised when they found out Barty Crouch was posing as Mad-Eye Moody? How do you think Harry felt about that? What about Ron and Hermione?"

This fourth book is rich with topics of conversation—bravery, friendship, decision-making, good versus evil, sportsmanship, respect for people of other cultures and races, relationships, outward appearances versus inner strengths and resources. Try asking your kids if any of the characters remind them of themselves—and see what they reveal!

Harry Potter and the Order of the Phoenix

Synopsis: Harry is back at the Dursleys for the summer, nervously anticipating news of destruction brought on by Voldemort following his restoration to power at the end of *Harry Potter and the Goblet of Fire.* Harry remains traumatized by the awful experience that led to Cedric Diggory's death. When Dudley teases Harry about crying out during recurring nightmares of the event, Harry, enraged, points his wand at Dudley's heart. In the next instant, dementors appear and attack the two boys. Harry courageously saves his bullish cousin's soul by calling upon his *patronus,* a grand silver stag that charges and defeats the soulless creatures. (Dementors, we learned in *Harry Potter and the Prisoner of Azkaban,* are the guards at Azkaban prison that can suck out a person's soul with a deadly kiss.) Aunt Petunia shocks Harry and her family with knowledge of the wizarding world. For the first time, Harry sees Petunia as his mother's sister and wonders how much she knows about magic.

Harry faces possible expulsion from Hogwarts for using magic illegally, even though it was to save himself and Dudley from dementors. A group of wizards, including Lupin and Mad-Eye Moody, escort him to London to await his hearing at the Ministry of Magic. Harry stays at the secret headquarters of the Order of the Phoenix, a group dedicated to fighting Voldemort and his evil Death Eaters. Dumbledore is Secret-Keeper of the Order. Headquarters is located in the childhood home of Harry's godfather, Sirius Black, who remains a fugitive since his escape from Azkaban prison. Harry is horrified to learn that Sirius is a pureblooded wizard related to the Malfoys, but also, mercifully, to Mrs. Weasley.

Arthur Weasley escorts Harry to his Ministry hearing—rescheduled and relocated at the last minute so that Harry almost misses it! Dumbledore, his defense witness, arrives in the knick of time with a witness to Harry's dementor attack, Mrs. Figg, a squib (non-magical member of a wizard family) who lives near the Dursleys. Harry is cleared of all charges and returns to school.

These are troubled times for Harry: he is hurt to learn that Ron and Hermione are the new Gryffindor House prefects; the wizard newspaper insinuates that he lies about his adventures; and many suspect he killed Cedric Diggory. And he is having extreme difficulty controlling his temper!

The new defense against the dark arts teacher, Delores Jane Umbridge, Senior Undersecretary to the Minister of Magic, is both a horrible teacher and a wicked witch. She votes against Harry at his Ministry hearing; then, at school, she kicks him off the Quidditch team and uses torture to punish him. In the classroom, she assigns readings on defense theory and denies students a chance to practice defense techniques. Meanwhile, the Ministry of Magic fears Dumbledore is raising an army to take over the wizarding world, so the headmaster is removed from many influential advisory roles. Fudge names Umbridge "Hogwarts High Inquisitor," a position of unprecedented authority in the school.

Hermione and Ron convince Harry to teach them defense against the dark arts, based on his experiences over the past four years. To Harry's surprise, twenty-five students show up for the first lesson! Dobby the House Elf shows Harry a meeting place—the Room of Requirement, which magically appears when needed and provides everything imaginable for its users. The group calls itself "Dumbledore's Army," making light of Ministry fears. Harry discovers that he loves to teach.

Neville Longbottom's wizarding skills improve dramatically during Harry's lessons. Raised by his formidable grandmother,

Neville shares many similarities with Harry, including the same birthday and a parentless childhood. However, unknown to the other students, Neville's parents, once highly skilled aurors, were utterly incapacitated by Voldemort's Death Eaters and remain in St. Mungo's Hospital. Neville's grandmother believes Neville is a far less gifted wizard than his parents, but the boy has always used his father's old wand. The old wand breaks near the end of this book, foreshadowing change for Neville and his wizarding abilities in future volumes.

Harry makes a new friend, Luna Lovegood, a free-spirited and brilliant Ravenclaw, who understands Harry and lightens his heart. Meanwhile, Cho Chang, Ravenclaw's seeker and the former girlfriend of Cedric Diggory, offers Harry his first kiss. The complex situation ties Harry in emotional knots.

<hr />

"I want to spend my heaven doing good upon earth."

— St. Thérèse of Lisieux

<hr />

Harry experiences dream-like visions in which he witnesses actual events, such as a snake attack on Arthur Weasley that Harry sees from the snake's point of view. While Arthur convalesces in the hospital, Harry and the Weasleys spend Christmas with Sirius, who delights in preparing the celebration. On Christmas Day, Harry, Ron, Ginny, and Hermione discover Neville visiting his parents. When the group sees Neville's broken mother, they are moved to pity for their friend.

Harry's dreams reveal that he shares experiences with Voldemort. A connection, forged when Voldemort gave Harry his scar, grew stronger when the Dark Lord drank Harry's blood. Unfortunately, Voldemort comes to realize this connection and manipulates Harry through the dreams.

Dumbledore assigns Professor Snape to teach Harry how to defend his mind against outside intrusion, as he experiences with Voldemort. Ultimately, Snape refuses to continue lessons because

Harry's dad, James Potter, tormented him in school. Snape's own scar runs too deep to forgive Harry the sins of his father. Meanwhile, Hagrid returns to Hogwarts, having failed in an attempt to ally wizards and giants. His face and body show signs of a fearsome struggle, which turns out to be from his effort to bring his little brother—a giant—back home with him. Hagrid's unconditional love and perseverance are unexpectedly rewarded in the story.

The plot thickens when ten Death Eaters escape Azkaban and Umbridge learns about Dumbledore's Army. She brings Harry before Fudge, but Dumbledore accepts the blame. Before Fudge can send him to Azkaban, Dumbledore flees with his phoenix, and Umbridge becomes Hogwarts headmistress.

Voldemort manipulates Harry in a dream to go to the Department of Mysteries to retrieve a prophecy concerning them both. Accompanied by Ron, Hermione, Ginny, Neville, and Luna, Harry faces Death Eaters led by Lucius Malfoy. The Order of the Phoenix arrives to save the day, but Sirius dies in battle and Voldemort escapes...until the next volume of Harry's continuing story.

Seeds of the Gospel: While much of this volume reveals human flaws and foibles—such as Harry's temper and his bitterness over all that Voldemort took away from him—it also draws theological parallels that are hard to miss.

This year, the Sorting Hat does more than sort students into houses at the beginning of the academic term. It sings about the four Hogwarts founders—how they wished that all the school's students could work together as one body—and about the divisive forces that are trying to tear Hogwarts apart, and that will fail only if students unite in a common purpose for good (chap. 11).

The passage offers a great opportunity to talk about the Church: we are all different—with different gifts, different styles of worship, different roles—and yet we all believe in the same God who loves us. For older kids or adults, the big question that is obvious at Hogwarts applies to the Church: "If our goals are the same, why do we fight one another? What would it take to become united? What do you think God would say about it?" The same questions apply to our society and our world.

In chapter twelve, Hermione recounts Dumbledore's belief that bonds of friendship and trust have as much power as Voldemort's bonds of discord and enmity and that these bonds allow the young wizards to defeat the evil that threatens Hogwarts. Talk about the ways friendship and trust make us strong: "How do good relationships help us to resist evil? How do your friends help you?" Also, talk about Dumbledore's call to world unity: "differences of habit and language are nothing at all if our aims are identical and our hearts are open." "What is Dumbledore talking about for the wizarding world?" you might begin. "How do you think we could bond with other cultures in our world?"

Neville's grandmother constantly compares him to his father, who lies incapacitated in the hospital with irreparable brain damage because of Voldemort. She claims Neville is less talented than his parents (chap. 23)—and yet she has saddled the lad with his father's old wand, a wand that apparently fails to suit him, given the results of much of his magic (chap. 35). Talk about each person's need to be what he or she is created to be, perhaps asking: "Why do you think Neville had so much trouble with that wand? What do you think will happen when he gets one that's perfect for him? Why is it important to learn about ourselves? How do you know what God wants you to be?" Discuss God's creative wisdom in making us all different and able to serve one another in different ways. Also, talk about the differences among people and their gifts and how what we are good at doing often leads us to discover what we are called to do with our lives.

Peeves the Poltergeist teases Harry about seeing visions and speaking in tongues (chap. 12). Our Christian saints often reported similar events. Discuss these gifts and their relevance in today's Church with this or a similar opener: "Why do you think God might allow some people to experience mystical events? What good does it do?"

The final chapters of *Order of the Phoenix* review and underscore every Christian theme that Rowling has presented in her story thus far. In speaking to Harry after the ordeal in the Department of Mysteries, Dumbledore points out that Harry has a great gift of discernment—he can detect Voldemort's presence (chap. 37). But Harry's gift is compromised by emotion (chap. 24). Talk about the need to learn self-control and how that helps us make good choices, perhaps beginning: "It's hard to know what to do when we're upset or excited or scared, isn't it? What can we do to calm down so that we can think clearly?" Also, ask kids how they know when something is not right and how that feels. Talk about ways to deal with fears as well as ways to trust and act on instincts that something harmful is near.

Dumbledore tells Harry that suffering is part of being human, and Harry responds that he doesn't want to be human if being human means experiencing suffering (chap. 37). Jesus, too, in the Garden of Gethsemane, faced the dreaded realization that suffering would be required in ridding the world of evil. If someone your child knows has suffered, talk about how it affected that person and those who love him or her. Ask how suffering might help to make a person stronger or to feel closer to God. Also, talk about Harry's suffering: "Why does Dumbledore say that suffering is part of being human? Do you think that's true? Why?"

Death is the prevailing theme of book five, but Rowling presents it in a way consistent with Christian teachings. Those who have died remain near us, "just beyond the veil," like Sirius. In the wizarding world, deceased persons live on in pictures, but are still capable of contributing to the events in the world. Talk about the Communion of Saints and what that means—the unity in Christ of all the redeemed, those on Earth and those who have died: "How do the people who have gone before us help us now on Earth? How can we tap into this reality?"

The fifth book in the *Harry Potter* series is dark and troubling. It causes us to worry about Harry's future and the destinies of his friends. But it is also full of seeds of the Gospel that can be cultivated in conversations with our kids. Since kids who read this book are generally older and more knowledgeable about their faith, and since, by now, you have gotten the hang of scratching beneath the surface of stories, relish this chance to talk about Harry and his adventures...and about your own child's adventures in our colorful world.

10

We're Off to See the Wizard

The universe is made of stories, not of atoms.
— Muriel Rukeyser
from her 1958 poem "The Speed of Darkness"

After delving into a number of popular works of children's fiction together, we can see that a number of stories share similar themes: friendship, human dignity, courage, compassion, and forgiveness, although the message may differ from story to story. Even if each story involved exactly the same themes, the settings, characters, and plots would impact the audience in a variety of ways, leading to varied and rich conversations about them.

Over the door of the library in Thebes, in ancient Greece, a wise lover of story inscribed these words: "Healing place of the soul." As parents, we are both healed and refreshed by approaching story in the company of our children. By reading and sharing many stories together, we discover pieces of wisdom to add to that great mosaic we assemble throughout our lives and which color our spirituality. From story we gain insight, solve problems, and learn about life beyond our own part of the world. In story we have a chance to pull together the fragments of our fast-paced whirl-of-life and become whole again.

⟫◆⟪

"Books, books, books!"
— Elizabeth Barrett Browning, *Aurora Leigh*

⟫◆⟪

What follows is a list of books that families can enjoy together. The titles are broken down into three groupings: preschool to second grade; third to fifth grades; and sixth to ninth grades. The list is by no means exhaustive; it's just a resource to get you started. The age groupings are not set in stone either. Since you know your child best of all, you will know if a picture book is still appropriate in fourth grade or if a complex story will work for your child at an earlier age than indicated on this list. Every now and again a kid's reading appetite may not fit within the "normal" boundaries; for example, a young friend of mine, now a bright high school student, tackled Michael Crichton's work with ease in seventh grade, and I read Margaret Mitchell's *Gone with the Wind* in fourth grade, just after I finished *A Wrinkle in Time.* So, use your best judgment in selecting story to read together and talk about, but encourage young readers to read age-appropriate materials whenever possible.

Since I often read books that were "too old" for me as a child, I can see in hindsight that I missed nuances in stories the first time around. As a result, I encourage you to consider suggestions for kids *younger* than your child when you choose stories to share, for stories with layers of meaning only become more meaningful as readers mature. As an adult, you will likely glean the most from your adventures into story to use in your own prayer life toward spiritual growth. Your insights will give you direction in helping your child to open the gates of imagination into a garden of wonder, where together you can unearth seeds of the Gospel through reflection and conversation.

Just as Jesus invited us to use our imaginations to enter into his stories and there discover truth and beauty, the Spirit calls us to enter into the stories that emerge from God's people and there, in the creative expressions of popular culture, discover meaning and nourishment for our journey. We have nothing to fear from exploring the art form called "children's literature," for we are marked with the sign of faith and share in the collaborative work of God's ongoing creation. Relax and enjoy the movement of the Spirit among and within us through the work of literary artists and the disarming observations of a child.

Stories for Young Ones

Preschool Through Second Grade

Adoption

> *Horton Hatches an Egg* by Dr. Seuss
> *The Water-Babies* by Charles Kingsley

Collections of Stories

> *The Book of Virtues* by William J. Bennett
> *Ladder of Angels* by Madeleine L'Engle (Note: Bible stories for children)
> *The Parables of Jesus* by Tomie dePaola
> *Rootabaga Stories* by Carl Sandburg
> *Stories for Children* by Isaac Bashevis Singer

Courage

> *Bears on Hemlock Mountain* by Alice Dalgliesh
> *The Biggest Bear* by Lynd Ward
> *Bringer of the Mystery Dog* by Ann Nolan Clark
> *Chitty Chitty Bang Bang* by Ian Fleming
> *Come a Tide* by George Ella Lyon

Courage by Bernard Waber

The Dragons of Blueland by Ruth Stiles Gannett

Jumanji by Chris Van Allsburg

My Father's Dragon by Ruth Stiles Gannett

Owl Moon by Jane Yolen

Pamela Camel by Bill Peet

Ramona the Brave by Beverly Cleary

St. George and the Dragon by Margaret Hodges

Swamp Angel by Anne Isaacs

Swimmy by Leo Lionni

Teddy in the Undersea Kingdom by Jan Mogensen

CThe Three Pigs by David Wiesner

The Year of the Perfect Christmas Tree by Barbara Cooney

Cultures, Tradition, and Tolerance

Abuela by Arthur Dorros

Abuela's Weave by Omar S. Casteneda

The Butter Battle by Dr. Seuss

Ceremony in the Circle of Life by White Deer of Autumn
(Gabriel Horn)

Chicken Sunday by Patricia Polacco

Crictor by Tomi Ungerer

Crow Boy by Taro Yashima

Dr. DeSoto by William Steig

Everybody Cooks Rice by Norah Dooley

The Girl Who Loved Wild Horses by Paul Goble

Grandpa Bear's Fantastic Scarf by Gillian Heal

Hairs/Pelitos by Sandra Cisneros

The Hundred Dresses by Eleanor Estes

In My Mother's House by Ann Nolan Clark

Joseph Had a Little Overcoat by Simms Taback

The Keeping Quilt by Patricia Polacco

Little Blue and Little Yellow by Leo Lionni

A Little Story About a Big Turnip by Tatiana Zunshine

Luba and the Wren by Patricia Polacco

Lyle, Lyle Crocodile by Bernard Waber
Mama, Do You Love Me? by Barbara Joosse
Not So Fast Songolo by Niki Daly
Old Turtle by Douglas Wood
The Rough-Face Girl by Rafe Martin
Sitti's Secrets by Naomi Shihab Nye
The Story About Ping by Marjorie Flack
Umbrella by Taro Yashima
When Clay Sings by Byrd Baylor
Who Came Down That Road by George Ella Lyon
Winnie-the-Pooh by A. A. Milne

Death and Loss

Annie and the Old One by Miska Miles
Betty Doll by Patricia Polacco
Bluebird Summer by Deborah Hopkinson

Discipline

The Boy Who Held Back the Sea by Thomas Locker
Curious George by H. A. and Margret Rey
The Great Gracie Chase: Stop That Dog by Cynthia Rylant
Pancakes, Pancakes by Eric Carle
Pierre by Maurice Sendak
Ramona series by Beverly Cleary
The Story About Ping by Marjorie Flack
Strega Nona by Tomie dePaola
The Tale of Peter Rabbit by Beatrix Potter
Two Bad Ants by Chris Van Allsburg
When Sophie Gets Angry, Really, Really Angry by Molly
   Garrett Bang
Where the Wild Things Are by Maurice Sendak
Wings: A Tale of Two Chickens by James Marshall

Encouragement

Amelia's Road by Linda Jacobs Altman

The Bee Tree by Patricia Polacco

Big Thoughts for Little People by Kenneth N. Taylor

Chrysanthemum by Kevin Henkes

A Color of His Own by Leo Lionni

Evan's Corner by Elizabeth Starr Hill

The Little Engine That Could by Watty Piper

The Mud Flat Olympics by James Stevenson

Nobody Is Perfick by Bernard Waber

Now One Foot, Now the Other by Tomie dePaola

Presents from Grandma by Jan Mark

The Remarkable Farkle McBride by John Lithgow

She Come Bringing Me That Baby Girl by Eloise Greenfield

Sing to the Stars by Mary Brigid Barrett

Spinky Sulks by William Steig

Swimmy by Leo Lionni

The Tale of Peter Rabbit by Beatrix Potter

Winnie-the-Pooh by A. A. Milne

You Look Ridiculous Said the Rhinoceros to the Hippopotamus by Bernard Waber

Faith

Adelita: A Mexican Cinderella Story by Tomie dePaola

The Amazing Story of Noah's Ark by Marcia Williams

The Carrot Seed by Ruth Krauss

Horton Hears a Who by Dr. Seuss

How the Grinch Stole Christmas by Dr. Seuss

The Legend of the Poinsettia by Tomie dePaola

The Night of Las Posadas by Tomie dePaola

Pascual and the Kitchen Angels by Tomie dePaola

The Polar Express by Chris Van Allsburg

Family and Belonging

Adelita: A Mexican Cinderella Story by Tomie dePaola

All the Places to Love by Patricia MacLachlan

All the Way Home by Lore Segal

Are We Almost There by James Stevenson

Are You My Mother by P. D. Eastman

Babushka Baba Yaga by Patricia Polacco

A Baby Sister for Frances by Russel Hoban

The Baby Sister by Tomie dePaola

A Bear Called Paddington by Michael Bond

Best Friends for Frances by Russel Hoban

The Best Nest by P. D. Eastman

Big Sister and Little Sister by Charlotte Zolotow

A Birthday for Frances by Russel Hoban

Blueberries for Sal by Robert McCloskey

Bread and Jam for Frances by Russel Hoban

Catwings series by Ursula LeGuin

Corduroy by Don Freeman

Dandelions by Eve Bunting

Do You Know What I'll Do? By Charlotte Zolotow

Evan's Corner by Elizabeth Starr Hill

Fanny's Dream by Caralyn and Mark Buehner

First Pink Light by Eloise Greenfield

The Five Chinese Brothers by Claire H. Bishop

Go and Hush the Baby by Betsy Byars

Grandfather's Journey by Allen Say

Grandmama's Joy by Eloise Greenfield

Grandpa Bear's Fantastic Scarf by Gillian Heal

Grandpa's Face by Eloise Greenfield

Hansel and Gretel by Rika Lesser

Harvey's Hideout by Russel Hoban

Have You Seen My Duckling by Nancy Tarfuri

Horton Hatches an Egg by Dr. Seuss

The House on East 88th Street by Bernard Waber

A Hug Goes Around by Laura Krauss Melmed

Ira Sleeps Over by Bernard Waber

Island Boy by Barbara Cooney

Jojo's Revenge by Mick Inkpen

The Keeping Quilt by Patricia Polacco

Leave Horatio Alone by Eleanor Lowenton Clymer

The Legend of the Bluebonnet by Tomie dePaola

Lovable Lyle by Bernard Waber

Luba and the Wren by Patricia Polacco

Lyle and the Birthday Party by Bernard Waber

Lyle Finds His Mother by Bernard Waber

Lyle, Lyle Crocodile by Bernard Waber

Make Way for Ducklings by Robert McCloskey

Mama, Do You Love Me? by Barbara M. Joosse

Midnight Teddies by Dana Kubick

My Grandson Lew by Charlotte Zolotow

My Mama Had a Dancing Heart by Libba Moore Gray

A New Coat for Anna by Harriet Ziefert

Nobody Is Perfick by Bernard Waber

Olivia by Ian Falconer

One Morning in Maine by Robert McCloskey

Owl Moon by Jane Yolen

Ox-Cart Man by Donald Hall

Penguin Pete by Marcus Pfister

Penguin Pete's New Friends by Marcus Pfister

Pete's a Pizza by William Steig

Peter's Chair by Ezra Jack Keats

A Pocket for Corduroy by Don Freeman

The Rag Coat by Lauren Mills

The Relatives Came by Cynthia Rylant

The Runaway Bunny by Margaret Wise Brown

The Scrambled States of America by Laurie Keller

Seven Little Monsters by Maurice Sendak

Simple Pictures Are Best by Nancy Willard

Sitti's Secrets by Naomi Shihab Nye

Snow Day by Barbara M. Joosse

Song and Dance Man by Karen Ackerman

Spinky Sulks by William Steig

Stellaluna by Janell Cannon

Sylvester and the Magic Pebble by William Steig

Theodore by Edward Ormondroyd
Theodore's Rival by Edward Ormondroyd
Time at the Top by Edward Ormondroyd
Time of Wonder by Robert McCloskey
When I Am Old with You by Angela Johnson
When I Was Young in the Mountains by Cynthia Rylant
Where the Wild Things Are by Maurice Sendak
William's Doll by Charlotte Zolotow
The Year of the Perfect Christmas Tree by Barbara Cooney
Yonder by Tony Johnston
You're Just What I Need (former title: *The Bundle Book*)
    by Ruth Krauss
Zathura by Chris Van Allsburg

Forgiveness and Reconciliation

Bartholomew and the Oobleck by Dr. Seuss
The Bear's Water Picnic by John Yeoman
Big Thoughts for Little People by Kenneth N. Taylor
Curious George by H. A. and Margret Rey
A Day's Work by Eve Bunting
Grandpa's Face by Eloise Greenfield
Little Bear's Trousers by Jane Hissey
Nobody Is Perfick by Bernard Waber
Tale of Three Trees by Angela Elwell Hunt
Where the Wild Things Are by Maurice Sendak
Why Mosquitoes Buzz in People's Ears by Verna Aardema

Friendship

Alexander and the Wind-Up Mouse by Leo Lionni
Amigo by Byrd Baylor Schweitzer
A Bad Case of Stripes by David Shannon
The Bear's Water Picnic by John Yeoman
Centerburg Tales by Robert McCloskey
Diary of a Worm by Doreen Cronin
Do You Want to Be My Friend? by Eric Carle

Fish Is Fish by Leo Lionni

Frog and Toad are Friends by Arnold Lobel

Frog and Toad Together by Arnold Lobel

Funny, Funny Lyle by Bernard Waber

George and Martha: The Complete Stories of Two Best Friends by James Marshall

The Golden Egg Book by Margaret Wise Brown

Goodnight Moon by Margaret Wise Brown

Henry and Mudge series by Cynthia Rylant

Homer Price by Robert McCloskey

Hug Me by Patti Stren

Ira Says Goodbye by Bernard Waber

Little Bear's Trousers by Jane Hissey

Lyle at the Office by Bernard Waber

Lyle, Lyle Crocodile by Bernard Waber

Madeline series by Ludwig Bemelmans

May I Bring a Friend by Beatrice S. De Regniers

Nobody Is Perfick by Bernard Waber

Old Henry by Joan W. Blos

The Old Woman Who Named Things by Cynthia Rylant

Penguin Pete's New Friends by Marcus Pfister

Peter Rabbit books by Beatrix Potter

Pocketful of Cricket by Rebecca Caudill

Rainbow Fish by Marcus Pfister

The Snowman by Raymond Briggs

The Snowy Day by Ezra Jack Keats

The Snuggle Bunny by Nancy Jewell

Thy Friend, Obadiah by Brinton Turkle

Together by George Ella Lyon

Winnie-the-Pooh by A. A. Milne

Goodnight Books

The Bed Book by Sylvia Plath

Big Red Barn by Margaret Wise Brown

Goodnight Moon by Margaret Wise Brown

How I Became a Pirate by Melinda Long

I Love You Mouse by Margaret Bloy Graham

The Napping House by Audrey Wood

The Sleepy Book by Charlotte Zolotow

You're Just What I Need (former title: *The Bundle Book*) by Ruth Krauss

Hope

Abuela's Weave by Omar S. Casteneda

The Amazing Bone by William Steig

Catwings series by Ursula LeGuin

A Color of His Own by Leo Lionni

Flip by Wesley Dennis

Imogene's Antlers by David Small

Jackalope by Janet Stevens and Susan Stevens Crummel

The Little Engine That Could by Watty Piper

The Little Wooden Doll by Margery Williams Bianco

Lyle, Lyle Crocodile by Bernard Waber

Roland the Minstrel Pig by William Steig

Shrek by William Steig

Song of the Swallows by Leo Politi

Swimmy by Leo Lionni

Sylvester and the Magic Pebble by William Steig

Where the Buffaloes Begin by Olaf Baker

Human Dignity

Paper Bag Princess by Robert Munsch

Jealousy

She Come Bringing Me That Baby Girl by Eloise Greenfield

Justice

Dr. DeSoto by William Steig

The Real Thief by William Steig

Kindness and Sharing

Bear Circus by William Pène du Bois

A Circle of Friends by Giora Carmi

Frederick by Leo Leonni

The Giving Tree by Shel Silverstein

The Grouchy Ladybug by Eric Carle

How the Grinch Stole Christmas by Dr. Seuss

It's Mine by Leo Lionni

Nathan's Fishing Trip by Lulu Delacre

Not So Fast Songolo by Niki Daly

The Old Woman Who Lived in a Vinegar Bottle
    by Rumer Godden

Rainbow Fish by Marcus Pfister

Rechenka's Eggs by Patricia Polacco

The Rough-Face Girl by Rafe Martin

Tico and the Golden Wings by Leo Lionni

Wee Gillis by Munro Leaf

Love and Concern

The Amazing Bone by William Steig

Baby Animals by Margaret Wise Brown

Bently and Egg by William Joyce

The Best-Loved Doll by Rebecca Caudill

Catwings series by Ursula LeGuin

A Chair for My Mother by Vera B. Williams

Clifford the Big Red Dog series by Norman Bridwell

Curious George by H. A. and Margret Rey

Dandelions by Eve Bunting

Fanny's Dream by Caralyn and Mark Buehner

The Five Chinese Brothers by Claire H. Bishop

The Go-Between by Amy Hest

Grandmama's Joy by Eloise Greenfield

Harry the Dirty Dog by Gene Zion

Higglety, Pigglety Pop: Or There Must Be More to Life
    by Maurice Sendak

Horton Hatches the Egg by Dr. Seuss

Horton Hears a Who by Dr. Seuss

The Little Engine That Could by Watty Piper

The Little House by Virginia Lee Burton

Lucy's Picture by Nicola Moon

Madeline series by Ludwig Bemelmans

The Mitten by Alvin Tresselt

The Mitten by Jan Brett

My Father's Dragon by Ruth Stiles Gannett

Nobody Is Perfick by Bernard Waber

Old Turtle and the Broken Truth by Douglas Wood

Play with Me by Marie H. Ets

Rapunzel by Paul O. Zelinksy

Rumpelstiltskin by Paul O. Zelinksy

Shrek by William Steig

St. George and the Dragon by Margaret Hodges

Sylvester and the Magic Pebble by William Steig

The Rough-Face Girl by Rafe Martin

The Steadfast Tin Soldier by Hans Christian Andersen

The Story About Ping by Marjorie Flack

Thy Friend, Obadiah by Brinton Turkle

When I Am Old with You by Angela Johnson

Where the Wild Things Are by Maurice Sendak

Who Wants Arthur by Amanda Graham

Whobody There by Charles and Ann Morse

Winnie-the-Pooh by A. A. Milne

Materialism, Selfishness, and Greed

Anansi and the Moss-Covered Rock by Eric A. Kimmel

The Chalk Doll by Charlotte Pomerantz

Chitty Chitty Bang Bang by Ian Fleming

Coyote Steals the Blanket: An Ute Tale by Janet Stevens

Crictor by Tomi Ungerer

Higglety, Pigglety Pop: Or There Must Be More to Life
    by Maurice Sendak

How the Grinch Stole Christmas by Dr. Seuss
The Hundred Dresses by Eleanor Estes
Joseph Had a Little Overcoat by Simms Taback
The Lorax by Dr. Seuss
Luba and the Wren by Patricia Polacco
A New Coat for Anna by Harriet Ziefert
The Rag Coat by Lauren Mills
Stone Soup by Marcia Brown
The Table Where Rich People Sit by Byrd Baylor
The Treasure by Uri Shulevitz
Tub Toys by Terry Miller Shannon and Timothy Warner
Two Bad Ants by Chris Van Allsburg
Wings: A Tale of Two Chickens by James Marshall
The Wolf's Chicken Stew by Keiko Kasza
Yertle the Turtle by Dr. Seuss

Mystery and Wonder

Abuela by Arthur Dorros
The Amazing Bone by William Steig
And to Think That I Saw It on Mulberry Street by Dr. Seuss
Bark, George by Jules Pfeiffer
Black and White by David Macauley
The Cat in the Hat by Dr. Seuss
The Cat in the Hat Comes Back by Dr. Seuss
A Dark, Dark Tale by Ruth Brown
The Fairy Doll by Rumer Godden
The Garden of Abdul Gasazi by Chris Van Allsburg
I Wonder If I'll See a Whale by Frances Ward Weller
Jumanji by Chris Van Allsburg
The Legend of the Poinsettia by Tomie dePaola
Magic Tree House series by Mary Pope Osborne
A New Coat for Anna by Harriet Ziefert
Once When I Was Scared by Helena Clare Pittman
The Paper Crane by Molly Bang
The Polar Express by Chris Van Allsburg

Snuggle Piggy and the Magic Blanket by Michele Stepto
The Rough-Face Girl by Rafe Martin
The Silver Pony by Lynd Ward
The Three Princes by Eric A. Kimmel
Tuesday by David Wiesner
Who Came Down That Road by George Ella Lyon
Why the Chicken Crossed the Road by David Macaulay

Perseverance

The Boy Who Held Back the Sea by Thomas Locker
Charlie Needs a Cloak by Tomie dePaola
Daisy's Taxi by Ruth Young
Dominic by William Steig
Elmer and the Dragon by Ruth Stiles Gannett
The 500 Hats of Bartholomew Cubbins by Dr. Seuss
Flip by Wesley Dennis
Galimoto by Karen Lynn Williams
The Goat in the Rug by Geraldine as told to Charles L. Blood
    and Martin Link
Homer Price by Robert McCloskey
Horton Hatches the Egg by Dr. Seuss
John Henry and His Hammer by H. W. Felton
Jumanji by Chris Van Allsburg
The Legend of the Indian Paintbrush by Tomie dePaola
The Legend of the Persian Carpet by Tomie dePaola
The Little Engine That Could by Watty Piper
*The Little Mouse, The Red Ripe Strawberry, and The Big
    Hungry Bear* by Don and Audrey Wood
A Little Story About a Big Turnip by Tatiana Zunshine
Mike Fink by Steven Kellogg
Mike Mulligan and His Steam Shovel by Virginia Lee Burton
Miss Rumphius by Barbara Cooney
Mother Goose Rhymes
Mouse Soup by Arnold Lobel
Ox-Cart Man by Donald Hall

Paul Bunyan by Steven Kellogg

Pecos Bill by Steven Kellogg

Pecos Bill: The Greatest Cowboy of All Time by James
Cloyd Bowman

Shrek by William Steig

The Steadfast Tin Soldier by Hans Christian Andersen

Wee Gillis by Munro Leaf

Poetry

Beatrix Potter's Nursery Rhyme Book

A Caribbean Dozen: Poems from Caribbean Poets (compiled
by John Agard and Grace Nichols)

A Child's Garden of Verses by Robert Louis Stevenson

Daydreamers by Eloise Greenfield

Good Night, Sleep Tight: A Poem for Every Night of the Year
(compiled by Ivan Jones)

Hailstones and Halibut Bones by Mary O'Neill

Hector Protector and As I Went Over the Water by Maurice
Sendak

Mary Had a Little Lamb by Sarah Joseph Hale (illustrated by
Tomie dePaola)

Mother Goose Rhymes

My Shadow by Robert Louis Stevenson (illustrated by
Glenna Lang)

The New Kid on the Block by Jack Pretlusky

Now We Are Six by A. A. Milne

The Owl and the Pussycat by Edward Lear (illustrated by
Jan Brett)

Poems for Children by Eleanor Farjeon

The Random House Book of Poetry for Children (compiled by
Jack Pretlusky)

Read-Aloud Rhymes for the Very Young by Jack Pretlusky

Sing a Song of Popcorn: Every Child's Book of Poems (compiled by Beatrice Schenk de Regniers, et al.)

The Slant Book by Peter Newell

Some of the Days of Everett Anderson by Lucille Clifton

Something Big Has Been Here by Jack Pretlusky

Stars Tonight by Sara Teasdale

The Sun Is So Quiet by Nikki Giovanni

Tomie dePaola's Book of Poems

Under the Sunday Tree by Eloise Greenfield

When We Were Very Young by A. A. Milne

You Be Good, and I'll Be Night by Eve Merriam

Pride

Chanticleer and the Fox by Geoffrey Chaucer,
     retold by Barbara Cooney

Many Moons by James Thurber

Mufaro's Beautiful Daughters by John Steptoe

Petunia by Roger Duvoisin

Rainbow Fish by Marcus Pfister

Responsibility

A Bear Called Paddington by Michael Bond

The Biggest Bear by Lynd Ward

Caps for Sale by Esphyr Slobodkina

The Cat in the Hat by Dr. Seuss

The Cat in the Hat Comes Back by Dr. Seuss

Cloudy with a Chance of Meatballs by Judi Barrett

A Day's Work by Eve Bunting

Flossie and the Fox by Patricia C. McKissack

Good Dog, Carl by Alexandra Day

Good Night Gorilla by Peggy Rathman

Horton Hears a Who by Dr. Seuss

I Am Not Going to Get Up Today by Dr. Seuss

Just So Stories by Rudyard Kipling

Little Bear's Trousers by Jane Hissey

The Lorax by Dr. Seuss

Many Moons by James Thurber

Mother Goose Rhymes

Officer Buckle and Gloria by Peggy Rathman
Ox-Cart Man by Donald Hall
Peppe the Lamplighter by Elisa Bartone
Strega Nona by Tomie dePaola

Stories for Young Readers

Third to Sixth Grade

Adoption

The Story of Holly and Ivy by Rumer Godden

Collections of Stories

All Around the Town by Phyllis McGinley
The Book of Dragons (ed. Michael Hague)
The Book of Virtues by William J. Bennett
The Cow Tail Switch and Other West African Stories
    by Harold Courlander
Cut from the Same Cloth: American Women in Myth,
    Legend, and Tall Tale by Robert D. San Souci
The Faber Book of North American Legends by Virginia
    Haviland
The Jack Tales by Richard Chase
My Brother Louis Measures Worms by Barbara Robinson
The People Could Fly by Virginia Hamilton
The Power of Light by Isaac Bashevis Singer
Shen of the Sea: Chinese Stories for Children by Arthur
    Bowie Chrisman
Tales from Shakespeare by Charles and Mary Lamb
Thistle and Thyme: Tales and Legends from Scotland
    by Sorche Nic Leodhas
Zlateh the Goat and Other Stories by Isaac Bashevis Singer

Compassion and Kindness

Black Beauty by Anna Sewell
Charlotte's Web by E. B. White

The Indian in the Cupboard by Lynn Reid Banks

Mama's Going to Buy You a Mockingbird by Jean Little

Courage

The Boy and the Ghost by Robert D. San Souci

Brave Irene by William Steig

Call It Courage by Armstrong Sperry

Cowardly Clyde by Bill Peet

Different Dragons by Jean Little

The Enchanted Castle by E. Nesbit

The House of Sixty Fathers by Meindert DeJong

Little House series by Laura Ingalls Wilder

Lon Po Po by Ed Young

Mine for Keeps by Jean Little

National Velvet by Enid Bagnold

Number the Stars by Lois Lowry

Peter Graves by William Pène du Bois

Poppy by Avi

Redwall series by Brian Jacques

Shiloh by Phyllis Reynolds Naylor

A Swiftly Tilting Planet by Madeleine L'Engle

Thee, Hannah by Marguerite de Angeli

Tucker's Countryside by George Selden

A Wind in the Door by Madeleine L'Engle

A Wrinkle in Time by Madeleine L'Engle

Cultures, Tradition, and Tolerance

All-of-a-Kind Family by Sydney Taylor

...And Now Miguel by Joseph Krumgold

Amos and Boris by William Steig

The Birchbark House by Louise Erdrich

Bright April by Marguerite de Angeli

The Borrowers series by Mary Norton

Call It Courage by Armstrong Sperry

Dragonwings by Lawrence Yep

The Giant by William Pène du Bois

The Good Master by Kate Seredy

Gypsy Girl (first published as *The Diddakoi*) by Rumer Godden

A Grain of Rice by Helena Clare Pittman

The House of Sixty Fathers by Meindert DeJong

Julie of the Wolves by Jean Craighead George

Mouse House by Rumer Godden

Number the Stars by Lois Lowry

Onion Tears by Diana Kidd

Seedfolks by Paul Fleischman

Sign of the Beaver by Elizabeth George Speare

The Singing Tree by Kate Seredy

Thee, Hannah by Marguerite de Angeli

Death and Loss

Because of Winn Dixie by Kate DiCamillo

Chasing Redbird by Sharon Creech

Gentle Ben by Walt Morey

Keeper of the Doves by Betsy Byars

Missing May by Cynthia Rylant

Mama's Going to Buy You a Mockingbird by Jean Little

Onion Tears by Diana Kidd

Sarah, Plain and Tall by Patricia MacLachlan

Discipline

The Adventures of Pinocchio by Carlo Collodi

Babushka's Doll by Patricia Polacco

The Best Christmas Pageant Ever by Barbara Robinson

The Best School Year Ever by Barbara Robinson

Bobby Baseball by Robert Kimmel Smith

Charlie and the Chocolate Factory by Roald Dahl

The Good Master by Kate Seredy

Henry and Ribsy by Beverly Cleary

Mary Poppins series by Pamela Travers

The Moffats by Eleanor Estes

Mrs. Piggle-Wiggle series by Betty MacDonald

Otis Spofford by Beverly Cleary

Ralph S. Mouse by Beverly Cleary

Encouragement

The Door in the Wall by Marguerite deAngeli

Frindle by Andrew Clement

The Golden Goblet by Eloise Jarvis McGraw

Harry Kitten and Tucker Mouse by George Selden

Oh, the Places You'll Go by Dr. Seuss

Ramona and Her Father by Beverly Cleary

Family and Belonging

About the B'nai Bagels by E. L. Konigsburg

...And Now Miguel by Joseph Krumgold

Across Five Aprils by Irene Hunt

The Barn by Avi

The Bells of Christmas by Virginia Hamilton

The Best Christmas Pageant Ever by Barbara Robinson

Bobby Baseball by Robert Kimmel Smith

By the Shores of Silver Lake by Laura Ingalls Wilder

The Cabin Faced West by Jean Fritz

Caddie Woodlawn by Carol Ryrie Brink

Charlie and the Chocolate Factory by Roald Dahl

Charlotte's Web by E. B. White

The Chestry Oak by Kate Seredy

The Doll's House by Rumer Godden

Ella Enchanted by Gail Carson Levine

Farmer Boy by Laura Ingalls Wilder

The First Four Years by Laura Ingalls Wilder

From the Mixed-Up Files of Mrs. Basil E. Frankweiler
    by E. L. Konigsburg

A Grain of Rice by Helena Clare Pittman

Granny Torrelli Makes Soup by Sharon Creech

Heidi by Johanna Spyri

Hello, Mrs. Piggle-Wiggle by Betty MacDonald

Henry and Ribsy by Beverly Cleary

Keeper of the Doves by Betsy Byars

Little House in the Big Woods by Laura Ingalls Wilder

Little House on the Prairie by Laura Ingalls Wilder

Little Men by Louisa May Alcott

Little Town on the Prairie by Laura Ingalls Wilder

Little Women by Louisa May Alcott

The Long Winter by Laura Ingalls Wilder

Look Through My Window by Jean Little

The Middle Moffat by Eleanor Estes

Miss Happiness and Miss Flower by Rumer Godden

The Moffat Museum by Eleanor Estes

The Moffats by Eleanor Estes

Morning Girl by Michael Dorris

Mrs. Piggle-Wiggle by Betty MacDonald

Mrs. Piggle-Wiggle's Farm by Betty MacDonald

Mrs. Piggle-Wiggle's Magic by Betty MacDonald

On the Banks of Plum Creek by Laura Ingalls Wilder

Owls in the Family by Farley Mowat

Ramona series by Beverly Cleary

Runaway Ralph by Beverly Cleary

Sarah, Plain and Tall by Patricia MacLachlan

The Secret Garden by Frances Hodgson Burnett

Sign of the Beaver by Elizabeth Speare George

The Singing Tree by Kate Seredy

Socks by Beverly Cleary

Stone Fox by John Reynolds Gardiner

Stuart Little by E. B. White

Summer of the Swans by Betsy Byars

Swiss Family Robinson by Johann D. Wyss

These Happy Golden Years by Laura Ingalls Wilder

Thimble Summer by Elizabeth Enright

The Trolls by Polly Horvath

Understood Betsy by Dorothy Canfield Fisher

A Wrinkle in Time by Madeleine L'Engle

Forgiveness and Reconciliation

At the Back of the North Wind by George MacDonald

The Bronze Bow by Elizabeth George Speare

A Christmas Carol by Charles Dickens

Henry Huggins by Beverly Cleary

Old Henry by Joan W. Blos

Otis Spofford by Beverly Cleary

The Phantom Tollbooth by Norton Juster

Ramona and Her Mother by Beverly Cleary

Shiloh Season by Phyllis Reynolds Naylor

The Tale of Despereaux by Kate DiCamillo

Friendship and Loyalty

Abel's Island by William Steig

About the B'nai Bagels by E. L. Konigsburg

Along Came a Dog by Meindert DeJong

Angelo by David Macauley

Because of Winn Dixie by Kate DiCamillo

Ben and Me by Robert Lawson

The BFG by Roald Dahl

The Borrowers by Mary Norton

Charlotte's Web by E. B. White

The Cricket in Times Square by George Selden

David and the Phoenix by Edward Ormondroyd

Different Dragons by Jean Little

The Dragon of Og by Rumer Godden

Ellen Tebbits by Beverly Cleary

The Facts and Fictions of Minna Pratt by Patricia MacLachlan

Gentle Ben by Walt Morey

The Giant by William Pène du Bois

The Giving Tree by Shel Silverstein

The Good Master by Kate Seredy

Harry Kitten and Tucker Mouse by George Selden

Harry Potter series by J. K. Rowling

Heidi by Johanna Spyri

Henry Huggins series by Beverly Cleary

The Hobbit by J. R. R. Tolkien

The Jungle Book by Rudyard Kipling

King of Shadows by Susan Cooper

Mama's Going to Buy You a Mockingbird by Jean Little

The Middle Moffat by Eleanor Estes

Mine for Keeps by Jean Little

The Mouse and the Motorcycle by Beverly Cleary

The Mysterious Island by Jules Verne

The Pigman by Paul Zindel

Ramona's World by Beverly Cleary

Rascal by Sterling North

The Secret Garden by Frances Hodgson Burnett

Shadow Spinner by Susan Fletcher

Tom's Midnight Garden by Philippa Pearce

Understood Betsy by Dorothy Canfield Fisher

The View from Saturday by E. L. Konigsburg

The Wind in the Willows by Kenneth Grahame

Where the Red Fern Grows by Wilson Rawls

White Fang by Jack London

The Wonderful Wizard of Oz by L. Frank Baum

The Young Merlin trilogy by Jane Yolen

Good Versus Evil

Peter Pan by J. M. Barrie

The Princess and the Curdie by George MacDonald

The Princess and the Goblin by George MacDonald

The Prydain Chronicles by Lloyd Alexander
> *The Black Cauldron*
> *The Castle of Llyr*
> *Taran Wanderer*
> *The High King*
> *The Foundling and Other Tales of Prydain*

Redwall series by Brian Jacques
A Swiftly Tilting Planet by Madeleine L'Engle
A Wind in the Door by Madeleine L'Engle
A Wrinkle in Time by Madeleine L'Engle

Hope

Abel's Island by William Steig
The Adventures of Pinocchio by Carlo Collodi
...And Now Miguel by Joseph Krumgold
Because of Winn Dixie by Kate DiCamillo
The Box of Delights by John Masefield
Emily's Runaway Imagination by Beverly Cleary
Everything on a Waffle by Polly Horvath
From the Mixed-Up Files of Mrs. Basil E. Frankweiler
    by E. L. Konigsburg
Ginger Pye by Eleanor Estes
Hans Brinker or the Silver Skates by Mary
    Mapes Dodge
The House of Sixty Fathers by Meindert DeJong
James and the Giant Peach by Roald Dahl
Little House series by Laura Ingalls Wilder
The Midnight Folk by John Masefield
Misty of Chincoteague by Marguerite Henry
The Mysterious Island by Jules Verne
National Velvet by Enid Bagnold
Oh, the Places You'll Go by Dr. Seuss
The Prince and the Pauper by Mark Twain
Seedfolks by Paul Fleischman
Shadrach by Meindert DeJong
The Story of Holly and Ivy by Rumer Godden
Strawberry Girl by Lois Lenski
The Tale of Despereaux by Kate DiCamillo
Thimble Summer by Elizabeth Enright
The Van Gogh Café by Cynthia Rylant
The Wheel on the School by Meindert DeJong

Human Dignity

The *Midwife's Apprentice* by Karen Cushman

Justice

The *Alley* by Eleanor Estes

Five Children and It by E. Nesbit

The *Pushcart War* by Jean Merrill

The *Three Policemen, or Young Bottsford of Farbe Island* by William Pène du Bois

The *Whipping Boy* by Sid Fleischman

Kindness, Generosity, and Sharing

The *BFG* by Roald Dahl

Caddie Woodlawn by Carol Ryrie Brink

A *Christmas Carol* by Charles Dickens

The *Dragon of Og* by Rumer Godden

The *Giant* by William Pène du Bois

The *Indian in the Cupboard* by Lynn Reid Banks

The *King's Chessboard* by David Birch

The *Mouse and the Motorcycle* by Beverly Cleary

Mouse House by Rumer Godden

The *Old Meadow* by George Selden

Pinky Pye by Eleanor Estes

Pippi Longstocking by Astrid Lindgren

Rabbit Hill by Robert Lawson

Shiloh by Phyllis Reynolds Naylor

Thee, Hannah by Marguerite de Angeli

Tough Winter by Robert Lawson

The *Voyages of Dr. Doolittle* by Hugh Lofting (1998, ed. Patricia and Fredrick McKissack)

The *Wind in the Willows* by Kenneth Grahame

Love and Concern

Abel's Island by William Steig

The *Barn* by Avi

The Bronze Bow by Elizabeth George Speare

The Castle in the Attic by Elizabeth Winthrop

A Grain of Rice by Helena Clare Pittman

Harry Cat's Pet Puppy by George Selden

Hurry Home, Candy by Meindert DeJong

King of the Wind: The Story of the Godolphin Arabian
    by Marguerite Henry

The Little Prince by Antoine de Saint-Exupè266ry

Ramona and Her Father by Beverly Cleary

Ramona and Her Mother by Beverly Cleary

Rascal by Sterling North

Sarah, Plain and Tall by Patricia MacLachlan

Shadrach by Meindert DeJong

Shiloh by Phyllis Reynolds Naylor

Shiloh Season by Phyllis Reynolds Naylor

The Tale of Despereaux by Kate DiCamillo

The Trumpet of the Swan by E. B. White

Where the Red Fern Grows by Wilson Rawls

A Wrinkle in Time by Madeleine L'Engle

Materialism, Greed, and Poverty

At the Back of the North Wind by George MacDonald

The Borrowers Afield by Mary Norton

The Borrowers Aloft by Mary Norton

The Borrowers by Mary Norton

Charlie and the Chocolate Factory by Roald Dahl

The Chocolate Touch by Patrick Skene Catling

A Christmas Carol by Charles Dickens

Ella Enchanted by Gail Carson Levine

The Golden Goblet by Eloise Jarvis McGraw

The Island of the Aunts by Eva Ibbotson

The Moffats by Eleanor Estes

Mouse House by Rumer Godden

Mr. Popper's Penguins by Richard and Florence Atwater

The Old Meadow by George Selden

The Prince and the Pauper by Mark Twain

The Pushcart War by Jean Merrill

Treasure Island by Robert Louis Stevenson

Mystery and Wonder

Alice's Adventures in Wonderland by Lewis Carroll

Alligator Case by William Pène du Bois

At the Back of the North Wind by George MacDonald

The Box of Delights by John Masefield

Charley and the Great Glass Elevator by Roald Dahl

Charlie and the Chocolate Factory by Roald Dahl

Chasing Redbird by Sharon Creech

The Enchanted Castle by E. Nesbit

The Fairy Books (ed. Andrew Lang)

The Five Children and It by E. Nesbit

From the Mixed-Up Files of Mrs. Basil E. Frankweiler
by E. L. Konigsburg

The Genie of Sutton Place by George Selden

Ginger Pye by Eleanor Estes

Half Magic by Edward Eager

Harry Potter series by J. K. Rowling

The Indian in the Cupboard by Lynn Reid Banks

The Island of the Aunts by Eva Ibbotson

James and the Giant Peach by Roald Dahl

The Little Princess by Frances Hodgson Burnett

Mary Poppins series by Pamela Travers

The Midnight Folk by John Masefield

The Mysterious Island by Jules Verne

The Phantom Tollbooth by Norton Juster

The Phoenix and the Carpet by E. Nesbit

The Princess and the Goblin by George MacDonald

The Railway Children by E. Nesbit

Sees Behind Trees by Michael Dorris

Shadow Spinner by Susan Fletcher

The Story of the Amulet by E. Nesbit

The Story of the Treasure Seekers by E. Nesbit

Thimble Summer by Elizabeth Enright

The Three Policemen, or Young Bottsford of Farbe Island
    by William Pène du Bois

Through the Looking Glass by Lewis Carroll

Time at the Top by Edward Ormondroyd

Tom's Midnight Garden by Philippa Pearce

The Van Gogh Café by Cynthia Rylant

The Voyages of Dr. Doolittle by Hugh Lofting (1998, ed.
    Patricia and Fredrick McKissack)

The Wizard of Oz series by L. Frank Baum

The Wonderful Flight to the Mushroom Planet
    by Eleanor Cameron

Perseverance

Abel's Island by William Steig

The Barn by Avi

The Borrowers Afloat by Mary Norton

Brave Irene by William Steig

The Cabin Faced West by Jean Fritz

Charley and the Great Glass Elevator by Roald Dahl

The Fledgling by Jane Langton

From Anna by Jean Little

A Grain of Rice by Helena Clare Pittman

Henry and Beezus by Beverly Cleary

The House of Sixty Fathers by Meindert DeJong

Julie of the Wolves by Jean Craighead George

Little House series by Laura Ingalls Wilder

The Midnight Folk by John Masefield

Miss Hickory by Carolyn Sherwin Bailey

Misty of Chincoteague by Marguerite Henry

Mr. Popper's Penguins by Richard and Florence Atwater

Paddle to the Sea by Clancy Holling

Pippi Longstocking by Astrid Lindgren

Stone Fox by John Reynolds Gardiner

Strawberry Girl by Lois Lenski

Tucker's Countryside by George Selden

Poetry

*And the Green Grass Grew All Around: Folk Poetry from
Everyone* by Alvin Schwartz

At the Crack of the Bat (compiled by Lillian Morrison)

Black Swan, White Crow, Haiku by J. Patrick Lewis

Candy Corn by James Stevenson

The Children's Own Longfellow
by Henry Wadsworth Longfellow

Corn Chowder by James Stevenson

Doodle Soup by John Ciardi

Falling Up by Shel Silverstein

The Flag of Childhood: Poems of the Middle East
by Naomi Shihab Nye

For Laughing out Loud: Poems to Tickle Your Funny Bone
(ed. Jack Pretlutsky)

Honey, I Love and Other Love Poems by Eloise Greenfield

Joyful Noise: Poems for Two Voices by Paul Fleischman

Jump Back, Honey by Paul Lawrence Dunbar

A Light in the Attic by Shel Silverstein

Love That Dog by Sharon Creech

The New Kid on the Block by Jack Pretlusky

The Pied Piper of Hamelin by Robert Browning

Piping Down the Valleys Wild (ed. Nancy Larrick)

Popcorn by James Stevenson

*Reflections on a Gift of Watermelon Pickle...and Other
Modern Verse* (compiled by Stephen Dunning,
Edward Lueders, and Hugh Smith)

Relatively Speaking: Poems about Family by Ralph Fletcher

Spin a Soft Black Song by Nikki Giovanni

Sweet Corn by James Stevenson

Where the Sidewalk Ends by Shel Silverstein

Windsong by Carl Sandburg

You Come Too by Robert Frost

Pride

The Ant and the Elephant by Bill Peet
The Borrowers Avenged by Mary Norton
The Borrowers by Mary Norton
Her Majesty Grace Jones by Jane Langton
The King's Chessboard by David Birch
The King's Equal by Katherine Paterson
One of Grain of Rice by Demi
The Pushcart War by Jean Merrill
Sees Behind Trees by Michael Dorris

Responsibility

The Borrowers series by Mary Norton
The Castle in the Attic by Elizabeth Winthrop
A Fine, Fine School by Sharon Creech
Henry and Beezus by Beverly Cleary
Henry and the Clubhouse by Beverly Cleary
Henry and the Paper Route by Beverly Cleary
The Indian in the Cupboard by Lynn Reid Banks
Kokopelli's Flute by Will Hobbs
Peter Pan by J. M. Barrie
The Prince and the Pauper by Mark Twain
Rabbit Hill by Robert Lawson
Ramona Quimby, Age 8 by Beverly Cleary
The Singing Tree by Kate Seredy
Summer of the Swans by Betsy Byars
Tough Winter by Robert Lawson
Understood Betsy by Dorothy Canfield Fisher

Truth

The Fighting Ground by Avi
Mrs. Frisby and the Rats of NIMH by Robert C. O'Brien
The Phantom Tollbooth by Norton Juster
The Pushcart War by Jean Merrill
The White Stag by Kate Seredy

Stories for Tweens to Teens

Sixth to Ninth Grade

Adoption

> *Anne of Green Gables* by Lucy Maud Montgomery
> *Dicey's Song* by Cynthia Voigt
> *The Wanderer* by Sharon Creech

Collections of Stories

> *Martin Pippin and the Apple Orchard* by Eleanor Farjeon
> *Martin Pippin in the Daisy Field* by Eleanor Farjeon
> *The Thurber Carnival* by James Thurber

Compassion and Kindness

> *Alpha Centauri* by Robert Siegel
> *Beauty: A Retelling of the Story of Beauty and the Beast*
>   by Robin McKinley
> *Rebecca of Sunnybrook Farm* by Kate Douglas Wiggin
> *Skellig* by David Almond
> *The Well: David's Story* by Mildred D. Taylor

Courage

> *The Amber Spyglass* by Philip Pullman
> *Arilla Sun Down* by Virginia Hamilton
> *An Episode of Sparrows* by Rumer Godden
> *The Black Arrow* by Robert Louis Stevenson
> *The Black Cauldron* by Lloyd Alexander
> *The Blue Sword* by Robin McKinley
> *The Book of Three* by Lloyd Alexander
> *The Castle of Llyr* by Lloyd Alexander
> *The Door in the Wall* by Marguerite de Angeli
> *Gib and the Grey Ghost* by Zilpha Keatley Snyder
> *Gib Rides Home* by Zilpha Keatley Snyder
> *The Golden Compass* by Philip Pullman
> *Harry Potter* series by J. K. Rowling

The High King by Lloyd Alexander

The Hobbit by J. R. R. Tolkien

Holes by Louis Sachar

The House of the Scorpion by Nancy Farmer

Island of the Blue Dolphins by Scott O'Dell

Jim Davis: A High Seas Adventure by John Masefield

Jip: His Story by Katherine Paterson

Johnny Tremain by Esther Forbes

Lord of the Rings trilogy by J. R. R. Tolkien

My Antonia by Willa Cather

Nory Ryan's Song by Patricia Reilly Giff

Old Ramon by Jack Schaefer

Old Yeller by Fred Gipson

Peter Graves by William Pène du Bois

Pinocchio by Carlo Collodi

Sarah Bishop by Scott O'Dell

Sing Down the Moon by Scott O'Dell

A Single Shard by Linda Sue Park

Smoky, the Cowhorse by Will James

The Subtle Knife by Philip Pullman

Taran Wanderer by Lloyd Alexander

The Trumpeter of Krakow by Eric P. Kelly

The Wanderer by Sharon Creech

Whale Rider by Witi Ihimaera

The Yearling by Marjorie Kinnan Rawlings

Zia by Scott O'Dell

Cultures, Traditions, and Tolerance

Anne of Green Gables by Lucy Maud Montgomery

At Her Majesty's Request by Walter Dean Myers

Black Star, Bright Dawn by Scott O'Dell

Bud, Not Buddy by Christopher Paul Curtis

The Cay by Theodore Taylor

The Devil's Arithmetic by Jane Yolen

Dobry by Monica Shannon

The Friendship by Mildred D. Taylor

A Jar of Dreams by Yoshiko Uchida

Haveli by Suzanne Fisher Staples

Island of the Blue Dolphins by Scott O'Dell

Maniac Magee by Jerry Spinelli

The Master Puppeteer by Katherine Paterson

The Moves Make the Man by Bruce Brooks

Nory Ryan's Song by Patricia Reilly Giff

Onion John by Joseph Krumgold

A Papa Like Everyone Else by Sydney Taylor

Roll of Thunder, Hear My Cry by Mildred D. Taylor

Running on Eggs by Anna Levine

Secret of the Andes by Ann Nolan Clark

Shabanu by Suzanne Fisher Staples

Sing Down the Moon by Scott O'Dell

A Single Shard by Linda Sue Park

Streams to the River, River to the Sea: A Novel of Sacagawea by Scott O'Dell

The Talking Earth by Jean Craighead George

Walk Two Moons by Sharon Creech

Water Sky by Jean Craighead George

Whale Rider by Witi Ihimaera

When Hitler Stole Pink Rabbit by Judith Kerr

Zia by Scott O'Dell

Death and Loss

After the Rain by Norma Fox Mazer

Anne's House of Dreams by Lucy Maud Montgomery

Belle Prater's Boy by Ruth White

Bridge to Terabithia by Katherine Paterson

A Day No Pigs Would Die by Robert Newton Peck

A Gathering of Days by Joan W. Blos

Hatchet by Gary Paulsen

Johnny Tremain by Esther Forbes

Lily's Crossing by Patricia Reilly Giff

Miracle's Boys by Jacqueline Woodson

The Pigman by Paul Zindel

The Red Pony by John Steinbeck

Rilla of Ingleside by Lucy Maud Montgomery

A Ring of Endless Light by Madeleine L'Engle

Sarah Bishop by Scott O'Dell

Silver Days by Soni Levitin

Skellig by David Almond

Tree by Leaf by Cynthia Voigt

Tuck Everlasting by Natalie Babbitt

Wish You Well by David Baldacci

Family and Belonging

Anne of Green Gables series by Lucy Maud Montgomery

Borrowed Children by George Ella Lyon

Caddie Woodlawn by Carol R. Brink

Charlotte's Web by E. B. White

Cheaper by the Dozen by Frank B. Gilbreth and Ernestine Gilbreth Carey

Dear Mr. Henshaw by Beverly Cleary

Dicey's Song by Cynthia Voigt

Dobry by Monica Shannon

A Gathering of Days by Joan W. Blos

Gib Rides Home by Zilpha Keatley Snyder

The Great Gilly Hopkins by Katherine Paterson

Haveli by Suzanne Fisher Staples

Heidi by Johanna Spyri

Homecoming by Cynthia Voigt

Hoot by Carl Hiaasen

Island of the Blue Dolphins by Scott O'Dell

Lily's Crossing by Patricia Reilly Giff

The Little House series by Laura Ingalls Wilder

Little Men by Louisa May Alcott

Little Women by Louisa May Alcott

A Long Way from Chicago by Richard Peck

M. C. Higgins the Great by Virginia Hamilton

The Matchlock Gun by Walter D. Edmonds

Miracle's Boys by Jacqueline Woodson

My Antonia by Willa Cather

My Side of the Mountain by Jean Craighead George

Nory Ryan's Song by Patricia Reilly Giff

Roll of Thunder, Hear My Cry by Mildred D. Taylor

The Secret Garden by Frances Hodgson Burnett

Secret of the Andes by Ann Nolan Clark

Shabanu by Suzanne Fisher Staples

Sounder by William H. Armstrong

*Streams to the River, River to the Sea: A Novel of
    Sacagawea* by Scott O'Dell

Stuart Little by E. B. White

Swiss Family Robinson by Johann D. Wyss

A Tree Grows in Brooklyn by Betty Smith

Turn Homeward, Hannalee by Patricia Beatty

The Watsons Go to Birmingham—1963
    by Christopher Paul Curtis

Walk Two Moons by Sharon Creech

When Hitler Stole Pink Rabbit by Judith Kerr

A Year Down Yonder by Richard Peck

Zia by Scott O'Dell

Forgiveness and Reconciliation

Freaky Friday by Mary Rodgers

A Girl of the Limberlost by Gene Stratton-Porter

Ida Early Comes over the Mountain by Robert Burch

The Devil's Arithmetic by Jane Yolen

Whirligig by Paul Fleischman

Freedom

Amos Fortune, Free Man by Elizabeth Yates

At Her Majesty's Request by Walter Dean Myers

Beauty: A Retelling of the Story of Beauty and the Beast
    by Robin McKinley

The Captive by Scott O'Dell

Catherine Called Birdy by Karen Cushman

The City of Gold and Lead by John Christopher

A Connecticut Yankee in King Arthur's Court by Mark Twain

Crispin: The Cross of Lead by Avi

The Earthsea Triology by Ursula LeGuin

The Giver by Lois Lowry

I Am David (previously published as *North to Freedom*)
     by Anne Holm

Johnny Tremain by Esther Forbes

The Pool of Fire by John Christopher

Sarah Bishop by Scott O'Dell

The Trumpeter of Krakow by Eric P. Kelly

The White Mountains by John Christopher

Friendship and Loyalty

The Adventures of Huckleberry Finn by Mark Twain

The Adventures of Tom Sawyer by Mark Twain

Afternoon of the Elves by Janet Taylor Lisle

Anne of the Island by Lucy Maud Montgomery

Anne of Windy Poplars by Lucy Maud Montgomery

Belle Prater's Boy by Ruth White

Bridge to Terabithia by Katherine Paterson

The Egypt Game by Zilpha Keatley Snyder

Gib and the Grey Ghost by Zilpha Keatley Snyder

The Golden Compass by Philip Pullman

Gray Boy by Jim Arnosky

The Gypsy Game by Zilpha Keatley Snyder

Harry Potter series by J. K. Rowling

Holes by Louis Sachar

Jip: His Story by Katherine Paterson

Lily's Crossing by Patricia Reilly Giff

The Lord of the Rings trilogy by J. R. R. Tolkien

Old Ramon by Jack Schaefer

Old Yeller by Fred Gipson

Onion John by Joseph Krumgold

Rainbow Valley by Lucy Maud Montgomery

Roll of Thunder, Hear My Cry by Mildred D. Taylor

Smoky, the Cowhorse by Will James

Sounder by William H. Armstrong

To the Edge of the World by Michelle Torrey

The Watsons Go to Birmingham—1963
    by Christopher Paul Curtis

Good Versus Evil

The Book of the Dun Cow by Walter Wangerin, Jr.

The Earthsea trilogy by Ursula LeGuin
    The Wizard of Earthsea
    The Tombs of Atuan
    The Farthest Shore

The Dark Is Rising sequence by Susan Cooper
    Over Sea, Under Stone
    Silver on the Tree
    The Grey King
    Greenwitch
    The Dark Is Rising

The Hero and the Crown by Robin McKinley

Perelandra by C. S. Lewis

The Strange Case of Dr. Jekyll and Mr. Hyde
    by Robert Louis Stevenson

The Westmark trilogy by Lloyd Alexander

Hope

Anne of Green Gables by Lucy Maud Montgomery

The Bears' House by Marilyn Sachs

Bud, Not Buddy by Christopher Paul Curtis

Dear Mr. Henshaw by Beverly Cleary

Hope Was Here by Joan Bauer

I Am David (previously published as *North to Freedom*)
    by Anne Holm

The Light Beyond the Forest by Rosemary Sutcliff
The Once and Future King by T. H. White
A Papa Like Everyone Else by Sydney Taylor
Silver Days by Soni Levitin
Strider by Beverly Cleary
Trouble River by Betsy Byars
The White Mountains by John Christopher

Human Dignity

The Adventures of Huckleberry Finn by Mark Twain
Beauty: A Retelling of the Story of Beauty and the Beast
    by Robin McKinley
The Captive by Scott O'Dell
A Connecticut Yankee in King Arthur's Court by Mark Twain
The Devil's Arithmetic by Jane Yolen
The Earthsea trilogy by Ursula LeGuin
An Episode of Sparrows by Rumer Godden
Esperanza Rising by Pam Muñoz Ryan
Eva by Peter Dickinson
The Friendship by Mildred D. Taylor
A Girl of the Limberlost by Gene Stratton-Porter
The Giver by Lois Lowry
Harry Potter series by J. K. Rowling
The House of the Scorpion by Nancy Farmer
Ida Early Comes over the Mountain by Robert Burch
A Jar of Dreams by Yoshiko Uchida
Onion John by Joseph Krumgold
The Slave Dancer by Paula Fox
Rebecca of Sunnybrook Farm by Kate Douglas Wiggin
20,000 Leagues Under the Sea by Jules Verne
The Well: David's Story by Mildred D. Taylor

Jealousy and Pride

The Black Pearl by Scott O'Dell
Haveli by Suzanne Fisher Staples
Jacob Have I Loved by Katherine Paterson

Shabanu by Suzanne Fisher Staples

The Wizard of Earthsea by Ursula LeGuin

Justice

The Adventures of Tom Sawyer by Mark Twain

Beyond the Western Sea by Avi

The Call of the Wild by Jack London

Crispin: The Cross of Lead by Avi

A Connecticut Yankee in King Arthur's Court by Mark Twain

Dear Mr. Henshaw by Beverly Cleary

The Friendship by Mildred D. Taylor

The Ghost in the Tokaido Inn by Dorothy Hoobler

The Giver by Lois Lowry

Holes by Louis Sachar

Roll of Thunder, Hear My Cry by Mildred D. Taylor

Love

The Adventures of Tom Sawyer by Mark Twain

After the Rain by Norma Fox Mazer

The Amber Spyglass by Philip Pullman

Anne of Green Gables series by Lucy Maud Montgomery

The Black Arrow by Robert Louis Stevenson

The Cay by Theodore Taylor

Gray Boy by Jim Arnosky

Harry Potter and the Sorcerer's Stone by J. K. Rowling

The Hero and the Crown by Robin McKinley

The Incredible Journey by Sheila Burnford

Jane Eyre by Charlotte Bronte

Midnight Hour Encores by Bruce Brooks

Old Yeller by Fred Gipson

The Once and Future King by T. H. White

Prairie Songs by Pam Conrad

Skellig by David Almond

Streams to the River, River to the Sea: A Novel of Sacagawea by Scott O'Dell

To the Edge of the World by Michelle Torrey
Tree by Leaf by Cynthia Voigt
Water Sky by Jean Craighead George
Whalesong by Robert Siegel
The Yearling by Marjorie Kinnan Rawlings

Materialism, Greed, and Poverty

Artemis Fowl by Eoin Colfer
The Black Pearl by Scott O'Dell
Captains Courageous by Rudyard Kipling
The Captive by Scott O'Dell
Catherine Called Birdy by Karen Cushman
Esperanza Rising by Pam Muñoz Ryan
Harry Potter series by J. K. Rowling
Ida Early Comes over the Mountain by Robert Burch
Kidnapped by Robert Louis Stevenson
The Kingdom series by Cynthia Voigt
The King's Fifth by Scott O'Dell
Lyddie by Katherine Paterson
The Master Puppeteer by Katherine Paterson
My Side of the Mountain by Jean Craighead George
The Slave Dancer by Paula Fox
Summer of the Monkeys by Wilson Rawls
Tuck Everlasting by Natalie Babbitt
A Tree Grows in Brooklyn by Betty Smith

Mystery and Wonder

Afternoon of the Elves by Janet Taylor Lisle
Alpha Centauri by Robert Siegel
Belle Prater's Boy by Ruth White
The Blue Sword by Robin McKinley
The Dark Is Rising sequence by Susan Cooper
The Devil's Arithmetic by Jane Yolen
Castaways on Long Ago by Edward Ormondroyd
Freaky Friday by Mary Rodgers

The Ghost in the Tokaido Inn by Dorothy Hoobler

Harry Potter series by J. K. Rowling

The Hero and the Crown by Robin McKinley

The Hobbit by J. R. R. Tolkien

Holes by Louis Sachar

Hoot by Carl Hiaasen

Lord of the Rings trilogy by J. R. R. Tolkien

Skellig by David Almond

The Sword in the Stone by T. H. White

The Trumpeter of Krakow by Eric P. Kelly

Tuck Everlasting by Natalie Babbitt

Whalesong by Robert Siegel

Wish You Well by David Baldacci

Perseverance and Discipline

The Adventures of Tom Sawyer by Mark Twain

Anne of Windy Poplars by Lucy Maud Montgomery

Arilla Sun Down by Virginia Hamilton

Around the World in Eighty Days by Jules Verne

The Bears' House by Marilyn Sachs

The Black Pearl by Scott O'Dell

Black Star, Bright Dawn by Scott O'Dell

The Call of the Wild by Jack London

Carry on, Mr. Bowditch by Jean Lee Latham

Hatchet by Gary Paulsen

The Hero and the Crown by Robin McKinley

The Incredible Journey by Sheila Burnford

Jim Davis: A High Seas Adventure by John Masefield

Lyddie by Katherine Paterson

My Side of the Mountain by Jean Craighead George

The Once and Future King by T. H. White

Summer of the Monkeys by Wilson Rawls

The Sword in the Stone by T. H. White

The Talking Earth by Jean Craighead George

To the Edge of the World by Michelle Torrey

Where the Red Fern Grows by Wilson Rawls

Poetry

The Dream Keeper and Other Poems by Langston Hughes

Ordinary Things: Poems from a Walk in Early Spring by Ralph Fletcher

Out of the Dust by Karen Hesse

Prayers from the Ark and The Creatures' Choir by Carmen Bernos Gasztold (trans. Rumer Godden)

Songs of Innocence and Songs of Experience by William Blake

Voices from the Field (compiled by S. Beth Atkin)

The Way of the Wolf by Martin Bell

Responsibility

Anne of Avonlea by Lucy Maud Montgomery

Anne of Windy Poplars by Lucy Maud Montgomery

Borrowed Children by George Ella Lyon

The City of Gold and Lead by John Christopher

The Dark Is Rising by Susan Cooper

A Day No Pigs Would Die by Robert Newton Peck

The Hero and the Crown by Robin McKinley

The Matchlock Gun by Walter D. Edmonds

My Friend Flicka by Mary O'Hara

The Pool of Fire by John Christopher

Rilla of Ingleside by Lucy Maud Montgomery

20,000 Leagues Under the Sea by Jules Verne

Whale Rider by Witi Ihimaera

The Yearling by Marjorie Kinnan Rawlings

Truth

Anne of Green Gables by Lucy Maud Montgomery

Beyond the Western Sea by Avi

The Dies Drear Chronicle by Virginia Hamilton
    House of Dies Drear
    The Mystery of Drear House
The Giver by Lois Lowry
The Haymeadow by Gary Paulsen
Lily's Crossing by Patricia Reilly Giff
Pictures of Hollis Woods by Patricia Reilly Giff
A Single Shard by Linda Sue Park
The Subtle Knife by Philip Pullman
Tangerine by Edward Bloor
The Witch of Blackbird Pond by Elizabeth George Speare

Notes

1. Joseph Campbell, *The Power of Myth* (New York: Doubleday, 1988), p. xvii.

2. Anthony J. de Mello, S.J., *One Minute Wisdom* (New York: Doubleday, 1986), p. 23.

3. Tony Veale, "Metaphor, Memory and Meaning: Symbolic and Connectionist Issues in Metaphor Interpretation" (Ph.D. diss., Trinity College, Dublin, 1995), http://www.compapp.dcu.ie/~tonyv/news_frame.html.

4. Raymond E. Brown, S.S., *The Gospel and Epistles of John* (Collegeville: The Liturgical Press, 1988), p. 36.

5. Don Tapscott, "Educating the Net Generation," *Integrating Technology into the Curriculum* 56, no. 5 (Feb. 1999). Association for Supervision and Curriculum, Development. http://www.ascd.org/articles/9902el_tapscott.html.

6. Pontifical Council for Social Communications, *Ethics in Communication* (Boston: Pauline Books & Media, 2000), no. 4.

7. William D. Romanowski, *Eyes Wide Open: Looking for God in Popular Culture* (Grand Rapids: Brazos Press, 2001), p. 32.

8. Pontifical Council for Social Communications, *Ethics in Communication*, no. 25.

9. *Catechism of the Catholic Church* (Washington, D.C.: United States Catholic Conference, 2000), no. 2519.

10. Second Vatican Council, *Gaudium et Spes* (Boston: Pauline Books & Media, 1965), no. 2.

11. John Paul II, *Crossing the Threshold of Hope* (New York: Knopf, 1994), p. 89.

12. Ibid., p. 113.

13. John Paul II, *Address to the Participants in the Plenary Meeting of the Pontifical Council for Social Communications, 4.*

14. Pontifical Council for Social Communications, *Ethics in Communication*, no. 9.

15. David J. Wolpe, *Teaching Your Children About God: A Modern Jewish Approach* (New York: Henry Holt and Co., 1993), p. 7.

16. Bernice E. Cullinan, *Literature and the Child,* 2d ed. (San Diego: Harcourt Brace Jovanovich, 1989), p. 11.

17. Bernice E. Cullinan, Mary K. Karrer, and Arlene M. Pillar, *Literature and the Child* (New York: Harcourt Brace Jovanovich, 1981), p. 12.

18. Ibid., p. 13.

19. Jean Piaget, "Commentary on Vygotsky's Criticisms of *Language and Thought of the Child* and *Judgment and Reasoning in the Child,*" trans. Leslie Smith, *New Ideas in Psychology,* 2–3 (March 2000): 241–59.

20. Stephen T. Kerr, "Why Vygotsky?," presented at the Annual Meeting of the American Association for the Advancement of Slavic Studies, Seattle, WA, Nov. 22, 1997.

21. Dr. C. George Boeree, "Personality Theories of Abraham Maslow," Shippensburg University, http://www.ship.edu/~cgboeree/maslow.html.

22. James W. Fowler, *The Stages of Faith* (San Francisco: Harper Collins, 1981), p. 121.

23. Harold Kent Straughn, "Stages of Faith: An Interview with James Fowler," Lifespiral Communications. http://www.lifespirals.com/TheMindSpiral/Fowler/fowler.html.

24. Fowler, *The Stages of Faith,* p. 136.

25. Ibid., p. 149.

26. Wolpe, *Teaching Your Child About God,* p. 9.

27. Fowler, *The Stages of Faith,* p. 172.

28. Bruno Bettelheim, *The Uses of Enchantment: The Meaning and Importance of Fairy Tales* (New York: Vintage Books, 1989), pp. 4–5.

29. Ibid., p. 179.

30. Fowler, *The Stages of Faith,* p. 133.

31. Robert Coles, *The Call of Stories: Teaching and the Moral Imagination* (Boston: Houghton Mifflin Co., 1989), pp. 67–69.

32. Roy E. Plotnick, "In Search of Watty Piper: A Brief History of the Little Engine Story," University of Illinois at Chicago, http://www.tigger.uic.edu/~plotnick/littleng.htm.

33. Scot Peacock, "Jane Hissey Autobiography," *Something About the Author: Facts and Pictures About Authors and Illustrators of Books for*

Young People, Vol. 130 (Farmington Hills, MI: The Gale Group, 2002), http://www.janehissey.com.

34. Bryan Sibley, introduction to *The Complete Chronicles of Narnia,* by C. S. Lewis (New York: Harper Collins, 1998), p. 2.

35. *CCC,* no. 1443.

36. Phyllis Bixler, *The Secret Garden: Nature's Magic* (New York: Twayne, 1996), pp. ix–xv.

37. Ibid., pp. xii–xiv.

38. *The Letters of J. R. R. Tolkien,* ed. Humphrey Carpenter, with the assistance of Christopher Tolkien (Boston: Houghton Mifflin, 2000), 142, p. 172.

39. Douglas A. Anderson, "Revised Note on the Text," *The Lord of the Rings* (Boston: Houghton Mifflin, 1994), p. xi.

40. Kristen Moran, "Scholastic to Release J. K. Rowling's Phenomenal Bestseller *Harry Potter and the Order of the Phoenix* in Paperback on August 10, 2004," news release, Scholastic Corporation, Feb. 2, 2004.

41. Jay Lyman, "*Harry Potter* Movie Ticket Sales Break Internet Records," *NewsFactor Enterprise I.T. Top Tech News,* Nov. 16, 2001, http://www.newsfactor.com/perl/story/14856.html.

42. Barry Davis, "*Harry Potter* Movie Breaks Local Records," *The Jerusalem Post (Internet Edition),* Dec. 3, 2001, http://www.jpost.com/Editions/2001/12/03/Culture/Music.39243.html.

43. Guylaine Cadorette, "Box Office Analysis: Spellbound by 'Azkaban,'" Hollywood.com News, http://www.hollywood.com/news/detail/article/1754782.

44. Catherine Jack Deavel and David Paul Deavel, "Character, Choice, and Harry Potter," *Logos: A Journal of Catholic Thought and Culture* (Vol. 5.4), Fall 2002, http://www.stthomas.edu/cathstudies/logos/vol5_4/deavel.html.

45. Anne LeVeque, "Harry Potter Author: 'I Believe in God, Not Magic,'" Catholic News Service/U.S. Catholic Conference, Jan. 5, 2000.

46. John Paul II, *Evangelium Vitae* (Boston: Pauline Books & Media, 1995), p. 96.

47. Catherine Jack Deavel and David Paul Deavel, "Character, Choice, and Harry Potter."

48. Zenit News Agency, "In Defense of Harry Potter: Professors Defend Fiction's Famous Wizard," March 16, 2003, ZE03031622.

49. Catherine Jack Deavel and David Paul Deavel, "Character, Choice, and Harry Potter."

50. Zenit News Agency, "Harry Potter Not a Problem, Says Church Figure," Feb. 2, 2003, ZE03020304.

51. Ibid.

52. Catherine Jack Deavel and David Paul Deavel, "Character, Choice, and Harry Potter."

53. Ibid.

54. Ibid.

55. J. K. Rowling, "A Good Scare: The Wizard of Harry Potter Explains What Kids Need to Know of the Dark Side," *Time,* Oct. 20, 2000, p. 108.

56. John Paul II, *Familiaris Consortio* (Boston: Pauline Books & Media, 1981), p. 4.

57. J. K. Rowling, "The Not Especially Fascinating Life So Far of J. K. Rowling," (Part 2), http://www.cliphoto.com/potter/rowling1.htm.

58. Malcom Jones, "The Return of Harry Potter," *Newsweek,* July 10, 2000, p. 60.

59. "The Author J. K. Rowling: The J. K. Rowling Interview As Presented by Stories from the Web," Birmingham Libraries, U.K., http://www.storiesfromtheweb.org/stories/rowling/interview1.asp.

60. The Second Vatican Council's *Lumen Gentium* states that "all Christians in any state or walk of life are called to the fullness of Christian life and to the perfection of love" (no. 40).

61. Stanton J. Linden, *Darke Hieroglyphicks: Alchemy in English Literature from Chaucer to the Restoration* (Lexington: University Press of Kentucky, 1996), pp. 154–5, 189–82, 210–11, 214–20.

62. Clarence H. Miller, "Christ as the Philosopher's Stone in George Herbert's 'The Elixir,'" *Notes and Queries* 45 (1998):1.39–41.19.03, http://www.geocities.com/Athens/Acropolis/6586/miller.html.

Bibliography

Andrews, Robert, et al. The Columbia World of Quotations. New York: Columbia University Press, 1996. Available from World Wide Web: http://www.bartleby.com/66/.

Armstrong, Chris. "Christian History Corner: Saint J. R. R. the Evangelist," *Christianity Today*, March 10, 2003. http://www.christianitytoday.com/ct/2003/110/54.0.html.

Bettelheim, Bruno. *The Uses of Enchantment: The Meaning and Importance of Fairy Tales*. New York: Vintage Books, 1989.

Birzer, Bradley J., and Mark Eddy Smith. "Does *The Lord of the Rings* Teach Salvation by Works: A Conversation Between Brad Birzer and Mark Eddy Smith (Part II)," *Christianity Today*, Dec. 16, 2002. http://www.christianitytoday.com/ct/2002/149/42.0.html.

Bixler, Phyllis. *The Secret Garden: Nature's Magic*. New York: Twayne, 1996.

Boeree, Dr. C. George. "Personality Theories of Abraham Maslow." Shippensburg University web site: http://www.ship.edu/~cgboeree/maslow.html.

Brown, Raymond E., S.S. *The Gospel and Epistles of John*. Collegeville: The Liturgical Press, 1988.

Bruner, Kurt. "Tapping Tolkien to Teach Teens," *Plugged In*, Dec. 2001.

Cadorette, Guylaine. "Box Office Analysis: Spellbound by 'Azkaban,'" Hollywood.com News; http://www.hollywood.com/news/detail/article/1754782.

Campbell, Joseph (with Bill Moyers). *The Power of Myth*. New York: Doubleday, 1988.

Carroll, Lewis. *Alice's Adventures in Wonderland*. New York: Artisan, 1996.

Cavanaugh, Brian, T.O.R. "Storytelling As Ministry," *The Priest*, Dec. 1994. Available from Appleseeds web site of Franciscan University of Steubenville: http://www.appleseeds.org/Art_min.htm.

Colebatch, Hal G. P. "The Lord of the Rings, Harry Potter, and Star Wars," *AD2000* (Vol. 15, No. 3), April 2002, p. 10.

Coles, Robert. *The Call of Stories: Teaching and the Moral Imagination*. Boston: Houghton Mifflin Company, 1989.

———. *The Moral Intelligence of Children*. New York: Random House, 1997.

Considine, David. "Some Principles of Media Literacy." http://www.ci.appstate.edu/programs/edmedia/medialit/article4.html.

Crosby, Michael H., O.F.M. Cap. *Sprituality of the Beatitudes*. Maryknoll: Orbis Books, 1981.

Crossan, John Dominic. *In Parables: The Challenges of the Historical Jesus*. New York: Harper and Row, 1973.

Cullinan, Bernice E. *Literature and the Child*. New York: Harcourt Brace Jovanovich, 1981.

———. *Literature and the Child (2nd ed.)* San Diego: Harcourt Brace Jovanovich, 1989.

Davis, Barry. "*Harry Potter* Movie Breaks Local Records," *The Jerusalem Post (Internet Edition)*, Dec. 3, 2001. http://www.jpost.com/Editions/2001/12/03/Culture/Music.39243.html.

Deavel, Catherine Jack, and David Paul Deavel. "Character, Choice, and Harry Potter," *Logos: A Journal of Catholic Thought and Culture* (Vol. 5.4), Fall 2002. http://www.stthomas.edu/cathstudies/logos/vol5_4/deavel.html.

De Mello, Anthony J., S.J. *One Minute Wisdom*. New York: Doubleday, 1986.

DeGaetano, Gloria. *Screen Smarts: A Family Guide to Media Literacy*. Boston: Houghton-Mifflin, 1996.

Duska, Ronald, and Mariellen Whelan. *Moral Development: A Guide to Piaget and Kohlberg*. New York: Paulist Press, 1975.

Duffy, James. "Moral Imagination: Filling Our Children with Good Things," *Lay Witness* (Vol. 21, No. 4), May 2000.

Fowler, James W. *The Stages of Faith: The Psychology of Human Development and the Quest for Meaning.* San Francisco: Harper Collins, 1981.

Gallagher, Maureen. *The Art of Catechesis: What You Need to Be, Know and Do.* New York: Paulist Press, 1998.

Gibbs, Nancy. "The Real Magic of Harry Potter," *Time,* June 23, 2003, pp. 60–67.

Granger, John. "Harry Potter and the Inklings: The Christian Meaning of *The Chamber of Secrets,*" *CSL: The Bulletin of the New York C. S. Lewis Society,* Nov./Dec. 2002.

Guroian, Vigen. "On Fairy Tales and the Moral Imagination," The Wilberforce Forum, BreakPoint Online. http://www.pfm.org/Content/ContentGroups/BreakPoint/Columns/Really_Human_Things/200217/On_Fairy_Tales_and_the_Moral_Imagination.htm.

———. *Tending the Heart of Virtue: How Classic Stories Awaken a Child's Moral Imagination.* New York: Oxford University Press, 1998.

Harris, Maria. "Enlarging the Religious Imagination: The Imagery of Time," *PACE 13.* Winona: St. Mary's Press, 1982–83.

Harris, Robert. "Metaphor," *A Handbook of Rhetorical Devices.* 2002. VirtualSalt web site: http://www.virtualsalt.com/rhetoric.htm#Metaphor.

The Henry J. Kaiser Family Foundation. *Kids and Media@ the New Millennium.* Menlo Park: The Henry J. Kaiser Family Foundation, 2001.

Horell, Harold Daly. "Harry Potter, Hope, and Holiness," *The Living Light* (Vol. 37, No. 3), Spring 2001.

Hunt, Gladys. *Honey for a Child's Heart (3rd ed.).* Grand Rapids: Zondervan, 1989.

Hurst, Carol Otis. "Reading with Your Child at Home," Carol Hurst's Children's Literature Site, http://www.carolhurst.com/profsubjects/reading/parentreading.html.

Hurst, Carol Otis. "Believing in Children as Readers, Learners and Teachers," Carol Hurst's Children's Literature Site: http://www.carolhurst.com/profsubjects/reading/parentreading.html.

"Interview with Mary Margaret Keaton," *My Friend,* May 2001, p. 18.

Jackson, Lisa. "The Return of Harry Potter," *Christian Parenting Today,* Sept./Oct. 2000, p. 44–47.

John Paul II. Address to the Participants in the Plenary Meeting of the Pontifical Council for Social Communications. March 2, 2002. Vatican website: http//www.vatican.va/holy_father/john_paul_ii /speeches/2002/march/documents/hf_-ii_spe_20020301_ pccs_en.html (accessed Oct. 19, 2004).

————. *Crossing the Threshold of Hope.* New York: Knopf, 1994.

————. *Evangelium Vitae.* Boston: Pauline Books & Media, 1995.

————. *Familiaris Consortio.* Boston: Pauline Books & Media, 1981.

————. *Letter to Artists.* Boston: Pauline Books & Media, 1999.

————. *Novo Millennio Ineunte.* Boston: Pauline Books & Media, 2001.

————. *Slavorum Apostoli.* Boston: Pauline Books & Media, 1985.

Jones, Malcolm. "The Return of Harry Potter," *Newsweek,* July 10, 2000, p. 60.

Keaton, Mary Margaret. "Harry Potter: A Tool for Sowing Seeds of the Gospel," *Catechist Magazine,* March 200, p. 37–39. (Also archived online at http://www.peterli.com/cat/archive/featured/11_01/harry_potter.cfm.)

Keyser, Elizabeth Lennox. "Frances Hodgson Burnett's *The Secret Garden,*" *Women Writers of Children's Literature* (ed. Harold Bloom). Philadelphia: Chelsea House, 1998, pp. 128–130.

King, Don W. "The Wardrobe as Christian Metaphor," *Mythlore* (Vol. 14), Autumn 1987, pp. 25-27.

Lakoff, George and Mark Johnson. *Metaphors We Live By.* Chicago: University of Chicago Press, 1980.

Le Guin, Ursula. "Where Do You Get Your Ideas From?" *Dancing at the Edge of the World.* New York: Grove Press, 1989.

Leo XIII. *Rerum Novarum.* Boston: Pauline Books & Media, 1891.

LeVeque, Anne. "Harry Potter Author: 'I Believe in God, Not Magic,'" Catholic News Service/U.S. Catholic Conference, Jan. 5, 2000.

Lussier, Ernest, S.S.S. *Christ's Farewell Discourse.* New York: Alba House, 1979.

Libreria Editrice Vaticana. *General Directory for Catechesis.* Washington, D.C.: United States Catholic Conference, 1998.

Linden, Stanton J. *Darke Hieroglyphicks: Alchemy in English Literature from Chaucer to the Restoration.* Lexington: University Press of Kentucky, 1996.

Lyman, Jay. "*Harry Potter* Movie Ticket Sales Break Internet Records," *NewsFactor Enterprise I.T. Top Tech News,* Nov 16, 2001. http://www.newsfactor.com/perl/story/14856.html.

Mattingly, Terry. "Harry Potter's Magic Recalls Medieval Christian Symbols," *The Daily Camera,* June 21, 2003.

McKenna, Megan. *Lent: The Daily Readings.* Maryknoll: Orbis Books, 1997.

Miller, Clarence H. "Christ as the Philosopher's Stone in George Herbert's 'The Elixir,'" *Notes and Queries* 45:1.39–41.19.03.1998, accessed at http://www.geocities.com/Athens/Acropolis/6586/miller.html.

Moran, Kristen. "Scholastic to Release J. K. Rowling's Phenomenal Best-Seller *Harry Potter and the Order of the Phoenix* in Paperback on August 10, 2004," Official news release, Scholastic Corporation, Feb. 2, 2004.

Pearce, Joseph. "Why Tolkien Says *The Lord of the Rings* Is Catholic," *National Catholic Register,* Jan. 12, 2003.

Pontifical Council for Culture. *Toward a Pastoral Approach to Culture.* Boston: Pauline Books & Media, 1999.

Pontifical Council for Social Communications. *Aetatis Novae.* Boston: Pauline Books & Media, 1992.

———. *The Church and Internet.* Boston: Pauline Books & Media. 2002.

———. *Communio et Progressio.* Boston: Pauline Books & Media, 1971.

———. *Ethics in Advertising.* Boston: Pauline Books & Media, 1997.

———. *Ethics in Communication.* Boston: Pauline Books & Media, 2000.

Reese, James, O.S.F.S. *Jesus, His Word and Work: The Gospels of Matthew, Mark, and Luke.* New York: Pueblo Publishing Company, 1978.

Riera, Michael, and Joseph Di Prisco. *Right from Wrong: Instilling a Sense of Integrity in Your Child.* Cambridge: Perseus Publishing, 2002.

Romanowski, William D. *Eyes Wide Open: Looking for God in Popular Culture.* Grand Rapids: Brazos Press, 2001.

Rowling, J. K. "A Good Scare: The Wizard of Harry Potter Explains What Kids Need to Know of the Dark Side," *Time,* Oct. 30, 2000; p. 108.

———. "The Not Especially Fascinating Life So Far of J. K. Rowling" (Part 2). http://www.cliphoto.com/potter/rowling1.htm.

Scholastic Books. "Potter Primers: An Expert Talks About Harry Potter," Harry Potter Companion, Family Matters Parent Guides, Scholastic.com http://www.scholastic.com/familymatters/parent-guides/potter/expert.htm.

Schulman, Michael, and Eva Mekler. *Bringing Up a Moral Child: Teaching Your Child to be Kind, Just, and Responsible.* New York: Doubleday, 1985.

Sealey, Geraldine. "Highfalutin Harry: Scholars Rev Up for Latest Potter Book," ABC News. http://abcnews.go.com/sections/us/Entertainment/potter030619.html.

Second Vatican Council. *Gaudium et Spes.* Boston: Pauline Books & Media, 1965.

———. *Lumen Gentium.* Boston: Pauline Books & Media, 1964.

———. *Inter Mirifica.* Boston: Pauline Books & Media, 1963.

Sterne, Laurence. "Sermon 20, The Prodigal Son." *The Sermons of Laurence Sterne: The Text.* Edited by Melvyn New. Gainesville: University Press of Florida, 1996.

Stories from the Web."The Author J. K. Rowling: The J. K. Rowling Interview as presented by Stories from the Web." Birmingham Libraries, U.K. http://www.storiesfromtheweb.org/stories/rowling/interview1.asp.

Straughn, Harold Kent. "Interview with James Fowler," *MPL Journal.* http://www.lifespirals.com/TheMindSpiral/ Fowler/fowler.html.

Sutherland, Zena, and May Hill Arbuthnot. *Children and Books.* New York: Harper Collins, 1991.

Tallim, Jane. "And Now a Word from Our Sponsor: Teachable Moment," Media Awareness Network, http://www.media-awareness.ca/english/resources/educational/teachable_moments/word_from_our_sponsor.cfm.

Tapscott, Don. "Educating the Net Generation," *Integrating Technology into the Curriculum* (Vol. 56, No. 5, Feb. 1999), Association for Supervision and Curriculum Development. http://www.ascd.org/articles/9902el_tapscott.html.

Tapscott, Don. *Growing Up Digital: The Rise of the Net Generation.* New York: McGraw-Hill, 1998.

Taylor, Alina Corday. "Master of Middle Earth," *Smithsonian Magazine,* Jan. 2002; pp. 77–82.

Turner, Bryan S. "The Body and Being Human," *The Hedgehog Review* (Vol. 3, No. 2), Summer 2001.

U.S. Department. of Education. "Helping Your Child Become a Reader," U.S. Department of Education, http://165.224.220.62/pubs/parents/Reader/index.html.

Veale, Tony. Metaphor, Memory and Meaning: Symbolic and Connectionist Issues in Metaphor Interpretation. Ph.D. diss., Trinity College, Dublin, 1995. Available from World Wide Web: http://www.compapp.dcu.ie/–tonyv/news_frame.html.

"Who Needs Imagination: An Interview with Professor Paul Harris," Harvard Graduate School of Education News, March 1, 2002. http://www.gse.harvard.edu/news/features/harris03012002.htm.

Wolpe, David. *Teaching Your Children About God: A Modern Jewish Approach.* New York: Henry Holt and Company, 1993.

Woodard, Emory H. IV, with Natalia Gridina. *Media in the Home 2000: The Fifth Annual Survey of Parents and Children.* Philadelphia: Annenberg Public Policy Center of the University of Pennsylvania, 2000.

Zenit News Agency. "Harry Potter Not a Problem, Says Church Figure," Feb. 2, 2003. ZE03020304.

Zenit News Agency. "In Defense of Harry Potter: Professors Defend Fiction's Famous Wizard," March 16, 2003. ZE03031622.

Zenit News Agency. "When Faith and Artistic Creativity Meet: First Congress Held on Poetry and Christianity," May 4, 2003. ZE03050421.

Index

love. *see also* compassion; unconditional love
in *Abel's Island*, 149–150
in *Adelita: A Mexican
Cinderella Story*, 113–114
in *The Big Wave*, 138–143
in *The Borrowers*, 166
in *Charlotte's Web*, 159
in *Curious George*, 92
in *Esperanza Rising*, 176–182
in *The Fellowship of the Ring*,
198
in *Grandpa's Face*, 95–97
in *Harry Potter* stories, 201–203,
204, 205, 214
in *Island of the Blue Dolphins*,
155
in *Mama, Do You Love Me?*, 94
Maslow's hierarchy of shared
human needs, 65
in *The Mitten*, 53
in *Pedro and the Monkey*,
115–117
in *The Secret Garden*, 190–192
in *Shrek*, 16
in *Sounder*, 184
in *The Velveteen Rabbit*,
134–136
in *Where the Wild Things Are*,
104
in *Winnie-the-Pooh*, 128, 131
in *A Wrinkle in Time*, 61–62
Luba and the Wren (Polacco),
117–120

M

Macrocarpaea apparata, 202
The Magician's Nephew (Lewis),
168–171
Mama, Do You Love Me? (Joosse),
87, 93–94
mandrakes, 220–222
Mann, Horace (quotation), 30
Mann, Thomas (quotation), 34
Martin, de Porres (saint), 156
Mary, Mother of God, 110
dolors of Mary, 111

in *Esperanza Rising*, 180–181
Our Lady of Guadalupe, 181
Our Lady of Sorrows, 111
visit with Elizabeth, 130
Mary Poppins (Travers), 80
values in, xviii
mask of God, story as, 4
Maslow, Abraham, 65–68
Mater et Magistra (Pope John
XXIII), 179
materialism
in *The Borrowers*, 164–165
in *The Hobbit*, 195
in *Luba and the Wren*, 119–120
in *The Rainbow Fish*, 121
Matthew, book of
Beatitudes, 36
Jesus calms the sea, 139
mustard seed story, 5
McGuffey's Reader, xiii
media. *see also* communication
balanced consumption of, 29–30
discerning outlook toward,
30–32
enjoyment of, 40–43, 79–80
importance of books, 78–79
influence of, 160–161
as reflection of culture, 28
spirituality in communications,
38
violence in, 31
Media Beware website, "Media
Concepts," 27
"Media Concepts" (Media Beware
website, Ontario Ministry of
Education), 27
media culture
ease of communication, 17–18
engaging, 18–20
and sense of adventure, 39–40
statistics, 21–22
media education. *see* media literacy
media literacy
in *Charlotte's Web*, 161
equipping children for, 26–32
principles of, 27
skills for, 31

Mary Margaret Keaton is a writer and speaker residing in the Virginia suburbs of Washington, D.C., and is currently completing graduate studies in theology and Sacred Scripture at the Washington Theological Union. A frequent speaker on the spirituality of saints and on finding God in popular literature and film, the former news director and reporter also serves as a communications consultant to businesses and non-profit organizations.

She has served as a parish catechist for more than twenty years. Her articles have appeared in My Friend, Catechist, The Sunday Journal, The Arlington Catholic Herald and other diocesan newspapers as well as many online publications. She scripted two DVDs for the Vincentian Center for Church and Society at St. John's University in New York.

Mary Margaret and her husband Joe have been married for eighteen years, and are the parents of three children.

BOOKS & MEDIA

The Daughters of St. Paul operate book and media centers at the following addresses. Visit, call or write the one nearest you today, or find us on the World Wide Web, www.pauline.org

CALIFORNIA
3908 Sepulveda Blvd, Culver City, CA 90230	310-397-8676
5945 Balboa Avenue, San Diego, CA 92111	858-565-9181
46 Geary Street, San Francisco, CA 94108	415-781-5180

FLORIDA
145 S.W. 107th Avenue, Miami, FL 33174	305-559-6715

HAWAII
1143 Bishop Street, Honolulu, HI 96813	808-521-2731
Neighbor Islands call:	866-521-2731

ILLINOIS
172 North Michigan Avenue, Chicago, IL 60601	312-346-4228

LOUISIANA
4403 Veterans Memorial Blvd, Metairie, LA 70006	504-887-7631

MASSACHUSETTS
885 Providence Hwy, Dedham, MA 02026	781-326-5385

MISSOURI
9804 Watson Road, St. Louis, MO 63126	314-965-3512

NEW JERSEY
561 U.S. Route 1, Wick Plaza, Edison, NJ 08817	732-572-1200

NEW YORK
150 East 52nd Street, New York, NY 10022	212-754-1110
78 Fort Place, Staten Island, NY 10301	718-447-5071

PENNSYLVANIA
9171-A Roosevelt Blvd, Philadelphia, PA 19114	215-676-9494

SOUTH CAROLINA
243 King Street, Charleston, SC 29401	843-577-0175

TENNESSEE
4811 Poplar Avenue, Memphis, TN 38117	901-761-2987

TEXAS
114 Main Plaza, San Antonio, TX 78205	210-224-8101

VIRGINIA
1025 King Street, Alexandria, VA 22314	703-549-3806

CANADA
3022 Dufferin Street, Toronto, ON M6B 3T5	416-781-9131

¡También somos su fuente para libros,
videos y música en español!